# FOLDING IN ARCHITECTURE

*Front Cover: Peter Eisenman, Center for the Arts, Emory University, Atlanta, Concept Model*

Published in Great Britain in 2004 by Wiley-Academy, a division of John Wiley & Sons Ltd

Copyright © 2004               John Wiley & Sons Ltd, The Atrium, Southern Gate, Chichester, West Sussex PO19 8SQ, England
                              Telephone   (+44) 1243 779777

Email (for orders and customer service enquiries): cs-books@wiley.co.uk
Visit our Home Page on www.wileyeurope.com or www.wiley.com

*Other Wiley Editorial Offices*
John Wiley & Sons Inc., 111 River Street, Hoboken, NJ 07030, USA

Jossey-Bass, 989 Market Street, San Francisco, CA 94103-1741, USA

Wiley-VCH Verlag GmbH, Boschstr. 12, D-69469 Weinheim, Germany

John Wiley & Sons Australia Ltd, 33 Park Road, Milton, Queensland 4064, Australia

John Wiley & Sons (Asia) Pte Ltd, 2 Clementi Loop #02-01, Jin Xing Distripark, Singapore 129809

John Wiley & Sons Canada Ltd, 22 Worcester Road, Etobicoke, Ontario, Canada M9W 1L1

Printed and bound in Italy

# FOLDING IN ARCHITECTURE

WILEY-ACADEMY

# FOLDING IN ARCHITECTURE

# Contents

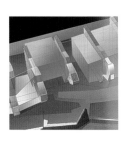

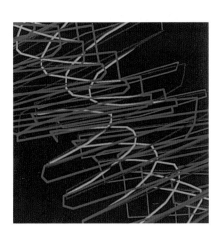

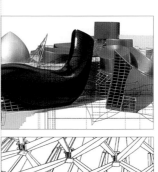

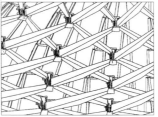

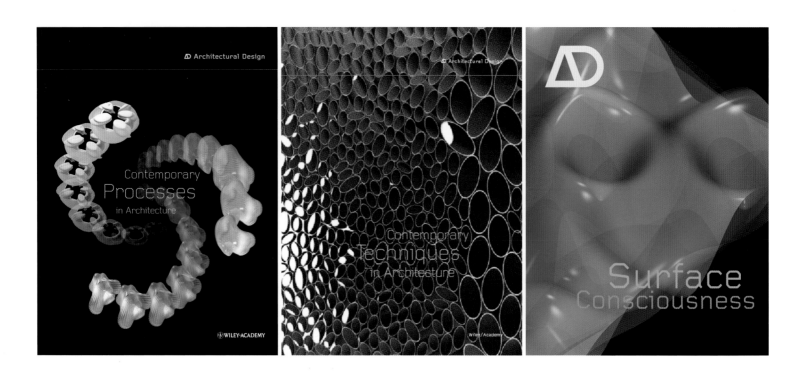

**Folding in Architecture** led the way for a whole new generation of *Architectural Design* titles. These most noteably include *Contemporary Processes in Architecture* (2000) and *Contemporary Techniques in Architecture* (2002), guest-edited by Ali Rahim, which brought the most current generative processes and techniques under theoretical consideration; *Surface Consciousness*, guest-edited by Mark Taylor, that made surface the main focus of an integrated architecture; and *Emergence: Morphogenetic Design Strategies* (2004), guest-edited by Michael Hensel, Achim Menges and Michael Weinstock, that is a full architectural exploration of the scientific model of Emergence.

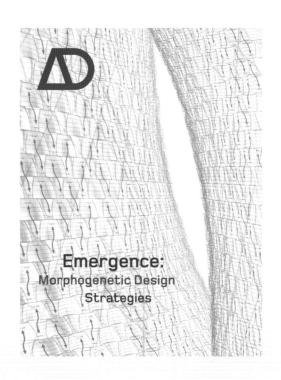

# PREFACE
## *HELEN CASTLE*

In the late 1980s and early 1990s, *AD* appeared in a small white format. The front cover image was framed within a squared-up box. Titles of issues reflected the most recent style machination – whether it be Post-Modernism, classicism or Modernism. By 1993, when *Folding in Architecture* was published, the publication's dimensions had been expanded to optimise on the visual drama of the shard, fragment and deconstructed image – black being the background colour of choice for Deconstruction. (Gloss and generous page layouts also being incited by the onset of desktop publishing.)

*Folding in Architecture* is most often acknowledged for the formative role that it played in the 'digital' revolution of architecture. It is, however, important not to overlook the original context in which this *Architectural Design* profile came out and the degree to which it was a catalyst for shifting more penetrating architectural preoccupations. For almost two decades, architecture had been the subject of what Lynn describes in his original introduction as 'formal conflicts', with endless debates over the 'right' or emergent style. It was a situation that had played itself out and was becoming increasingly tedious, with its constant internalising, for those both inside and outside architecture. Deconstruction was the ultimate conclusion of all these musings and discussions centred on form – as collaged form was artfully exploded into shards. Interestingly enough, Lynn chose *AD*, the publication that was most closely identified with the 1980s and Jencks's Post-Modernism and stylistic jostlings, as well as Deconstruction, to expound 'an alternative smoothness' for architecture. Rather than identifying and highlighting the differences between formal systems, Lynn's 'architectural curvilinearity' aspired to an intensive integration of differences in an architecture of 'the folded, the pliant and the supple'. In his new introduction to this revised edition of *Folding in Architecture*, Lynn

acknowledges the perceptual and conceptual changes that the issue pioneered when he says: 'For me, it is calculus that was the subject of the issue and it is the discovery and implementation of calculus by architects that continues to drive the field in terms of formal and constructed complexity. The loss of the module in favour of the infinitesimal component and the displacement of the fragmentary collage by the intensive whole are the legacy of the introduction of the calculus.' With its generative, conceptual and constructional effects, the application of calculus represents far more than a technological advancement, representing the same sort of full-scale perceptual and tectonic shift that was experienced in the Renaissance when Brunelleschi applied perspective in his drawing of the Florentine Baptistery and buildings started to be conceived in three-dimensional form on paper.

Greg Lynn and Mario Carpo, with their new thought-provoking additions to this publication, have coherently laid out the relevance of *Folding* to current thinking in architecture. In the development of this revised edition, Carpo, an architectural historian, was particularly mindful that this new book should be (bar some original typos he helped to eradicate) a historical document. With its original cover and graphics, it is a strong reminder of what the contained ideas and work were responding to, as well as where they were going.

**Helen Castle** *is Editor of* Architectural Design *and Executive Commissioning Editor of Wiley-Academy books.*

Folding in Architecture *was originally published as part of Academy's* Architectural Design *series. For further information about forthcoming books in this series, or to find out how you can subscribe please visit www.ArchDesignJournal.com or email architecture@wiley.co.uk.*

# INTRODUCTION
## *GREG LYNN*

As I argued in the original *Folding in Architecture* essay, since Robert Venturi and Denise Scott Brown's influential *Complexity and Contradiction in Architecture* (1966), it has been important for architecture to define compositional complexity. Ten years ago, the collected projects and essays in the first edition of this publication were an attempt to move beyond Venturi's pictorial collage aesthetics and the formal and spatial collage aesthetics that then constituted the vanguard of complexity in architecture, as epitomized by Johnson and Wigley's 'Deconstructivist Architecture' exhibition at MoMA in 1988. The desire for architectural complexity in both composition and construction continues today and can be characterised by several distinct streams of thought, three of which have connections to the projects and arguments first laid out in the *Architectural Design* issue of *Folding in Architecture*: voluptuous form, stochastic and emergent processes, and intricate assemblages. At the moment of the book's publication there were two distinct tendencies among architectural theorists and designers. The first was a shift from the linguistic and representational focus of both Post-Modernism and Derridean Deconstruction towards the spatial, artistic and mathematical models of Deleuze, Foucault, Whitehead and even, to some degree, Lacan. Of these initial experiments it was the Deleuzian focus on spatial models, most of which were derived from Leibniz's monadology that took hold in the field. The second tendency was an interest in scientific models of complexity, initially those derived from the work of René Thom and later those of the Santa Fe Institute, among others. The combination of the discovery, for the first time by architects, of a 300-year-old mathematical and spatial invention, that is calculus, and the introduction of a new cosmological and scientific model of emergence, chaos and complexity, made for an extremely provocative and incoherent moment in architectural experimentation. Today, a decade later, these interests have shaken out into more or less discrete schools of thought.

Intricacy connotes a new model of connectionism composed of extremely small–scale and incredibly diverse elements. Intricacy is the fusion of disparate elements into continuity, the becoming whole of components that retain their status as pieces in a larger composition. Unlike simple hierarchy, subdivision, compartmentalisation or modularity, intricacy involves a variation of the parts that is not reducible to the structure of the whole. The term intricacy is intended to move away from this understanding of the architectural detail as an isolated fetishised instance within an otherwise minimal framework. Detail need not be the reduction or concentration of architectural design into a discrete moment. In an intricate network, there are no details *per se*. Detail is everywhere, ubiquitously distributed and continuously variegated in collaboration with formal and spatial effects. Instead of punctuating volumetric minimalism with discrete details, intricacy implies complexity all over without recourse to

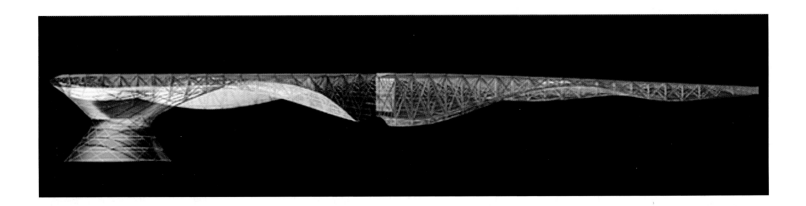

**Above** Coop Himmelb(l)au, BMW Welt, Munich, Germany (2001 - 2006)

**Opposite** Frank Gehry, Interactive Corp's Headquarters, New York, USA (2003 - 2006)

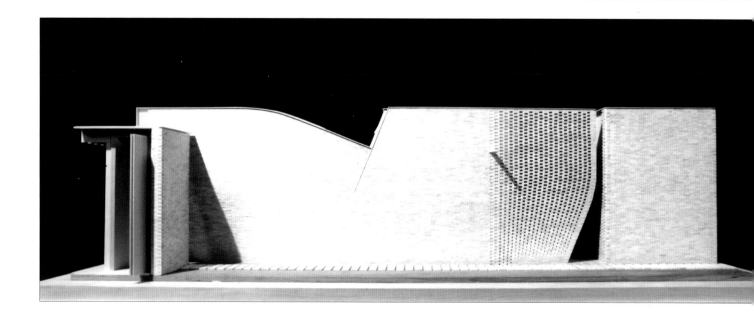

compositional contrast. Intricacy occurs where macro- and micro-scales of components are interwoven and intertwined. The major connection of the term intricacy to the concepts present in *Folding in Architecture* is that the term is a derivative of "pli", much like the other terms – complex, complicated, pliant – all of which imply compositional practices of weaving, folding and joining.

What is probably most interesting about *Folding in Architecture* is not the theoretical directions of the architects showcased in the publication but the fact – or a more blunt fact – that these practices were collected at the instant before they would be completely transformed by the computer. The focus, in the issue, on compositional, organisational, visual and material sensibilities, rather than on theories of digital design, was only possible at that moment before the digital waves of software-sponsored discourse that soon swept over the field and which only now are beginning to recede. The projects in *Folding* were in some cases facilitated by, often were mimicking in anticipation

of, or were asking for the assistance from, digital tools, but none of them could be simply reducible to digital design, visualisation or manufacturing tools. It is significant that the architects included in this publication, had all formed their ambitions for a new model of formal and spatial complexity before the advent of inexpensive, ubiquitous, spline modelling software. Instead of being confronted with the possibilities for an expedient realisation of forms and spaces that would otherwise be too complicated, messy or convoluted to produce, these architects made a claim towards new forms that would only later be facilitated digitally.

Because these architects were the first generation to adapt to the new digital medium, initially they were, by definition, the most amateur and inexperienced in their use. They were also the most experimental. At the time, none of these objects relied on digital process as a validation or explanation of their genesis. It would be inappropriate to make claims of expertise and refinement of their medium at the time, where now one can speculate on calculus based and digitally engendered qualities of the medium

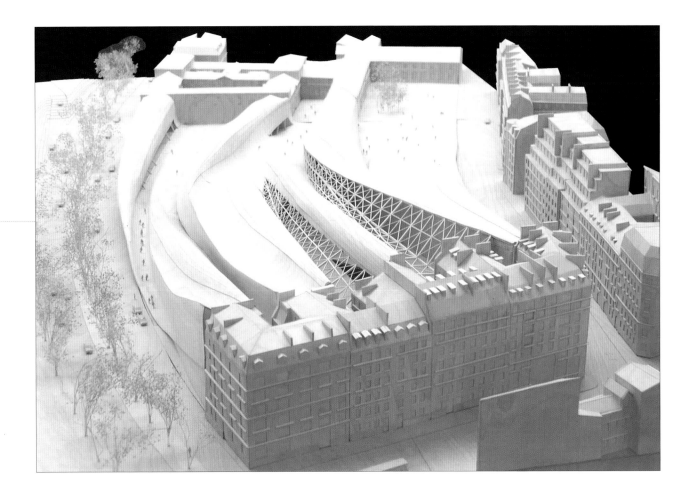

such as new forms of expertise including elegance, rigour and, I dare say, beauty.

Some used metaphors of folding, and even mechanical folding operations, to explain their morphology but none took recourse to digital visualisation and mapping as an explanation for their shape or form. Later, this would become a norm for some and this is the school of stochastic emergence and what some architects refer to as the digital gothic. Happy accidents and automatic processes are certainly the precursors to fine grain, detailed, continuous compositions as well as continuously variegated forms. The latter demands a fusion that is not possible without a theory of synthesis and unity that maintains detail as a discrete moment that participates intensively in the construction of a new kind of whole. In this way, a theory of intricate form is derived from Leibniz's logic of monadology and Deleuze's subsequent theories of 'le pli', or the fold.

For me, it is calculus that was the subject of the issue and it is the discovery and implementation of calculus by architects that continues to drive the field in terms of formal and constructed complexity. The loss of the module in favour of the infinitesimal component and the displacement of the fragmentary collage by the intensive whole are the legacy of the introduction of calculus. This is still being debated and explored. The works in *Folding* ten years ago pointed to several directions along the calculus path

of research into continuity, subdivision and a more generalised mathematics of curvature. A multifaceted approach towards detail, structure and form, relying on slippages between complex interconnectedness and singularity, between homogeneity at a distance and near formal incoherence in detail, between disparate interacting systems and monolithic wholes, and finally between mechanical components and voluptuous organic surfaces, is all part and parcel of the shift from whole number and fractional dimensions to formal and material sensibilities of the infinitesimal.

The drift from monolithic objects to infinitesimally scaled components explains the technical interest in the use of CNC controlled robotic technologies for construction. More important than the fact of the CNC device is the idea of intricacy, for example. There is little more banal or uninteresting than a new machine that is capable of producing mere variety, something with which we are mindlessly inundated at a greater velocity by the day. So to celebrate CNC for its ability to give us one-of-a-kind customised variety is to celebrate an aspect without much intellectual or creative merit. It is important to imbue digital technologies with some creative and intellectual force that engages the history or architectural problems and ambitions. The architects included in *Folding in Architecture* were laying out those problems and concerns in advance of the technology and it is they,

along with many other new practices, that are engaging with the problems of form and construction critically and creatively because of their investment in the field of ideas and theory. The intricacy of a calculus defined collection of elements in space evokes a particular kind of cohesion, continuity, wholism and even organicity. Intricate structures are continuously connected and intertwined through fine grain local linkages such that a totality or whole is operative. Intricate compositions are organic in the sense that each and every part and piece is interacting and communicating simultaneously so that every instance is affected by every other instance.

*Folding in Architecture* captured a moment before the discovery of a new kind of drafting machine, a much more vital machine than the compasses, adjustable triangles and rubber spline curves with which most of the projects were conceived. Much has been made of mechanical reproduction in art and architecture. Like mechanical reproduction and its modern vision of identical glossy modules, intricate reproduction is still dependent on a model of the machine. But instead of a mechanism of simple

repetition, an intricate reproduction machine is a wet machine charged with free energy, variation, and subtlety. Where the mechanical is characterised by rote, encoded, repetitive operations on a sequence of identical modular units, a different form of reproduction characterises the biological. In a word, an intricate machine is a vital rather than mechanical construct. Intricacy evokes an eroticism for the machine and a desire to make it reproduce organically, both in the variation of subtly variegated brothers and sisters as well as a differentiated complex of discrete organs that nonetheless coheres into a beautifully synthesised whole. These works move from the identical asexual reproduction of simple machines to the differential sexual reproduction of intricate machines. Not merely a theoretical difference, this gives these works their erotic dimension.

**Greg Lynn** *is Professor, Universität für angewandte Kunst Wien; Davenport Visiting Professor Yale University (2004); and Studio Professor, UCLA. He has professional practices in Los Angeles (Greg Lynn FORM) and New York (United Architects).*

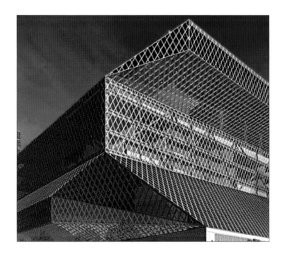

**Above** and **Opposite**  Frank Gehry, Interactive Corp's Headquarters, New York, USA

**Left**  Monica Ponce de Leon and Nader Tehrani of Office dA, Tongxian Arts Centre, Beijing, China

# TEN YEARS OF FOLDING
## *MARIO CARPO*

*F*olding in Architecture, first published in 1993 as a 'Profile' of *Architectural Design*, ranks as a classic of end-of-millennium architectural theory.[1] It is frequently cited and generally perceived as a crucial turning point. Some of the essays in the original publication have taken on lives of their own, and have been reprinted and excerpted – out of context, however, and often without reference to their first appearance in print. This ahistoric approach is characteristic of all works in progress: so long as a tradition is still active and alive, it tends to acquire a timeless sort of internal consistency, where chronology does not matter. In Antiquity and in the Middle Ages such phases could last for centuries. But we have been living in times of faster change for quite a while now – we even had to invent a new philosophy of history in the nineteenth century to take this into account – and ten years are quite a stretch in Internet time. This is one reason why the editors of this volume decided that the original 1993 issue of *Folding in Architecture* should be reprinted in facsimile, verbatim and figuratim, complete and unabridged: only some typographical errors have been edited out. Indeed, *Folding in Architecture* is now a classic – not a timeless one, however, but time specific.

More than would be customary in other trades and professions, many architects and architectural historians still believe in historical progress and in the pursuit of innovation. Any reasonable architectural thinker of our days, if asked, would disparage such a primitive theory of history, but theory and practice are here curiously at odds. Regardless of much discourse on long durations, the directionlessness of time, time warps, the end of time, and perhaps even the death of the author, it is a fact that events and people are still banally and routinely singled out to acquire historical status in architecture when they are thought to have started something. *Folding in Architecture* is no exception. In the common lore, this publication is now seen as seminal because it was the catalyst for a wave of change that marked the decade and climaxed towards the turn of the millennium, when, for a short spell of time, the new avant-garde that evolved out of it came to be known as 'topological', and was regarded as the quintessential architectural embodiment of the new digital technologies that were booming at the time.

Art historians, sociologists and psychologists will at some point reconstruct the story of architectural folding in the nineties and, as art historians frequently do, they will not fail to identify a trend towards curvilinearity that reversed a preceding trend towards angularity of form. Indeed, forms have a tendency to swing from the angular to the curvilinear, from parataxis to syntax, and art historians, following a pattern inaugurated in 1915 by Heinrich Wölfflin, have since brought this interpretive model to bear in a number of circumstances.[2] Obviously, the nineties started angular and ended curvilinear.[3] By the end of the decade, with few exceptions, curvilinearity was ubiquitous. It dominated industrial design, fashion, furniture, body culture, car design, food, critical theory in the visual arts, sex appeal, the art of discourse, even architecture. Admittedly one of the most influential architectural writers of the decade, Rem Koolhaas, kept designing in an angular mode, but the most iconic building of the time, Gehry's Bilbao, was emphatically curvilinear. In spite of the many varieties and competing technologies of curves that followed, curvilinear folds were and still are often seen as the archetypal and foundational figure of architecture in the age of digital pliancy. Yet, even cursory scrutiny of the essays and projects presented in this volume shows that digital technologies were but a marginal component of the critical discourse of the time. Likewise, most of the illustrations in this book feature strikingly angular, disjunctive forms. How can fractures, ridges and edges represent formal continuity? Where are the folds?

### 1. The formative years: philosophy, flaccidity, and infinity
At the beginning of the last decade of the century, architectural theory was busily discussing deconstructivism, and its eminently angular avatars in building. For reasons too long to explain, and perhaps inexplicable, American critical theory of the time was driving under the influence of some Parisian thinkers – some of them virtually ignored in their homeland. When Gilles Deleuze's impervious book on *The Fold, Leibniz and the Baroque* was first published in France in 1988, it failed to excite critical acclaim in the immediate surroundings of Boulevard Raspail.[4] Yet the Deleuzian fold was granted a second lease on life when Peter Eisenman – starting with the first publications on his Rebstock project in 1991 – began to elaborate an architectural version of it.[5]

Deleuze's book was on Leibniz, on folds, on the baroque and on many other things as well. Most of it can be read as a vast hermeneutic of continuity which Deleuze applied to Leibniz's theory of ideas (including his notorious monadology), to Leibniz's mathematics (differential calculus in particular) and to various expressions of the baroque in the arts: the fold, a unifying figure whereby different segments and planes are joined and merge in continuous lines and volumes, is both the emblem and the object of Deleuze's discourse. Folds avoid fractures, overlay gaps, interpolate. Eisenman's reading of Deleuze's fold, in this early stage, retained and emphasized this notion of forms that can change, morph and move: a new category of objects defined not by what they are, but by the way they change and by the laws that describe their continuous variations. Eisenman also related this differential notion of objects to a new age of electronic technologies and digital images (with no reference, however, to computer-aided design: Eisenman's writings of the time frequently cite fax technology as the harbinger of a new paradigm of electronic reproducibility, alternative and opposed to all paradigms of the mechanical age and destined to obliterate the Benjaminian distinction between original and reproduction).[6]

Eisenman's essays prior to 1993 also bear witness to a significant topical shift which evolved from a closer, often literal interpretation of Deleuze's arguments (in 1991 Eisenman even borrowed Deleuze's notion of the 'objectile', on which more will be said later),[7] to more architecturally inclined adaptations, including the use of René Thom's diagrams as design devices for generating architectural folds – a short circuit of sorts, as Thom's topological diagrams are themselves folds, and Thom actually itemized several categories of folding surfaces.[8] In his perhaps most accomplished essay on the matter, 'Folding in Time', Eisenman dropped Deleuze's conception of the "objectile", which he replaced with the contiguous and also Deleuzian concept of 'object-event': the breaking up of the Cartesian and perspectival grids of the classical tradition, prompted and promoted by the moving and morphing images of the digital age, requires architectural forms capable of continuous variation – forms that move in time.[9] Several stratagems, such as Thom's folding diagrams, may help to define them, but the 'folding' process remains purely generative,[10] and it does not relate to the actual form of the end product. Forms do not fold (actually, in all Eisenman's projects featured in *Folding in Architecture* in 1993 they fracture and break), because most buildings do not move: when built, architectural forms can at best only represent, symbolize or somehow evoke the continuity of change or motion.

This stance of Eisenman's would be extensively glossed over, rephrased and reformulated in the years that followed,[11] but in the context it seems unequivocal: folding is a process, not a product; it does not necessarily produce visible folds (although it would later on); it is about creating built forms, necessarily motionless, which can nevertheless induce the perception of motion by suggesting the 'continual variation' and 'perpetual development' of a 'form "becoming".'[12] Again, art historians might relate such forms to a long tradition of expressionist design. Eisenman himself, at this early stage in the history of folding, defined folding as a 'strategy for dislocating vision.'[13]

In 1993, Lynn's prefatory essay to *Folding in Architecture* eloquently argued for continuities of all types: visual, programmatic, formal, technical, environmental, socio-political and symbolic.

The list of suitable means to this end is also remarkably diverse: topological geometry, morphology, morphogenesis, Thom's catastrophe theory, Deleuze's theory of the fold and the 'computer technology of both the defense and Hollywood film industry.'[14] Nonetheless, a survey of the essays and projects featured in *Folding in Architecture* reveals some puzzling anomalies. Ten years later, many of the issues and topics that were so obviously prominent in 1993 seem to be accidental leftovers of a bygone era. Today, they simply don't register. In other cases, we can see why certain arguments were made – as we can see that from there, they led nowhere. Yet this panoply of curiosities and antiques also includes vivid anticipations of the future. That much can be said without risk, as a significant part of that future has already come to pass.

Were Henry Cobb's lanky and somewhat philistine skyscrapers the predecessors of many folds and blobs to come? How does a philosophical and almost ontological quest for continuity in motion and form relate to Chuch Hobermans' humungous mechanical contrivances: buildings that actually move with cranky hinges, sliding metal panels, pivoting bolts and rivets? Jules Verne would have loved them. Why include the translation of the first chapter of Deleuze's *The Fold* , an opaque and vaguely misleading tirade on the organic and the mechanical in the seventeenth-century philosophy of nature, and not the second chapter, on Leibniz's law of continuity, differential calculus and the mathematical definition of the fold? What do Bahram Shirdel's ridges and creases (with explicit reference to Thom's diagrams) have in common with some of the earliest cucumiform epiphanies by Frank Gehry? The commentary blandly states that Gehry's irregular geometries were made possible 'by 3-D computer modelling.'[15] Digital technologies for design and manufacturing are mentioned by both Lynn and Kipnis as one tool among others that can help create 'smooth transformations,'[16] but the one essay entirely devoted to computing, Stephen Perrella's, is on morphing and computer animation in the making of the movie *Terminator 2* (the film's special effects director is quoted as saying 'we also used a programme called Photoshop').[17] Yet Lynn's presentation of Shoei Yoh's 'topological' roof for the Odawara Sports Complex includes a stunningly perceptive analysis of the new tectonic, formal and economic potentials brought about by the merging of computerized design, construction and fabrication. To date, little more has been said on the topic, which remains a central issue of the now ubiquitous debate on non-standard manufacturing.

The reason why some of the topics that emerged from the architectural discourse on folding of the early 1990s now seem so distant and outlandish, whereas others do not, is that something happened to separate them from us: a catastrophic event of sorts, a drastic environmental change followed by a typically Darwinian selection. As a result, many of those issues dropped out of sight. But those that remained thrived, and some were hugely magnified.

## 2. Maturity: mathematics, and the digital turn

Most architects in the early 1990s knew that computers could easily join dots with segments. But as CAD software quickly evolved, the graphic capabilities and processing speed of the machines grew, and the price of the new technologies declined, it soon appeared that computers could just as easily connect dots with continuous lines, and sometimes even extrapolate mathematical functions from them. Conversely, given a mathematical function, computers can visualize an almost infinite family of curves that share the same algorithm, with parameters that can be changed at will. Smoothness, first defined as a visual category by theorists of the picturesque at the end of the eighteenth century, turned out also to be a mathematical function derived from standard differential calculus.[18] Topological surfaces and topological deformations are equally described by mathematical functions – a bit unwieldy perhaps for manual operations, but already in the mid-nineties well within the grasp of any moderately priced desktop computer.

In this context, it stands to reason that the original quest for ontological continuity in architectural form should take a new turn. Computers, mostly indifferent to queries on the nature of Being, can easily deliver tools for the manipulation of mathematical continuity. These could be directly applied to the conception, the representation and the production of objects. And they were. In the late nineties, Bernard Cache could conclude that 'mathematics has effectively become an object of manufacture',[19] and Greg Lynn remarked that computer-aided design had 'allowed architects to explore calculus-based forms for the first time'.[20] To a large extent, our calculus is still Leibniz's: Lynn also added that Leibniz's monads contained integrals and equations.[21] As Leibniz's monads famously had no windows, this is hard to prove. Yet at this point Lynn was getting significantly closer to Deleuzes's original reading of Leibniz.

The mathematical component of Deleuze's work on Leibniz, prominent but previously ignored, now sprang to the forefront – together with the realization that Leibniz's differential calculus was for the most part the language still underlying the families of continuous forms that computers could now so easily visualize and manipulate. Indeed, as Deleuze had remarked, Leibniz's mathematics of continuity introduced and expressed a new idea of the object: differential calculus does not describe objects, but their laws of change – their infinite, infinitesimal variations. Deleuze even introduced a new terminology for his new two-tiered definition of the object: he called 'objectile' a function that virtually contains an infinite number of objects.[22] Each different and individual object eventualizes the mathematical algorithm, or objectile, common to all; in Aristotelian terms, as Leibniz might have used, an objectile is one form in many events. Deleuze's fold is itself a figure of differential calculus: it can be described geometrically as a point of inflection (the point that separates concavity and convexity in a curved line, or the point where the tangent crosses the line).[23] However, in good old calculus (as old as Leibniz, in fact), a point of inflection is in fact a maximum or a minimum in the first derivative of the function of the original curve. Deleuze mentions Bernard Cache with regard to both the mathematical definition of the fold and the concept of the objectile (which, however, he does not attribute to his gifted student).[24] Bernard Cache's essay, *Earth Moves*, where both notions are developed, did not appear in print until 1995 – and in English. The original French manuscript is cited in the English version as having been drafted in 1983.[25]

So we see how an original quest for formal continuity in architecture, born in part as a reaction against the deconstructivist cult of the fracture, ran into the computer revolution of the mid-nineties and turned into a theory of mathematical continuity. By a quirk of history, a philosophical text by Gilles Deleuze accompanied, fertilized and at times catalysed each of the different stages of this process. Without this preexisting pursuit of continuity in architectural forms and processes, of which the causes must be found in cultural and societal desires, computers in the nineties would most likely not have inspired any new geometry of forms. Likewise, without computers this cultural demand for continuity in the making of forms would soon have petered out and disappeared from our visual landscape. The story of folding, and in particular of the way folding went digital at a time when computers were becoming such a pivotal component of architectural design, once again suggests that only a dialectical interaction – a feedback loop of sorts – between technology and society can bring about technical and societal change: including, in this case, change in architectural form.

The notion of a direct causal correspondence between digital technologies and complex geometries (including the most general of all, topology) was built on a truism, but generalised into a fallacy. True, without computers some of those complex forms could not have been conceived, designed, measured, or built. However, computers per se do not impose shapes, nor do they articulate aesthetic preferences. One can use computers to design boxes or folds, indifferently. In fact, the story that we have been tracing indicates that the theory of folding created a cultural demand for digital design, and an environment conducive to it. Consequently, when digital design tools became available, they were embraced and adopted – and immediately put to use to process what many architects at the time most needed and wanted: folds. If we look at *Folding in Architecture* now, we cannot fail to notice that digital technologies were then the main protagonist *in absentia*. Not surprisingly, they would not remain absent for long: computers are much better at generating folds than Thom's clumsy topological diagrams. In the process, folding evolved towards a *seconda maniera* of fully digital, smooth curvilinearity. Folds became blobs.[26]

### 3 - Senility? Technologists and visionaries

As suggested above, *Folding in Architecture* contains the seeds of many developments that would mark the 1990s, and issues that were prefigured there are still actively debated. As it now appears, mathematical continuity in design and in manufacturing can be the springboard for different and, in some cases, divergent endeavors. A continuous sequence of endless variations in time may be used to capture a still frame: a one-off, a synecdoche of sorts, which can be made to stand for the rest of the sequence, and evoke the invisible. This was Eisenman's stance ten years ago and, if the forms may have changed, the principles underpinning them have not. Eisenman's frozen forms were meant to suggest movement. Similar formal statements today – regardless of some rudimentary qualities of motion and interactivity that recent technologies can confer upon buildings – are more frequently read as metaphors or figurative reminders of the new modes of making things: they may give visible form to the mostly invisible logic at work, which in time will change our production and manufacturing techniques. Architects often prefigure technical change, and artistic invention may anticipate forthcoming techno-social conventions. Such visionary anticipations of a future, digitally made environment were markedly smooth and curvilinear in the late nineties; and they may remain so for some time to come. Considering the technology for which they stand, this is not inappropriate: these technical objects should been seen as presentations, not as prototypes.

Yet, alongside this metaphor of technological change, which architectural invention may represent and even memorialize, real technological change is happening, although perhaps not so fast as the 'irrational exuberance' of the late 1990s may have led us to believe.[27] The new technological paradigm is also predicated upon continuous variations, but instead of producing one variance out of many, it posits that many variants may be produced simultaneously or sequentially. Thus, the same tools for processing mathematical continuity can be used to mass-produce the infinite variants of the same 'objectile' – at no additional cost. Continuity in this case is not set in a chronological sequence, but in a manufacturing series. At a small scale, some such technologies already exist – they are in use and they produce things. How and when they might become relevant to the general process of building remains to be seen. When this happens, for the first time in the history of the machine-made environment, forms of all types (within the limits of the objectile/object paradigm) may be mass-produced on demand, indifferently, and at the same unit price. New, non-standard, custom-made and infinitely variable

and adaptable forms will follow programs as never before. Better and cheaper objects and buildings will be made available to more people. And if this agenda may recall the moral ambitions of 20th Modernism, the architectural forms that will come out of it will most certainly not.

In a coda to his brief presentation of Shoei Yoh's topological roofs, published in 1997 in an illustrated monograph of Yoh's work, Lynn extended his interpretation of Yoh's continuity of form obtained through a multiplicity of minor variations.[28] Yoh's structures can endlessly change, morph and adapt as they are built by the assembly of non-standard parts. Let's compare with the most eloquent example of the opposite: in any given structure, whether horizontal or vertical, Mies's I-beams were all the same size, regardless of load; hence, as many engineers are keen to point out, if one section fits the load, then all others are by necessity oversized. In contrast, each individual component in Yoh's 3-D latticed trusses is only as big as it needs to be. At Mies's time, the waste of building materials caused by oversizing might have been compensated by the economies of scale obtained trough the mass-production of identical parts: one doubts that this argument might have ever been prominent in Mies's mind, but Mies's aesthetics to some extent sublimated that technical condition. Today, digital file-to-factory production systems can generate the same economies of scale with no need to mass-produce identical beams: beams can be all different – within some limits – and still be mass-produced. Economies of scale can thus be compounded by a more economical use of materials.

As Lynn points out, Yoh's use of advanced technologies and off-site prefabrication is paralleled by his adaptation of traditional building materials and artisanal modes of production. For example, some of Yoh's buildings use wood or bamboo frames and match local building know-how with computer-based design technologies. Although Yoh himself never seems to have investigated the theoretical implications of this practice, the alliance between artisanal (pre-mechanical) and digital (post-mechanical) technologies is based on solid facts and figures. The artisanal mode of production is mostly foreign to economies of scale: 2000 identical Doric capitals, or 2000 variations of the same Doric capital, come at the same unit price, as each capital is hand-made. In the digital mode, industrial economies of scale are obtained regardless of product standardisation. In both cases, the result is the same: identical reproduction has no technical rationale, nor any economic justification. When pursued manually or digitally, standardisation does not generate cheaper products, nor better-built ones. Of course one may cherish identicality for a number of other reasons, unrelated to cost or functioning. But let's put it another way. There was a time when identical reproduction, or standardization, was eminently justified: the more identical pieces one could make, the less their unit cost would be. Standardisation was then an inescapable moral and social imperative. This age of the industrial standard began with the mechanical phase of the Industrial Revolution – and ended with it.

However, as it happens, the end of the mechanical era has been proclaimed on many occasions. One of the most propitious times to proclaim the end of the first machine age was in the early 1930s of the last century, and with some logic: in 1929 the machine age seemed to have imploded – spontaneously, so to speak: a sudden but natural death. In *Technics and Civilization*, first published in 1934, Lewis Mumford disparaged all that had gone wrong with the machine age that had just crashed, which he characterized as 'paleotechnic', and heralded an imminent golden age of new machines, the 'neotechnic' age, where the evil machines of old would be replaced by new and better ones, not hard but soft machines – organic instruments of a new biotechnic economy, where man would no longer be obliged to adapt itself to the mechanical rhythm of the machine, but machines would learn to adapt themselves the dynamic flow of organic life.[29] Mumford's discourse was tantalizingly self-contradictory and included streaks of viscerally anti-modern propaganda, but in writing of an age of new machines, 'smaller, faster, brainer [sic], and more adaptable' than those of the earlier mechanical age, he seems even more than a preacher – he sounds prophetic.[30] Around the same time, Frank Lloyd Wright – then almost on the same wavelength as Mumford, and probably inspired by him – presented his anti-European blueprint for a 'disappeared city', and insisted that the industrialisation of building need not result in the standardisation of form: all buildings should be machine-made, but no two homes need be alike.[31]

In 1932 and 1934, respectively, Wright and Mumford were were probably running a little ahead of the technology of their time. Yet it is one of the most significant legacies of the publication of *Folding in Architecture* that, since 1993, we have no reason not to be aware that this time around, non-standard production has opened for business and is here to stay.

*Mario Carpo*, architectural historian and critic, is currently the Head of the Study Centre at the Canadian Centre for Architecture in Montréal. His prize-winning Architecture in the Age of Printing, *published in English by the MIT Press in 2001, is translated into several languages. Mario Carpo is the author of several books on the history of architectural theories, and of essays and articles on early-modern and contemporary topics.*

**Notes**

1 *Folding in Architecture*, Greg Lynn (ed), *Architectural Design*, Profile 102, 63, 3-4 (1993).

2 In his *Principles of Art History*, first published in 1915, the historian and philosopher of art Heinrich Wölfflin defended a cyclical view of the evolution of man-made forms, which swing from classical sobriety to Baroque fancifulness, then back to reason and so on ad infinitum. Wölfflin never characterised the Baroque, either the time specific or the timeless version of it, as an age of decline or degeneracy. Instead, he used sets of oppositions (linear and painterly, plane and recession, closed and open form, etc) through which he defined classical and Baroque phases. Heinrich Wölfflin, *Kunstgeschichtliche Grundbegriffe* (1915); English translation: *Principles of Art History*, trans MD Hottinger from seventh revised German edition (1929), G Bell and Sons (London), 1932, pp 230–5. See also Michael Podro, *The Critical Historians of Art*, Yale University Press (New Haven and London), 1982, p 140.

3 Luis Fernández-Galiano has compared the 'sharp folds of the F-117 Nighthawk Lockheed's stealth fighter' and the 'undulating profile' of the later B-2 stealth fighter made by Northrop Grumman, considering the former as representative of the 'fractured forms of deconstructivism that initiated the nineties under the wings of Derrida', and the latter as representative 'of the warped volumes of the formless current that are wrapping up the decade, referring back to Deleuze or Bataille'. Luis Fernández-Galiano, 'Split-screen. La décennie numérique', *Architecture d'Aujourd'hui*, no 325 (December 1999), pp 28–31: 30. Oddly, the technical specifications – aerodynamics and the avoidance of radar detection – would have been the same for both of these fighter planes. As architectural curvilinearity has been conspicuously ebbing and flowing in recent times, the rise of architectural flaccidity in the digital environment of the late 1990s has prompted a critical reassessment of antecedents, including some that had been overlooked until very recently. For a thorough survey of pre-blob, space-age ovoids in the 1960s and their biomorphic and technological underpinnings (mostly related to the development of plastics technology) see Georges Teyssot, 'Le songe d'un environnement bioréaliste. Ovoïdes et sphéroïdes dans l'architecture des années soixante' in *Architectures expérimentales, 1950–2000*, Collection du FRAC Centre, Éditions HYX (Orléans), 2003, pp 39–43.

4 Gilles Deleuze, *Le pli: Leibniz et le baroque*, Éditions de Minuit (Paris), 1988; English translation: *The Fold: Leibniz and the Baroque*, foreword and translation by Tom Conley, University of Minnesota Press (Minneapolis), 1993.

5 Peter D Eisenman, 'Unfolding Events: Frankfurt Rebstock and the Possibility of a New Urbanism' in Eisenman Architects, Albert Speer and Partners and Hanna/Olin, *Unfolding Frankfurt*, Ernst and Sohn (Berlin), 1991, pp 8–18; 'Oltre lo sguardo. L'architettura nell'epoca dei media elettronici' (Visions' Unfolding: Architecture in the Age of Electronic Media), *Domus*, no 734 (January 1992), pp 17–24 (frequently reprinted, most recently in Luca Galofaro, *Digital Eisenman: An Office of the Electronic Era*, Birkhauser (Basel), 1999, pp 84–9); and 'Folding in Time: The Singularity of Rebstock', *Folding in Architecture* (1993), pp 22–6.

6 See in particular Eisenman, 'Unfolding Events', p 9; 'Visions' Unfolding' (1992), p 21; and 'Folding in Time' (1993), p 24.

7 Eisenman, 'Unfolding Events', p 14.

8 Greg Lynn, 'Architectural Curvilinearity: The Folded, the Pliant and the Supple', *Folding in Architecture* (1993), pp 8–15. See in particular p 13 on 'the catastrophe diagram used by Eisenman in the Rebstock Park project … by Kipnis in the Briey project, and Shirdel in the Nara Convention Hall'.

9 Deleuze 'argues that in the mathematical studies of variation, the notion of object is change. This new object for Deleuze is no longer concerned with the framing of space, but rather a temporal modulation that implies a continual variation of matter. … No longer is an object defined by an essential form. He calls this idea of an object, an "object event". The idea of event is critical to the discussion of singularity. Event proposes a different kind of time which is outside of narrative time or dialectical time.' Eisenman, 'Folding in Time' (1993), p 24.

10 'These typologies, introduced into the system of the Fold, allow the Fold to reveal itself; the folding apparatus is invisible, purely a conceptual drawing, until it is activated by something cast into it.' Eisenman, 'Unfolding Events', p 16.

11 For a recapitulation of this discussion in essays by Michael Speaks, Greg Lynn, Jeffrey Kipnis and Brian Massumi, see Giuseppa di Cristina, 'The Topological Tendency in Architecture' in *Architecture and Science*, Wiley-Academy (London), 2001, pp 6–14, in particular p 10 and footnotes 15–18; Michael Speaks, 'It's Out There … The Formal Limits of the American Avant-garde', Hypersurface Architecture, Stephen Perella (ed), *Architectural Design*, Profile 133, 68, 5–6 (1998), pp 26–31, in particular p 29: 'Why does [Lynn's] architecture not move? … Why does his architecture stop moving when it is no longer design technique and becomes architecture?'

12 Eisenman, 'Alteka Office Building', *Folding in Architecture* (1993), p 28.

13 'Folding is only one of perhaps many strategies for dislocating vision.' Eisenman, 'Visions' Unfolding', (1992), p 24.

14 Lynn, 'Architectural Curvilinearity', p 8.

15 Frank Gehry and Philip Johnson, 'Lewis Residence, Cleveland, Ohio', *Folding in Architecture* (1993), p 69.

16 Lynn, 'Architectural Curvilinearity', p 12; Jeffrey Kipnis, 'Towards a New Architecture', *Folding in Architecture* (1993), pp 40–9: 47.

17 Stephen Perrella, 'Interview with Mark Dippe. Terminator 2', *Folding in Architecture* (1993), pp 90–93: 93.

18 See in particular Edmund Burke, *Philosophical Enquiry* (1757); William Gilpin, *Observations … relative chiefly to picturesque beauty* (1782) and *Three essays: On picturesque beauty; On picturesque travel; and On sketching landscape: to which is added a poem On landscape painting* (1792). In mathematical terms, the quality of smoothness of a line or surface is defined by the function that designates the angular coefficients of the tangents to each point of it (that is, by the first derivative of the function that describes the original line or surface).

19 Bernard Cache, 'Objectile. The Pursuit of Philosophy by Other Means', *Hypersurface Architecture II*, Stephen Perella (ed), *Architectural Design*, Profile 141, 69, 9–10 (1999), pp 67–71: 67.

20 For centuries, architects had been drawing with algebra, but now, 'CAD software enables architects to draw and sketch using calculus' Greg Lynn, *Animate Form*, Princeton Architectural Press (New York), 1999, pp 16–18.

21 Lynn, Animate Form, pp 15–16.

22 Deleuze, *Le pli*, p 26.

23 Deleuze, *Le pli*, pp 20–5.

24 Deleuze, *Le pli*, pp 22, 26.

25 Bernard Cache, *Earth Moves. The Furnishing of Territories*, transl. by Anne Boyman, ed. by Michael Speaks, MIT Press (Cambridge MA and London), 1995, p iii. 26. The official date of birth of architectural blobs (of blobs defined as such) appears to be May 1996. See Greg Lynn, 'Blobs (or Why Tectonics is Square and Topology is Groovy)', ANY 14 (May 1996), pp 58–62. For a survey of blob developments in the late 1990s see Peter Cachola Schmal (ed), *Digital Real. Blobmeister: erste gebaute Projecte*, Birkhäuser (Basel), 2001. On the early history of space-age ovoids in the 1960s, and the eponymous film that popularised the blob in 1958, see Georges Teyssot, 'Le songe d'un environnement bioréaliste', p 40.

27 See Mario Carpo, 'Post-Hype Digital Architecture. From Irrational Exuberance to Irrational Despondency', *Grey Room* 14 (forthcoming in 2004).

28 'In all of these [Shoei Yoh's] projects there is a response to the shift in the economies and techniques of construction from one of assembly-line production of a standard to the assembly-like production of a series of singular units. These projects articulate an approach to standardisation and repetition that combines a generic system of construction with slight variations of each member. This attribute is reminiscent of historic methods of craftmanship where every element could be generic in some regard while given a distinct identity in each instance … Through both manual construction and industrial fabrication [these projects] exploit the economy of what is often referred to as "custom assembly-line production".' Greg Lynn, 'Classicism and Vitality' in Anthony Iannacci (ed) *Shoei Yoh*, L'Arca Edizioni (Milan), 1997, pp 13–16: 15. See also Lynn's 'Odawara Municipal Sports Complex' in *Shoei Yoh*, pp 67–70; and 'Shoei Yoh, Odawara Municipal Sports Complex', *Folding in Architecture* (1993), p 79.

29 Lewis Mumford, *Technics and Civilization*, George Routledge and Sons (London) and Harcourt, Brace and Co (New York), 1934, especially Chapter VIII, sections 1 ('The Dissolution of "The Machine"') and 2 ('Toward an Organic Ideology'), pp 364–72.

30 'In the very act of enlarging its dominion over human thought and practice, the machine [Mumford here means the earlier, 'paleotechnic' machine] has proved to a great degree self-eliminating … This fact is fortunate for the race. It will do away with the necessity, which Samuel Butler satirically pictured in Erewhon, for forcefully extirpating the dangerous troglodytes of the earlier mechanical age. The old machines will in part die out, as the great saurians died out, to be replaced by smaller, faster, brainer [sic], and more adaptable organisms, adapted not to the mine, the battlefield and the factory, but to the positive environment of life.' Mumford, *Technics and Civilization*, p 428.

31 Frank Lloyd Wright, *The Disappearing City*, William Farquhar Payson (New York), 1932, pp 34, 45.

Architectural Design

# FOLDING IN ARCHITECTURE

*OPPOSITE:* HENRY COBB, DETAIL OF THE FIRST INTERSTATE BANK TOWER; *ABOVE:* FRANK GEHRY & PHILIP JOHNSON, LEWIS
RESIDENCE, BIRD'S-EYE VIEW OF MODEL

ACADEMY EDITIONS • LONDON

# KENNETH POWELL
## *UNFOLDING FOLDING*

During the last quarter of a century the certainties which appeared to underlay the hegemony of modernism in architecture have been under constant attack, so that what seemed beyond question – a set of immutable 'truths' – is now largely discredited. The Modern Movement was born at the CIAM Congress of 1928, when Corbusier and Gropius hammered out a persuasive, but essentially exclusive programme for architectural revolution.

Revolutionaries often end up as tyrants. What began as a liberating force became a rigid orthodoxy. In a recent exposé of the failings of the 'functionalist' gospel (*AA Files*, Autumn, 1992) Colin St John Wilson quotes Alvar Aalto to the effect that 'one of the ways to arrive at a more and more humanely built environment is to expand the concept of the 'Rational'. Aalto is identified – with Wright, Asplund, Scharoun and others – as part of 'the other tradition' of modern architecture.

Venturi's *Complexity and Contradiction* (1966) stands at the head of a series of key texts which undermined homogeneity and orthodoxy in favour of an honest acceptance of the discontinuity and disjunction which are part of all human life. More recently, Deconstruction has been seen as a basis for the revival of the humane art of architecture. With a strong philosophical base the Deconstructivist 'movement' (if ever such) was libertarian, permissive, dynamic, but rooted in the conflict which its adherents have seen as the dominant characteristic of modern urban life. As Mark Wigley put it, Deconstructivist architecture is 'devious' and 'slippery' – and disturbing. It had to disturb, to be subversive, in order to break the hold of the old order.

Deconstruction has done its job. Its jagged discordancies were shocking enough. But five years ago, when the work of seven allegedly Deconstructivist architects was shown at MOMA in New York,

none of those represented (with the exception of Frank Gehry) had built on any scale. Now all are building extensively. The new architecture of the end of the 20th century faces the problem of reconciling (as Greg Lynn suggests) the opposing goals of conflict and contradiction and of unity and reconstruction. In practice, architecture cannot be engaged in a process of permanent revolution. It has practical and formal, as well as speculative and philosophical ends to pursue.

The work reviewed here has significance as the product of a generation of architects who had previously espoused Deconstruction but now seek to address issues (especially those related to the life of the city) in which confrontation cannot be all. They have taken up the challenge of making their architecture a power on the streets, not just in the gallery and the pages of the specialist journals.

Peter Eisenman is a key figure in all this. His definition of 'weak form' paved the way for a flexible and flowing, soft-edged approach to architectural design. Eisenman now seeks a new philosophical basis for an architecture which, were it not for the inescapable Wrightian overtones, one might categorise as 'organic'.

On reflection, 'organic' is not so inappropiate as an adjective where the projects included are concerned. Just as Baroque architecture grew out of an age of conflict and violence and yet was characterised by its richly decorative, highly expressive sense of conviction, the new expressive architecture of today is moving towards a sculptural drama which is powerfully present in projects such as that of Bahram Shirdel for the Nara Convention Center ('a complex spatial unity guided by the theme of the symbiosis of history and the future'), Eisenman's Wexner Center and Emory University Arts Center, and a number of recent and forthcoming schemes by

Frank Gehry. (In this respect, the Vitra Museum was a harbinger of things to come.) There are no obvious historical references to suggest a borrowing from the Baroque, yet there are uncanny links.

In particular, as Baroque architects transformed Rome and Prague, while respecting the existing form of those cities, the new organic architects of the 1990s are passionate urbanists. Urban transformation without violent upheaval is perhaps the central theme of their work. All these architects question the relevance of post-modernist and classicist formulae for urban survival/revival, while maintaining their defiance of the old modernism.

Seen in this light, the new architecture which has evolved out of the Deconstructivist episode is vastly important for its celebration of diversity. Post-Modernism rediscovered the city but its analysis of urban form and urban life, largely in the theory of collage, has proved inadequately retrograde. Gehry, Eisenman, Shirdel and others are seeking for nothing less than a reinstatement of the expressive power of architecture which underlies its cultural and social role. Lynn's project for 'reconfiguring' the Sears Tower as part of the fabric of Chicago reflects a desire for unity and harmony through rich diversity.

This issue explores just one theme, one approach to a new pliant, flowing architecture. It is an approach that has already produced rich rewards. Yet it is merely a start. Architects, confident in their role as social artists in the best sense, will increasingly reject the old constraints in favour of an inclusive and organic way of designing which is in tune with the man-made and natural world. These projects are far from being a re-run of history: they could play a part in making history.

*Carsten Juel-Christiansen, The Passage*

# GREG LYNN
## *ARCHITECTURAL CURVILINEARITY*
## *The Folded, the Pliant and the Supple*

For the last two decades, beginning with Robert Venturi's *Complexity and Contradiction in Architecture*,[1] and Colin Rowe and Fred Koetter's *Collage City*,[2] and continuing through Mark Wigley and Philip Johnson's *Deconstructivist Architecture*, architects have been primarily concerned with the production of heterogeneous, fragmented and conflicting formal systems. These practices have attempted to embody the differences within and between diverse physical, cultural and social contexts in formal conflicts. When comparing Venturi's *Complexity and Contradiction* or *Learning from Las Vegas* with Wigley and Johnson's *Deconstruction Architecture* it is necessary to overlook many significant and distinguishing differences in order to identify at least one common theme.

Both Venturi and Wigley argue for the deployment of discontinuous, fragmented, heterogeneous and diagonal formal strategies based on the incongruities, juxtapositions and oppositions within specific sites and programmes. These disjunctions result from a logic which tends to identify the potential contradictions between dissimilar elements. A diagonal dialogue between a building and its context has become an emblem for the contradictions within contemporary culture. From the scale of an urban plan to a building detail, contexts have been mined for conflicting geometries, materials, styles, histories and programmes which are then represented in architecture as internal contradictions. The most paradigmatic architecture of the last ten years, including Robert Venturi's Sainsbury Wing of the National Gallery, Peter Eisenman's Wexner Center, Bernard Tschumi's La Villette park or the Gehry House, invests in the architectural representation of contradictions. Through contradiction, architecture represents difference in violent formal conflicts.

Contradiction has also provoked a reactionary response to formal conflict. Such resistances attempt to recover unified architectural languages that can stand against heterogeneity. Unity is constructed through one of two strategies: either by reconstructing a continuous architectural language through historical analyses (Neo-Classicism or Neo-Modernism) or by identifying local consistencies resulting from indigenous climates, materials, traditions or technologies (Regionalism). The internal orders of Neo-Classicism, Neo-Modernism and Regionalism conventionally repress the cultural and contextual discontinuities that are necessary for a logic of contradiction. In architecture, both the reaction to and representation of heterogeneity have shared an origin in contextual analysis. Both theoretical models begin with a close analysis of contextual conditions from which they proceed to evolve either a homogeneous or heterogeneous urban fabric. Neither the reactionary call for unity nor the avant-garde dismantling of it through the identification of internal contradictions seems adequate as a model for contemporary architecture and urbanism.

In response to architecture's discovery of complex, disparate, differentiated and heterogeneous cultural and formal contexts, two options have been dominant; either conflict and contradiction or unity and reconstruction. Presently, an alternative smoothness is being formulated that may escape these dialectically opposed strategies. Common to the diverse sources of this post-contradictory work – topological geometry, morphology, morphogenesis, Catastrophe Theory or the computer technology of both the defence and Hollywood film industry – are characteristics of smooth transformation involving the intensive integration of differences within a continuous yet heterogeneous system. Smooth mixtures are made up of disparate elements which maintain their integrity while being blended within a continuous field of other free elements.

Smoothing does not eradicate differences but incorporates[3] free intensities through fluid tactics of mixing and blending. Smooth mixtures are not homogeneous and therefore cannot be reduced. Deleuze describes smoothness as 'the continuous variation' and the 'continuous development of form'.[4] Wigley's critique of pure form and static geometry is inscribed within geometric conflicts and discontinuities. For Wigley, smoothness is equated with hierarchical organisation: 'the volumes have been purified – they have become smooth, classical – and the wires all converge in a single, hierarchical, vertical movement.'[5] Rather than investing in arrested conflicts, Wigley's 'slipperiness' might be better exploited by the alternative smoothness of heterogeneous mixture. For the first time perhaps, complexity might be aligned with neither unity nor contradiction but with smooth, pliant mixture.

Both pliancy and smoothness provide an escape from the two camps which would either have architecture break under the stress of difference or stand firm. Pliancy allows architecture to become involved in complexity through flexibility. It may be possible to neither repress the complex relations of differences with fixed points of resolution nor arrest them in contradictions, but sustain them through flexible, unpredicted, local connections. To arrest differences in conflicting forms often precludes many of the more complex possible connections of the forms of architecture to larger cultural fields. A more pliant architectural sensibility values alliances, rather than conflicts, between elements. Pliancy implies first an internal flexibility and second a dependence on external forces for self-definition.

If there is a single effect produced in architecture by folding, it will be the ability to integrate unrelated elements within a new continuous mixture. Culinary theory has developed both a practical and precise definition for at least three types of mixtures. The first involves the manipulation of homogeneous elements; beating, whisking and whipping change the volume but not the nature of a liquid through agitation. The second method of incorporation mixes two or more disparate elements; chopping, dicing, grinding, grating, slicing, shredding and mincing eviscerate elements into fragments. The first method agitates a single uniform ingredient, the second eviscerates disparate ingredients. Folding, creaming and blending mix smoothly multiple ingredients 'through repeated gentle overturnings without stirring or beating' in such a way that their individual characteristics are maintained.[6] For instance, an egg and chocolate are folded together so that each is a distinct layer within a continuous mixture.

Folding employs neither agitation nor evisceration but a supple layering. Likewise, folding in geology involves the sedimentation of mineral elements or deposits which become slowly bent and compacted into plateaus of strata. These strata are compressed, by external forces, into more or less continuous layers within which heterogeneous deposits are still intact in varying degrees of intensity.

A folded mixture is neither homogeneous, like whipped cream, nor fragmented, like chopped nuts, but smooth and heterogeneous. In both cooking and geology, there is no preliminary organisation which becomes folded but rather there are unrelated elements or pure intensities that are intricated through a joint manipulation. Disparate elements can be incorporated into smooth mixtures through various manipulations including fulling:

'Felt is a supple solid product that proceeds altogether differently, as an anti-fabric. It implies no separation of threads, no intertwining, only an entanglement of fibres obtained by fulling (for example, by rolling the block of fibres back and forth). What becomes entangled are the microscales of the fibres. An aggregate of intrication of this kind is in no way homogeneous; nevertheless, it is smooth and contrasts point by point with the space of fabric (it is in principle infinite, open and uninhibited in every direction; it has neither top, nor bottom, nor centre; it does not assign fixed or mobile elements but distributes a continuous variation).'[7]

The two characteristics of smooth mixtures are that they are composed of disparate unrelated elements and that these free intensities become intricated by an external force exerted upon them jointly. Intrications are intricate connections. They are intricate, they affiliate local surfaces of elements with one another by negotiating interstitial rather than internal connections. The heterogeneous elements within a mixture have no proper relation with one another. Likewise, the external force that intricates these elements with one another is outside of the individual elements control or prediction.

## Viscous Mixtures

Unlike an architecture of contradictions, superpositions and accidental collisions, pliant systems are capable of engendering unpredicted connections with contextual, cultural, programmatic, structural and economic contingencies by vicissitude. Vicissitude is often equated with vacillation, weakness[8] and indecisiveness but more importantly these characteristics are frequently in the service of a tactical cunning.[9] Vicissitude is a quality of being mutable or changeable in response to both favourable and unfavourable situations that occur by chance. Vicissitudinous events result from events that are neither arbitrary nor predictable but seem to be accidental. These events are made possible by a collision of internal motivations with external forces. For instance, when an accident occurs the victims immediately identify the forces contributing to the accident and begin to assign blame. It is inevitable however, that no single element can be made responsible for any accident as these events occur by vicissitude; a confluence of particular influences at a particular time makes the outcome of an accident possible. If any element participating in such a confluence of local forces is altered the nature of the event will change. In *A Thousand Plateaus*, Spinoza's concept of 'a thousand vicissitudes' is linked with Gregory Bateson's 'continuing plateau of intensity' to describe events which incorporate unpredictable events through intensity. These occurrences are difficult to localise, difficult to identify.[10] Any logic of vicissitude is dependent on both an intrication of local intensities and the exegetic pressure exerted on those elements by external contingencies. Neither the intrications nor the forces which put them into relation are predictable from within any single system. Connections by vicissitude develop identity through the exploitation of local adjacencies and their affiliation with external forces. In this sense, vicissitudinous mixtures become cohesive through a logic of viscosity.

Viscous fluids develop internal stability in direct proportion to the external pressures exerted upon them. These fluids behave with two types of viscidity. They exhibit both internal cohesion and adhesion to external elements as their viscosity increases. Viscous fluids begin to behave less like liquids and more like sticky solids as the pressures upon them intensify. Similarly, viscous solids are capable of yielding continually under stress so as not to shear.

Viscous space would exhibit a related cohesive stability in response to adjacent pressures and a stickiness or adhesion to adjacent elements. Viscous relations such as these are not reducible to any single or holistic organisation. Forms of viscosity and pliability cannot be examined outside of the *vicissitudinous* connections and forces with which their deformation is intensively involved. The nature of pliant forms is that they are sticky and flexible. Things tend to adhere to them. As pliant forms are manipulated and deformed the things that stick to their surfaces become incorporated within their interiors.

## Curving away from Deconstructivism

Along with a group of younger architects, the projects that best represent pliancy, not coincidentally, are being produced by many of the same architects previously involved in the valorisation of contradictions. Deconstructivism theorised the world as a site of differences in order that architecture could represent these contradictions in form. This contradictory logic is beginning to soften in order to exploit more fully the particularities of urban and cultural contexts. This is a reasonable transition, as the Deconstructivists originated their projects with the internal discontinuities they uncovered within buildings and sites. These same architects are beginning to employ urban strategies which exploit discontinuities, not by representing them in formal collisions, but by affiliating them with one another through continuous flexible systems.

Just as many of these architects have already been inscribed within a Deconstructivist style of diagonal forms, there will surely be those who would enclose their present work within a Neo-Baroque or even Expressionist style of curved forms. However, many of the formal similitudes suggest a far richer 'logic of curvilinearity'[11] that can be characterised by the involvement of outside forces in the development of form. If internally motivated and homogeneous systems were to extend in straight lines, curvilinear developments would result from the incorporation of external influences. Curvilinearity can put into relation the collected projects in this publication, Gilles Deleuze's *The Fold: Leibniz and the Baroque* and René Thom's catastrophe diagrams. The smooth spaces described by these continuous yet differentiated systems result from curvilinear sensibilities that are capable of complex deformations in response to programmatic, structural, economic, aesthetic, political and contextual influences. This is not to imply that intensive curvature is more politically correct than an uninvolved formal logic, but rather, that a cunning pliability is often more effective through smooth incorporation than contradiction and conflict. Many cunning tactics are aggressive in nature. Whether insidious or ameliorative these kinds of cunning connections discover new possibilities for organisation. A logic of curvilinearity argues for an active involvement with external events in the folding, bending and curving of form.

Already in several Deconstructivist projects are latent suggestions of smooth mixture and curvature. For instance, the Gehry House is typically portrayed as representing materials and forms already present within, yet repressed by, the suburban neighbourhood: sheds, chain-link fences, exposed plywood, trailers, boats and recreational vehicles. The house is described as an 'essay on the convoluted relationship between the conflict within and between forms . . . which were not imported to but emerged from within the house.'[12] The house is seen to provoke conflict within the neighbourhood due to its public representation of hidden aspects of its context. The Gehry House violates the neighbourhood from within. Despite the dominant appeal of the house to contradictions, a less contradictory and more pliant reading of the house is possible as a new organisation emerges between the existing house and Gehry's addition. A dynamic stability develops with the mixing of the original and the addition. Despite the contradictions between elements possible points of connection are exploited. Rather than valorise the conflicts the house engenders, as has been done in both academic and popular publications, a more pliant logic would identify, not the degree of violation, but the degree to which new connections were exploited. A new intermediate organisation occurs In the Gehry House by vicissitude from the affiliation of the existing house and its addition. Within the discontinuities of Deconstructivism there are inevitable unforeseen moments of cohesion.

Similarly, Peter Eisenman's Wexner Center is conventionally portrayed as a collision of the conflicting geometries of the campus, city and armoury which once stood adjacent to the site. These contradictions are represented by the diagonal collisions between the two grids and the masonry towers. Despite the disjunctions and discontinuities between these three disparate systems, Eisenman's project has suggested recessive readings of continuous non-linear systems of connection. Robert Somol[13] identifies such a system of Deleuzian rhizomatous connections between armoury and grid. The armoury and diagonal grids are shown by Somol to participate in a hybrid L-movement that organises the main gallery space. Somol's schizophrenic analysis is made possible by, yet does not emanate from within, a Deconstructivist logic of contradiction and conflict. The force of this Deleuzian schizo-analytic model is its ability to maintain multiple organisations simultaneously. In Eisenman's project the tower and grid need not be seen as mutually exclusive or in contradiction. Rather, these disparate elements may be seen as distinct elements co-present within a composite mixture. Pliancy does not result from and is not in line with the previous architectural logic of contradiction, yet it is capable of exploiting many conflicting combinations for the possible connections that are overlooked. Where *Deconstructivist Architecture* was seen to exploit external forces in the familiar name of contradiction and conflict, recent pliant projects by many of these architects exhibit a more fluid logic of connectivity.

## Immersed in Context

The contradictory architecture of the last two decades has evolved primarily from highly differentiated, heterogeneous contexts within which conflicting, contradictory and discontinuous buildings were sited. An alternative involvement with heterogeneous contexts could be affiliated, compliant and continuous. Where complexity and contradiction arose previously from inherent contextual conflicts, present attempts are being made to fold smoothly specific locations, materials and programmes into architecture while maintaining their individual identity.

This recent work may be described as being compliant; in a state of being plied by forces beyond control. The projects are formally folded, pliant and supple in order to incorporate their contexts with minimal resistance. Again, this characterisation should not imply flaccidity but a cunning submissiveness that is capable of bending rather than breaking. Compliant tactics, such as these, assume neither an absolute coherence nor cohesion between discrete elements but a system of provisional, intensive, local connections between free elements. Intensity describes the dynamic internalisation and incorporation of external influences into a pliant system. Distinct from a whole organism – to which nothing can be added or subtracted – intensive organisations continually invite external influences within their internal limits so that they might extend their influence through the affiliations they make. A two-fold deterritorialisation, such as this, expands by internalising external forces. This expansion through incorporation is an urban alternative to either the infinite extension of International Modernism, the uniform fabric of Contextualism or the conflicts of Post-Modernism and Deconstructivism. Folded, pliant and supple architectural forms invite exigencies and contingencies in both their deformation and their reception.

In both *Learning from Las Vegas* and *Deconstructivist Architecture*, urban contexts provided rich sites of difference. These differences are presently being exploited for their ability to engender multiple lines of local connections rather than lines of conflict. These affiliations are not predictable by any contextual orders but occur by vicissitude. Here, urban fabric has no value or meaning beyond the connections that are made within it. Distinct from earlier urban sensibilities that generalised broad formal codes, the collected projects develop local, fine grain, complex systems of intrication. There is no general urban strategy common to these projects, only a kind of tactical mutability. These folded, pliant and supple forms of urbanism are neither in deference to nor in defiance of their contexts but exploit them by turning them within their own twisted and curvilinear logics.

## The Supple and Curvilinear

1 supple\ *adj* [ME *souple*, fr OF, fr L *supplic-*, *supplex* submissive, suppliant, lit, bending under, fr *sub* + *plic-* (akin to *plicare* to fold) - more at PLY] 1a: compliant often to the point of obsequiousness b: readily adaptable or responsive to new situations 2a: capable of being bent or folded without creases, cracks or breaks: PLIANT b: able to perform bending or twisting movements with ease and grace: LIMBER c: easy and fluent without stiffness or awkwardness.[14]

At an urban scale, many of these projects seem to be somewhere between contexturalism and expressionism. Their supple forms are neither geometrically exact nor arbitrarily figural. For example, the curvilinear figures of Shoei Yoh's roof structures are anything but decorative but also resist being reduced to a pure geometric figure. Yoh's supple roof structures exhibit a logic of curvilinearity as they are continuously differentiated according to contingencies. The exigencies of structural span lengths, beam depths, lighting, lateral loading, ceiling height and view angles influence the form of the roof structure. Rather than averaging these requirements within a mean or minimum dimension they are precisely maintained by an anexact yet rigorous geometry. Exact geometries are eidetic; they can be reproduced identically at any time by anyone. In this regard, they must be capable of being reduced to fixed mathematical quantities. Inexact geometries lack the precision and rigor necessary for measurement.

Anexact geometries, as described by Edmund Husserl,[15] are those geometries which are irreducible yet rigorous. These geometries can be determined with precision yet cannot be reduced to average points or dimensions. Anexact geometries often appear to be merely figural in this regard. Unlike exact geometries, it is meaningless to repeat identically an anexact geometric figure outside of the specific context within which it is situated. In this regard, anexact figures cannot be easily translated.

Jeffrey Kipnis has argued convincingly that Peter Eisenman's Columbus Convention Center has become a canonical model for the negotiation of differentiated urban fringe sites through the use of near figures.[16] Kipnis identifies the disparate systems informing the Columbus Convention Center including: a single volume of inviolate programme of a uniform shape and height larger than two city blocks, an existing fine grain fabric of commercial buildings and network of freeway interchanges that plug into the gridded streets of the central business district. Eisenman's project drapes the large rectilinear volume of the convention hall with a series of supple vermiforms. These elements become involved with the train tracks to the north-east, the highway to the south-east and the pedestrian scale of High Street to the west. The project incorporates the multiple scales, programmes and pedestrian and automotive circulation of a highly differentiated urban context. Kipnis' canonisation of a form which is involved with such specific contextual and programmatic contingencies seems to be frustrated from the beginning. The effects of a pliant urban mixture such as this can only be evaluated by the connections that it makes. Outside of specific contexts, curvature ceases to be intensive. Where the Wexner

Center, on the same street in the same city, represents a monumental collision, the Convention Center attempts to disappear by connection between intervals within its context; where the Wexner Center de-stabilises through contradictions the Convention Center does so by subterfuge.

In a similar fashion Frank Gehry's Guggenheim Museum in Bilbao, Spain covers a series of orthogonal gallery spaces with flexible tubes which respond to the scales of the adjacent roadways, bridges, the Bilbao River and the existing medieval city. Akin to the Vitra Museum, the curvilinear roof forms of the Bilbao Guggenheim integrate the large rectilinear masses of gallery and support space with the scale of the pedestrian and automotive contexts.

The unforeseen connections possible between differentiated sites and alien programmes require conciliatory, complicit, pliant, flexible and often cunning tactics. Presently, numerous architects are involving the heterogeneities, discontinuities and differences inherent within any cultural and physical context by aligning formal flexibility with economic, programmatic and structural compliancy. A multitude of *pli* based words – folded, pliant, supple, flexible, plaited, pleated, plicating, complicitous, compliant, complaisant, complicated, complex and multiplicitous to name a few – can be invoked to describe this emerging urban sensibility of intensive connections.

## The Pliant and Bent

pliable\ *adj* [ME fr *plier* to bend, fold-more at PLY] 1a: supple enough to bend freely or repeatedly without breaking b: yielding readily to others: COMPLAISANT 2: adjustable to varying conditions: ADAPTABLE *syn* see PLASTIC *ant* obstinate.[17]

John Rajchman, in reference to Gilles Deleuze's book *Le Pli* has already articulated an affinity between complexity, or *plex*-words, and folding, or plic-words, in the Deleuzian paradigm of 'perplexing plications' or 'perplication'.[18] The plexed and the plied can be seen in a tight knot of complexity and pliancy. Plication involves the folding in of external forces. Complication involves an intricate assembly of these extrinsic particularities into a complex network. In biology, complication is the act of an embryo folding in upon itself as it becomes more complex. To become complicated is to be involved in multiple complex, intricate connections. Where Post-Modernism and Deconstructivism resolve external influences of programme,

use, economy and advertising through contradiction, compliancy involves these external forces by knotting, twisting, bending and folding them within form.

Pliant systems are easily bent, inclined or influenced. An anatomical 'plica' is a single strand within multiple 'plicae'. It is a multiplicity in that it is both one and many simultaneously. These elements are bent along with other elements into a composite, as in matted hair(s). Such a bending together of elements is an act of multiple plication or multiplication rather than mere addition. Plicature involves disparate elements with one another through various manipulations of bending, twisting, pleating, braiding and weaving through external force. In RAA Um's Croton Aqueduct project a single line following the subterranean water supply for New York City is pulled through multiple disparate programmes which are adjacent to it and which cross it. These programmatic elements are braided and bent within the continuous line of recovered public space which stretches nearly 20 miles into Manhattan. In order to incorporate these elements the line itself is deflected and reoriented, continually changing its character along its length. The seemingly singular line becomes populated by finer programmatic elements. The implications of *Le Pli* for architecture involve the proliferation of possible connections between free entities such as these.

A plexus is a multi-linear network of interweavings, intertwinings and intrications; for instance, of nerves or blood vessels. The complications of a plexus – what could best be called complexity – arise from its irreducibility to any single organisation. A *plexus* describes a multiplicity of local connections within a single continuous system that remains open to new motions and fluctuations. Thus, a plexial event cannot occur at any discrete point. A multiply plexed system – a complex – cannot be reduced to mathematical exactitude, it must be described with rigorous probability. Geometric systems have a distinct character once they have been plied; they exchange fixed co-ordinates for dynamic relations across surfaces.

## Alternative types of transformation

Discounting the potential of earlier geometric diagrams of probability, such as Buffon's *Needle Problem*,[19] D'Arcy Thompson provides perhaps the first geometric description of variable deformation as an instance of discontinuous morphological development. His cartesian deformations, and their use of flexible topological rubber sheet geometry, suggest an alternative to the static morphological transformations of autonomous architectural types. A comparison of the typological and transformational systems of Thompson and Rowe illustrates two radically different conceptions of continuity. Rowe's is fixed, exact, striated, identical and static, where Thompson's is dynamic, anexact, smooth, differentiated and stable.

Both Rudolf Wittkower – in his analysis of the Palladian villas of 1949[20] – and Rowe – in his comparative analysis of Palladio and Le Corbusier of 1947[21] – uncover a consistent organisational type: the nine-square grid. In Wittkower's analysis of 12 Palladian villas the particularities of each villa accumulate (through what Edmund Husserl has termed variations) to generate a fixed, identical spatial type (through what could best be described as phenomenological reduction). The typology of this 'Ideal Villa' is used to invent a consistent deep structure underlying Le Corbusier's Villa Stein at Garche and Palladio's Villa Malcontenta. Wittkower and Rowe discover the exact geometric structure of this type in all villas in particular. This fixed type becomes a constant point of reference within a series of variations.

Like Rowe, Thompson is interested in developing a mathematics of species categories, yet his system depends on a dynamic and fluid set of geometric relations. The deformations of a provisional type define a supple constellation of geometric correpondences. Thompson uses the initial type as a mere provision for a dynamic system of transformations that occur in connection with larger environmental forces. Thompson's method of discontinuous development intensively involves external forces in the deformation of morphological types. The flexible type is able to both indicate the general morphological structure of a species while indicating its discontinuous development through the internalisation of heretofore external forces within the system.[22] For instance, the enlargement of a fish's eye is represented by the flexing of a grid. This fluctuation, when compared to a previous position of the transformational type, establishes a relation between water depth and light intensity as those conditions are involved in the formal differences between fish. The flexing grid of relations cannot be arrested

at any moment and therefore has the capacity to describe both a general type and the particular events which influence its development. Again, these events are not predictable or reducible to any fixed point but rather begin to describe a probable zone of co-present forces; both internal and external. Thompson presents an alternative type of inclusive stability, distinct from the exclusive stasis of Rowe's nine-square grid. The supple geometry of Thompson is capable of both bending under external forces and folding those forces internally. These transformations develop through discontinuous involution rather than continuous evolution.

The morphing effects used in the contemporary advertising and film industry may already have something in common with recent developments in architecture. These mere images have concrete influences on space, form, politics and culture; for example, the physical morphing of Michael Jackson's body, including the transformation of his form through various surgeries and his surface through skin bleaching and lightening. These physical effects and their implications for the definition of gender and race were only later represented in his recent video *Black & White*. In this video multiple genders, ethnicities and races are mixed into a continuous sequence through the digital morphing of video images. It is significant that Jackson is not black *or* white but black *and* white, not male *or* female but male *and* female. His simultaneous differences are characteristic of a desire for smoothness; to become heterogeneous yet continuous. Physical morphing, such as this, is monstrous because smoothness eradicates the interval between what Thompson refers to as discriminant characteristics without homogenising the mixture. Such a continuous system is neither an assembly of discrete fragments nor a whole.[23] With Michael Jackson, the flexible geometric mechanism with which his video representation is constructed comes from the same desire which aggressively reconstructs his own physical form. Neither the theory, the geometry or the body proceed from one another; rather, they participate in a desire for smooth transformation. Form, politics and self-identity are intricately connected in this process of deformation.

A similar comparison might be made between the liquid mercury man in the film *Terminator 2* and the Peter Lewis House by Frank Gehry and Philip Johnson. The Hollywood special effects sequences allow

the actor to both become and disappear into virtually any form. The horror of the film results not from ultra-violence, but from the ability of the antagonist to pass through and occupy the grids of floors, prison bars and other actors. Computer technology is capable of constructing intermediate images between any two fixed points resulting in a smooth transformation. These smooth effects calculate with probability the interstitial figures between fixed figures. Furthermore, the morphing process is flexible enough that multiple between states are possible. Gehry's and Johnson's Peter Lewis House is formulated from multiple flexible forms. The geometry of these forms is supple and can accommodate smooth curvilinear deformation along their length. Not only are these forms capable of bending to programmatic, structural and environmental concerns, as is the roof of Shoei Yoh's roof structures, but they can deflect to the contours and context of the site, similar to Peter Eisenman's Columbus Convention Center and RAA Um's Croton Aqueduct project.    Furthermore, the Lewis House maintains a series of discrete figural fragments – such as boats and familiar fish – within the diagrams of D'Arcy Thompson, which are important to both the morphing effects of Industrial Light and Magic and the morphogenetic diagrams of René Thom. Gehry's supple geometry is capable of smooth, heterogeneous continuous deformation. Deformation is made possible by the flexibility of topological geometry in response to external events, as smooth space is intensive and continuous. Thompson's curvilinear logic suggests deformation in response to unpredictable events outside of the object. Forms of bending, twisting or folding are not superfluous but result from an intensive curvilinear logic which seeks to internalise cultural and contextural forces within form. In this manner events become intimately involved with particular rather than ideal forms. These flexible forms are not mere representations of differential forces but are deformed by their environment.

## Folding and other catastrophes for architecture

3 fold vb [ME *folden*, fr. OE *foaldan*; akin to OHG *faldan* to fold, Gk di *plasios* twofold] vt 1: to lay one part over another part, 2: to reduce the length or bulk of by doubling over, 3: to clasp together: ENTWINE, 4: to clasp or em-brace closely: EMBRACE, 5: to bend (as a rock) into folds 6: to incorporate (a food ingredient) into a mixture by repeated gentle overturnings without stirring or beating, 7: to bring to an end.[24]

Philosophy has already identified the displacement presently occurring to the Post-Modern paradigm of complexity and contradiction in architecture, evidenced by John Rajchman's *Out of the Fold* and *Perplications*. Rajchman's text is not a manifesto for the development of new architectural organisations, but responds to the emergence of differing kinds of complexity being developed by a specific architect. His essays inscribe spatial innovations developed in architecture within larger intellectual and cultural fields. Rajchman both illuminates Peter Eisenman's architectural practice through an explication of *Le Pli* and is forced to reconsider Deleuze's original argument concerning Baroque space by the alternative spatialities of Eisenman's Rebstock Park project. The dominant aspect of the project which invited Rajchman's attention to folding was the employment of one of René Thom's catastrophe diagrams in the design process.

Despite potential protestations to the contrary, it is more than likely that Thom's catastrophe nets entered into the architecture of Carsten Juel-Christiansen's Die Anhalter Faltung, Peter Eisenman's Rebstock Park, Jeffrey Kipnis' Unite de Habitation at Briey installation and Bahram Shirdel's Nara Convention Hall as a mere formal technique. Inevitably, architects and philosophers alike would find this in itself a catastrophe for all concerned. Yet, their use illustrates that at least four architects simultaneously found in Thom's diagrams a formal device for an alternative description of spatial complexity. The kind of complexity engendered by this alliance with Thom is substantially different than the complexity provided by either Venturi's decorated shed or the more recent conflicting forms of Deconstructivism. Topological geometry in general, and the catastrophe diagrams in particular, deploy disparate forces on a continuous surface within which more or less open systems of connection are possible.

'Topology considers superficial structures susceptible to continuous transformations which easily change their form, the most interesting geometric properties common to all modification being studied. Assumed is an abstract material of ideal deformability which can be deformed, with the exception of disruption.'

These geometries bend and stabilise with viscosity under pressure. Where one would expect that an architect looking at catastrophes would be interested in conflicts, ironically, architects are finding new forms of dynamic stability in these diagrams. The mutual interest in Thom's diagrams points to a desire to be involved with events which they cannot predict. The primary innovation made by those diagrams is the geometric modelling of a multiplicity of possible co-present events at any moment. Thom's morphogenesis engages seemingly random events with mathematical probability.

Thom's nets were developed to describe catastrophic events. What is common to these events is an inability to define exactly the moment at which a catastrophe occurs. This loss of exactitude is replaced by a geometry of multiple probable relations. With relative precision, the diagrams define potential catastrophes through cusps rather than fixed co-ordinates. Like any simple graph, Thom's diagrams deploy X and Y forces across two axes of a gridded plane. A uniform plane would provide the potential for only a single point of intersection between any two X and Y co-ordinates. The supple topological surface of Thom's diagrams is capable of enfolding in multiple dimensions. Within these folds, or cusps, zones of proximity are contained. As the topological surface folds over and into itself multiple possible points of intersection are possible at any moment in the Z dimension. These co-present Z-dimensional zones are possible because the topological geometry captures space within its surface. Through proximity and adjacency various vectors of force begin to imply these intensive event zones. In catastrophic events there is not a single fixed point at which a catastrophe occurs but rather a zone of potential events that are described by these cusps. The cusps are defined by multiple possible interactions implying, with more or less probability, multiple fluid thresholds. Thom's geometric plexus organises disparate forces in order to describe possible types of connections.

If there is a single dominant effect of the French word *pli*, it is its resistance to being translated into any single term. It is precisely the formal manipulations of folding that are capable of incorporating manifold external forces and elements within form, yet *Le Pli* undoubtedly risks being translated into architecture as mere folded figures. In architecture, folded forms risk quickly becoming a sign for catastrophe. The success of the architects who are folding should not be based on their ability to represent catastrophe theory in architectural form. Rather, the topological

geometries, in connection with the probable events they model, present a flexible system for the organisation of disparate elements within continuous spaces. Yet, these smooth systems are highly differentiated by cusps or zones of co-presence. The catastrophe diagram used by Eisenman in the Rebstock Park project destabilises the way that the buildings meet the ground. It smooths the landscape and the building by turning both into one another along cusps. The diagrams used by Kipnis in the Briey project, and Shirdel in the Nara Convention Hall, develop an interstitial space contained simultaneously within two folded cusps. This geometrically blushed surface exists within two systems at the same moment and in this manner presents a space of co-presence with multiple adjacent zones of proximity.

Before the introduction of either Deleuze or Thom to architecture, folding was developed as a formal tactic in response to problems presented by the exigencies of commercial development. Henry Cobb has argued in both the *Charlottesville Tapes* and his *Note on Folding* for a necessity to both dematerialise and differentiate the massive homogeneous volumes dictated by commercial development in order to bring them into relation with finer grain heterogeneous urban conditions. His first principle for folding is a smoothing of elements across a shared surface. The facade of the John Hancock Tower is smoothed into a continuous surface so that the building might disappear into its context through reflection rather than mimicry. Any potential for replicating the existing context was precluded by both the size of the contiguous floor plates required by the developer and the economic necessity to construct the building's skin from glass panels. Folding became the method by which the surface of a large homogeneous volume could be differentiated while remaining continuous. This tactic acknowledges that the existing fabric and the developer tower are essentially of different species by placing their differences in mixture, rather than contradiction, through the manipulation of a pliant skin.

Like the John Hancock Building, the Allied Bank Tower begins with the incorporation of glass panels and metal frames into a continuous folded surface. The differentiation of the folded surface, through the simultaneous bending of the glass and metal, brings those elements together on a continuous plane. The manipulations of the material surface proliferate folding and bending effects in the massing of the building. The alien building becomes a continuous surface of disappearance that both diffracts and reflects the context through complex manipulations of folding. In the recent films *Predator* and *Predator II*, a similar alien is capable of disappearing into both urban and jungle environments, not through cubist camouflage[25] but by reflecting and diffracting its environment like an octopus or chameleon. The contours between an object and its context are obfuscated by forms which become translucent, reflective and diffracted. The alien gains mobility by cloaking its volume in a folded surface of disappearance. Unlike the 'decorated shed' or 'building board' which mimics its context with a singular sign, folding diffuses an entire surface through a shimmering reflection of local adjacent and contiguous particulari- ties. For instance, there is a significant difference between a small fish which represents itself as a fragment of a larger fish through the figure of a large eye on its tail, and a barracuda which becomes like the liquid in which it swims through a diffused reflection of its context. The first strategy invites deceitful detection where the second uses stealth to avoid detection. Similarly, the massive volume of the Allied Bank Tower situates itself within a particular discontinuous locale by cloaking itself in a folded reflected surface. Here, cunning stealth is used as a way of involving contex- tual forces through the manipulation of a surface. The resemblance of folded architecture to the stealth bomber results not from a similarity between military and architectural technologies or intentions but rather from a tactical disappearance[26] of a volume through the manipulation of a surface. This disappearance into the fold is neither insidious nor innocent but merely a very effective tactic.

Like Henry Cobb, Peter Eisenman introduces a fold as a method of disappear- ing into a specific context. Unlike Cobb, who began with a logic of construction, Eisenman aligns the fold with the urban contours of the Rebstock Park. The repeti- tive typologies of housing and office buildings are initially deployed on the site in a more or less functionalist fashion; then a topological net derived from Thom's Butterfly net is aligned to the perimeter of the site and pushed through the typological bars. This procedure differentiates the uniform bars in response to the global morphology of the site. In this manner the manifestation of the fold is in the incorpora-

tion of differences – derived from the morphology of the site – into the homogene- ous typologies of the housing and office blocks. Both Eisenman's local differentia- tion of the building types by global folding, and Cobb's local folding across construc- tional elements which globally differentiates each floor plate and the entire massing of the building are effective. Cobb and Eisenman 'animate' homogeneous organi- sations that were seemingly given to the architect – office tower and *siedlung* – with the figure of a fold. The shared principle of folding identified by both Eisenman and Cobb, evident in their respective texts, is the ability to differentiate the inherited homogeneous organisations of both Modernism (Eisenman's *seidlung*) and commercial development (Cobb's tower). This differentiation of known types of space and organisation has something in common with Deleuze's delimitation of folding in architecture within the Baroque. Folding heterogeneity into known typologies renders those organisations more smooth and more intensive so that they are better able to incorporate disparate elements within a continuous system. Shirdel's use of Thom's diagrams is quite interesting as the catastrophe sections do not animate an existing organisation. Rather, they begin as merely one system among three others. The convention halls float within the envelope of the building as they are supported by a series of transverse structural walls whose figure is derived from Thom's nets. This mixture of systems, supported by the catastrophe sections, generates a massive residual public space at the ground floor of the building. In Shirdel's project the ma- nipulations of folding, in both the catastro- phe sections and the building envelope, incorporate previously unrelated elements into a mixture. The space between the theatres, the skin and the lateral structural walls is such a space of mixture and intrication.

With structure itself, Chuck Hoberman is capable of transforming the size of domes and roofs through a folding structural mechanism. Hoberman develops adjust- able structures whose differential move- ments occurs through the dynamic transfor- mation of flexible continuous systems. The movements of these mechanisms are determined both by use and structure. Hoberman's structural mechanisms develop a system of smooth transformation in two ways. The Iris dome and sphere projects transform their size while maintain- ing their shape. This flexibility of size within

the static shape of the stadium is capable of supporting new kinds of events. The patented tiling patterns transform both the size and shape of surfaces, developing local secondary pockets of space and enveloping larger primary volumes.

So far in architecture, Deleuze's, Cobb's, Eisenman's and Hoberman's discourse inherits dominant typologies of organisation into which new elements are folded. Within these activities of folding it is perhaps more important to identify those new forms of local organisation and occupation which inhabit the familiar types of the Latin cross church, the *siedlung*, the office tower and the stadium, rather than the disturbances visited on those old forms of organisation. Folding can occur in both the organisations of old forms and the free intensities of unrelated elements, as is the case with Shirdel's project. Likewise, other than folding, there are several manipulations of elements engendering smooth, heterogene- ous and intensive organisation.

Despite the differences between these practices, they share a sensibility that resists cracking or breaking in response to external pressures. These tactics and strategies are all com*pli*ant to, com*pli*cated by, and com*pli*cit with external forces in manners which are: submissive, suppliant, adaptable, contingent, responsive, fluent, and yielding through involvement and incorporation. The attitude which runs throughout this collection of projects and essays is the shared attempt to place seemingly disparate forces into relation through strategies which are externally plied. Perhaps, in this regard only, there are many opportunities for architecture to be effected by Gilles Deleuze's book *Le Pli*. The formal characteristics of pliancy – anexact forms and topological geometries primarily – can be more viscous and fluid in response to exigencies. They maintain formal integrity through deformations which do not internally cleave or shear but through which they connect, incorporate and affiliate productively. Cunning and viscous systems such as these gain strength through flexible connections that occur by vicissitude. If the collected projects within this publication do have certain formal affinities, it is as a result of a folding out of formalism into a world of external influ- ences. Rather than speak of the forms of folding autonomously, it is important to maintain a logic rather than a style of curvilinearity. The formal affinities of these projects result from their pliancy and ability to deform in response to particular contingencies. What is being asked in different ways by the group of architects and theorists in this publication is: How can architecture be configured as a complex system into which external particularities are already found to be plied?

**Notes**

1 Venturi, Robert *Complexity and Contradiction in Architecture* (New York: Museum of Modern Art Papers on Architecture, 1966).

2 Two ideas were introduced in this text that seem extremely relevant to contemporary architecture: typological deformation and the continuity between objects and contexts. Both of these concepts receded when compared with the dominant ideas of *collision cities* and the dialectic of urban *figure/ground* relationships. Curiously, they illustrate typological deformations in both Baroque and early modern architecture: 'However, Asplund's play with assumed contingencies and assumed absolutes, brilliant though it may be, does seem to involve mostly strategies of response; and, in considering problems of the object, it may be useful to consider the admittedly ancient technique of deliberately *distorting* what is also presented as the *ideal* type. So the reading of Saint Agnese *continuously fluctuates between* an interpretation of the building as *object* and the building as *texture* . . . Note this type of strategy combines local concessions with a declaration of independence from anything local and specific.' p77.

3 See Sanford Kwinter and Jonathan Crary 'Foreword' *Zone 6: Incorporations* (New York: Urzone Books, 1992), pp12-15.

4 Deleuze, Gilles *A Thousand Plateaus: Capitalism and Schizophrenia* (Minneapolis: University of Minnesota Press, 1987), p478.

5 Wigley, Mark *Deconstructivist Architecture*, p15.

6 Cunningham, Marion *The Fannie Farmer Cookbook*, 13th edition (New York: Alfred A Knopf, 1990) pp41-47.

7 Deleuze, Gilles *Plateaus*, pp475-6.

8 An application of vicissitude to Kipnis' logic of undecidability and weak form might engender a cunning logic of non-linear affiliations. This seems apt given the reference to both undecidability and weakness in the definition of vicissitudes.

9 Ann Bergren's discussions of the *metis* in architecture is an example of cunning manipulations of form. For an alternative reading of these tactics in Greek art also see Jean-Pierre Vernant.

10 Deleuze, *Plateaus*, p256.

11 This concept has been developed by Leibniz and has many resonances with Sanford Kwinter's discussions of biological space and epigenesis as they relate to architecture and Catherine Ingraham's logic of the swerve and the animal lines of beasts of burden.

12 Wigley, Mark *Deconstructivist Architecture*, p22.

13 See 'O-O' by Robert Somol in the *Wexner Center for the Visual Arts* special issue of *Architectural Design* (London: Academy Editions, 1990).

14 *Webster's New Collegiate Dictionary* (Springfield, Mass: G&C Merriam Company, 1977), p1170.

15 Husserl, Edmund '*The Origin of Geometry*' *Edmund Husserl's Origin of Geometry: An Introduction* by Jacques Derrida (Lincoln: University of Nebraska Press, 1989).

16 See *Fetish* edited by Sarah Whiting, Edward Mitchell & Greg Lynn (New York: Princeton Architectural Press, 1992), pp158-173.

17 *Webster's*, p883.

18 Rajchman identifies an inability in contexualism to 'Index the complexifications of urban space'. Rajchman, John, 'Perplications: On the Space and Time of Rebstock Park,' *Unfolding Frankfurt* (Berlin: Ernst & Sohn Verlag, 1991), p21.

19 A similar exchange, across disciplines through geometry, occurred in France in the mid-18th century with the development of probable geometries. Initially there was a desire to describe chance events with mathematical precision. This led to the development of a geometric model that subsequently opened new fields of study in other disciplines. The mathematical interests in probability of the professional gambler Marquis de Chevalier influenced Comte de Buffon to develop the geometric description of the *Needle Problem*. This geometric model of probability was later elaborated in three-dimensions by the geologist Dellese and became the foundation for nearly all of the present day anatomical descriptions that utilise serial transactions: including CAT scan, X-Ray and PET technologies. For a more elaborate discussion of these exchanges and the impact of related probable and anexact geometries on architectural space refer to my forthcoming article in *NY Magazine no 1* (New York: Rizzoli International, 1993).

20 Wittkower, Rudolf, *Architectural Principles in the Age of Humanism* (New York: WW Norton & Co 1971).

21 Rowe, Colin *Mathematics of the Ideal Villa and Other Essays* (Cambridge: MIT Press, 1976).

22 For an earlier instance of discontinuous development based on environmental forces and co-evolution, in reference to dynamic variation, see William Bateson, *Materials for the Study of Variation: Treated with Especial Regard to Discontinuity in the Origin of Species* (Baltimore: John Hopkins University Press, 1894).

23 Erwin Panofsky has provided perhaps the finest example of this kind of heterogeneous smoothness in his analyses of Egyptian statuary and the Sphinx in particular: 'three different systems of proportion were employed – an anomaly easily explained by the fact that the organism in question is not a homogeneous but a heterogeneous one.'

24 *Webster's*, p445.

25 In Stan Allen's introduction to the work of Douglas Garofalo forthcoming in *assemblage 19* (Cambridge, Mass: MIT Press, 1992) a strategy of camouflage is articulated which invests surfaces with alternatives to the forms and volumes they delimit. The representation of other known figures is referred to as a logic of plumage. For instance, a butterfly wing representing the head of a bird invites a deceitful detection. This differs from the disappearance of a surface by stealth which resists any recognition.

26 This suggests a reading of Michael Hays' text on the early Mies van der Rohe Friedrichstrasse Tower as a tactic of disappearance by proliferating cacophonous images of the city. Hays' work on Hannes Meyer's *United Nations Competition Entry* is perhaps the most critical in the reinterpretation of functional contingencies in the intensely involved production of differentiated, heterogeneous yet continuous space through manipulations of a surface.

# GILLES DELEUZE
## *THE FOLD - LEIBNIZ AND THE BAROQUE*
### *The Pleats of Matter*

The Baroque refers not to an essence but rather to an operative function, to a trait. It endlessly produces folds. It does not invent things: there are all kinds of folds coming from the East, Greek, Roman, Romanesque, Gothic, Classical folds. . . Yet the Baroque trait twists and turns its folds, pushing them to infinity, fold over fold, one upon the other. The Baroque fold unfurls all the way to infinity. First, the Baroque differentiates its folds in two ways, by moving along two infinities, as if infinity were composed of two stages or floors: the pleats of matter, and the folds in the soul. Below, matter is amassed according to a first type of fold, and then organised according to a second type, to the extent its part constitutes organs that are 'differently folded and more or less developed'. [1] Above, the soul sings of the glory of God inasmuch as it follows its own folds, but without succeeding in entirely developing them, since 'this communication stretches out indefinitely'. [2] A labyrinth is said, etymologically, to be multiple because it contains many folds. The multiple is not only what has many parts but also what is folded in many ways. A labyrinth corresponds exactly to each level: the continuous labyrinth in matter and its parts, the labyrinth of freedom in the soul and its predicates. [3] If Descartes did not know how to get through the labyrinth, it was because he sought its secret of continuity in rectilinear tracks, and the secret of liberty in a rectitude of the soul. He knew the inclension of the soul as little as he did the curvature of matter. A 'cryptographer' is needed, someone who can at once account for nature and decipher the soul, who can peer into the crannies of matter and read into the folds of the soul. [4]

Clearly the two levels are connected (this being why continuity rises up into the soul). There are souls down below, sensitive animal; and there even exists a lower level in the souls. The pleats of matter surround and envelop them. When we learn that souls cannot be furnished with windows opening onto the outside, we must first, at the very least, include souls upstairs,

reasonable ones, who have ascended to the other level ('elevation'). It is the upper floor that has no windows. It is a dark room or chamber decorated only with a stretched canvas 'diversified by folds,' as if it were a living dermis. Placed on the opaque canvas, these folds, cords or springs represent an innate form of knowledge, but solicited by matter they move into action. Matter triggers 'vibrations or oscillations' at the lower extremity of the cords, through the intermediary of 'some little openings' that exist on the lower level. Leibniz constructs a great Baroque montage that moves between the lower floor, pierced with windows, and the upper floor, blind and closed, but on the other hand resonating as if it were a musical salon translating the visible movements below into sounds up above. [5]

It could be argued that this text does not express Leibniz's thought, but instead the maximum degree of its possible conciliation with Locke. The text also fashions a way of representing what Leibniz will always affirm: a correspondence and even a communication between the two levels, between the two labyrinths, between the pleats of matter and the folds in the soul. A fold between the two folds? And the same image, that of veins in marble, is applied to the two under different conditions. Sometimes the veins are the pleats of matter that surround living beings held in the mass, such that the marble tile resembles a rippling lake that teems with fish. Sometimes the veins are innate ideas in the soul, like twisted figures or powerful statues caught in the block of marble. Matter is marbled, of two different styles.

Wölfflin noted that the Baroque is marked by a certain number of material traits: horizontal widening of the lower floor, flattening of the pediment, low and curved stairs that push into space; matter handled in masses or aggregates, with the rounding of angles and avoidance of perpendiculars; the circular acanthus replacing the jagged acanthus, use of limestone to produce spongy, cavernous shapes, or to constitute a vortical form always put in motion by

renewed turbulence, which ends only in the manner of a horse's mane or the foam of a wave; matter tends to spill over in space, to be reconciled with fluidity at the same time fluids themselves are divided into masses. [6]

Huygens develops a Baroque mathematical physics whose goal is curvilinearity. With Leibniz the curvature of the universe is prolonged according to three other fundamental notions: the fluidity of matter, the elasticity of bodies and the motivating spirit as a mechanism. First, matter would clearly not be extended following a twisted line. Rather, it would follow a tangent. [7] But the universe appears compressed by an active force that endows matter with a curvilinear or spinning movement, following an arc that ultimately has no tangent. And the infinite division of matter causes the compressive force to return all portions of matter to the surrounding areas, to the neighbouring parts that bathe and penetrate the given body, and that determine its curvature. Dividing endlessly, the parts of matter form little vortices in a maelstrom, and in these are found even more vortices, even smaller, and even more are spinning in the concave intervals of the whirls that touch one another.

Matter thus offers an infinitely porous, spongy or cavernous texture without emptiness, caverns endlessly contained in other caverns: no matter how small, each body contains a world pierced with irregular passages, surrounded and penetrated by an increasingly vaporous fluid, the totality of the universe resembling 'a pond of matter in which there exist different flows and waves'. [8] From this, however, we could not conclude, in the second place, that even the most refined matter is perfectly fluid and thus loses its texture (according to a thesis that Leibniz imputes to Descartes). Descartes' error probably concerns what is to be found in different areas. He believed that the real distinction between parts entailed separability. What specifically defines an absolute fluid is the absence of coherence or cohesion; that is, the separability of parts, which in fact applies only to a passive and abstract matter.[9] According to Leibniz, two parts of really distinct matter can be inseparable, as shown not only by the action of surrounding forces that determine the curvilinear movement of a body, but also by the pressure of surrounding forces that determine its hardness (coherence, cohesion) or the inseparability of its parts. Thus it must be stated that a body has a degree of hardness as well as a degree of fluidity, or that it is essentially elastic, the elastic force of bodies being the expression of the active compressive force exerted on matter. When a boat reaches a certain speed a wave becomes as hard as a wall of marble. The atomistic hypothesis of an absolute hardness and the Cartesian hypothesis of an absolute fluidity are joined all the more because they share the error that posits separable minima, either in the form of finite bodies or in infinity in the form of points (the Cartesian line as site of its points, the analytical punctual equation).

This is what Leibniz explains in an extraordinary piece of writing: a flexible or an elastic body still has cohering parts that form a fold, such that they are not separated into parts of parts but are rather divided to infinity in smaller and smaller folds that always retain a certain cohesion. Thus a continuous labyrinth is not a line dissolving into independent points, as flowing sand might dissolve into grains, but resembles a sheet of paper divided into infinite folds or separated into bending movements, each one determined by the consistent or conspiring surrounding. 'The division of the continuous must not be taken as that of sand dividing into grains, but as that of a sheet of paper or of a tunic in folds, in such a way that an infinite number of folds can be produced, some smaller than others, but without the body ever dissolving into points or minima'.[10] A fold is always folded within a fold, like a cavern in a cavern. The unit of matter, the smallest element of the labyrinth, is the fold, not the point which is never a part, but a simple extremity of the line. That is why parts of matter are masses or aggregates, as a correlative to elastic compressive force. Unfolding is thus not the contrary of folding, but follows the fold up to the following fold. Particles are 'turned into folds,' that a 'contrary effort changes over and again'.[11] Folds of winds, of waters, of fire and earth, and subterranean folds of veins of ore in a mine. In a system of complex interactions, the solid pleats of 'natural geography' refer to the effect first of fire, and then of waters and winds on the earth; and the veins of metal in mines resemble the curves of conical forms, sometimes ending in a circle or an ellipse, sometimes stretching into a hyperbola or a parabola.[12] The model for the sciences of matter is the 'origami', as the Japanese philosopher might say, or the art of folding paper.

Two consequences result that provide a sense of the affinity of matter with life and organisms. To be sure, organic folds have their own specificity, as fossils demonstrate. But on the one hand, the division of parts in matter does not go without a decomposition of bending movement or of flexions. We see this in the development of the egg, where numerical division is only the condition of morphogenic movements, and of invagination as a pleating. On the other hand, the formation of the organism would remain an improbable mystery, or a miracle, even if matter were to divide to infinity into independent points. But it becomes increasingly probable and natural when an infinity of indeterminate states is given (already folded over each other), each of which includes a cohesion at its level, somewhat like the improbability of forming a word by chance with separate letters, but with far more likelihood with syllables or inflections.[13]

In the third place, it is evident that motivating force becomes the mechanism of matter. If the world is infinitely cavernous, if worlds exist in the tiniest bodies, it is because everywhere there can be found 'a spirit in matter,' which attests not only to the infinite division of parts but also to progressivity in the gain and loss of movement all while the conservation of force is realised. The matter-fold is a matter-time; its characteristics resemble the continuous discharge of an 'infinity of wind-muskets'.[14] And there still we can imagine the affinity of matter for life insofar as a muscular conception of matter inspires force in all things. By invoking the propagation of light and 'the explosion into luminosity', by making an elastic, inflammable, and explosive spirit from animal spirits, Leibniz turns his back on cartesianism. He renews the tradition of Van Helmont and is inspired by Boyle's experimentation.[15] In short, to the extent that folding is not opposed to unfolding, such is also the case in the pairs tension-release and contraction-dilation (but not condensation-rarefaction, which would imply a void).

The lower level or floor is thus also composed of organic matter. An organism is defined by the endogenous folds, while inorganic matter has exogenous folds that are always determined from without or by the surrounding environment. Thus, in the case of living beings, an inner formative fold is transformed through evolution, with the organism's development. Whence the necessity of a preformation. Organic matter is not, however, different from inorganic matter (here, the distinction of a first and a second matter is irrelevant). Whether organic or inorganic, matter is all one; but active forces are not the only ones exerted upon it. To be sure, these are perfectly material or mechanical forces, where indeed souls cannot be made to intervene: for the moment, vitalism is a strict organism. Material forces, which account for the organic fold. have only to be distinguished from the preceding forces, and be added to it; they must suffice, where they are exerted, to transform raw matter into organic matter. In contrast to compressive or elastic forces, Leibniz calls them 'plastic forces'. They organise masses but, although the latter prepare organisms or make them possible by means of motivating drive, it is impossible to go from masses to organisms, since organs are always based on these plastic forces that preform them, and are distinguished from forces of mass, to the point where every organ is born from a pre-existing organ.[16] Even fossils in matter are not explained by our faculty of imagination: when, for example, we see that the head of Christ we fancy in the spots on a wall refers to plastic forces that wind through organisms that already exist.

If plastic forces can be distinguished, it is not because living matter exceeds mechanical processes, but because mechanisms are not sufficient to be machines. A mechanism is faulty not for being too artificial to account for living matter, but for not being mechanical enough, for not being adequately machined. Our mechanisms are in fact organised into parts that are not in themselves machines, while the organism is infinitely machined, a machine whose every part or piece is a machine, but only 'transformed by different folds that it receives'.[17] Plastic forces are thus more machinelike than they are mechanical, and they allow for the definition of Baroque machines. It might be claimed that mechanisms of inorganic nature already stretch to infinity because the motivating force is of an already infinite composition, or that the fold always refers to other folds. But it requires that each time, an external determination, or the direct action of the surroundings, is needed in order to pass from one level to another; without this we would have to stop, as with our mechanisms. The living organism, on the contrary, by virtue of preformation has an internal destiny that makes it move from fold to fold, or that makes machines from machines all the way to infinity. We might say that between organic and inorganic things there exists a difference of vector, the latter going toward increasingly greater masses in which statistical mechanisms are operating, the former toward increasingly smaller, polarised masses in which the force of an individuating machinery, an internal individuation, is applied. Is this Leibniz's premonition of several aspects that will come true only much later?[18] No doubt, for Leibniz, internal individuation will only be explained at the level of souls: organic interiority is only derivative, and has but one container of coherence or cohesion (not of inherence or 'inhesion'). It is an interiority of space, and not yet of motion; also, an internalisation of the outside, an invagination of the outside that could not occur all alone if no true interiorities did not exist *elsewhere*. It remains the case that the organic body thus confers an interior on matter, by which the principle of individuation is applied to it: whence the figure of the leaves of a tree, two never being exactly alike because of their veins or folds.

Folding-unfolding no longer simply means tension-release, contraction-dilation, but enveloping-developing, involution-evolution. The organism is defined by its ability to fold its own parts and to unfold them, not to infinity, but to a degree of development assigned to each species. Thus an organism is enveloped by organisms one within another (interlocking of germinal matter), like Russian dolls. The first fly contains the seeds of all flies to come, each being called in its turn to unfold its own parts at the right time. And when an organism dies, it does not really vanish, but folds in upon itself, abruptly involuting into the again newly dormant seed by skipping all intermediate stages. The simplest way of stating the point is by saying that to unfold is to increase, to grow; whereas to fold is to diminish, to reduce, to 'withdraw into the recesses of a world'.[19] Yet a simple metric change would not account for the difference between the organic and the inorganic, the machine and its motive force. It would fail to show that movement does not simply go from one greater or smaller part to another, but from fold to fold. When a part of a machine is still a machine, the smaller unit is not the same as the whole. When Leibniz invokes Harlequin's layers of clothing, he means that his underwear is not the same as his outer garments. That is why metamorphosis or 'metaschematism' pertains to more than mere change of dimension: every animal is double – but as a heterogeneous or heteromorphic creature, just as the butterfly is folded into the caterpillar that will soon unfold. The double will even be simultaneous to the degree that the ovule is not a mere envelope but furnishes one part whose other is in the male element.[20] In fact, it is the inorganic that repeats itself, with a difference of proximate dimension, since it is always an exterior site which enters the body; the organism, in contrast, envelops an interior site that contains necessarily *other* species of organisms, those that envelop in their turn the interior sites containing yet other organisms: 'Each portion of matter may be conceived as a garden full of plants, and as a pond full of fish. But every branch of each plant, every member of each animal, and every drop of their liquid parts is in itself likewise a similar garden or pond.'[21] Thus the inorganic fold happens to be simple and direct, while the organic fold is always composite, alternating and indirect (mediated by an interior surrounding).[22]

Matter is folded twice, once under elastic forces, a second time under plastic forces, but one is not able to move from the first to the second. Thus the universe is neither a great living being, nor is it in itself an Animal: Leibniz rejects this hypothesis as much as he rejects that of a universal Spirit. Organisms retain an irreducible individuality, and organic descendants retain an irreducible plurality. It remains that the two kinds of force, the two kinds of folds – masses and organisms – are strictly co-extensive. There are no *fewer* living beings than parts of inorganic matter.[23] Clearly an exterior site is not a living being; rather, it is a lake, a pond or a fish hatchery. Here the figure of the lake or pond acquires a new meaning, since the pond – and the marble tile – no longer refer to elastic waves that swim through them like inorganic folds, but to fish that inhabit them like organic folds. And in life itself the inner sites contained are even more hatcheries full of other fish: a 'swarm'. Inorganic folds of sites move between two organic folds. For Leibniz, as for the Baroque, the principles of reason are veritable cries: Not everything is fish, but fish are teeming everywhere . . . Universality does not exist, but living things are ubiquitous.

It might be said that the theory of preformation and duplication, as observations made through the microscope confirm, has long been abandoned. The meaning of development or evolution has turned topsy-turvy since it now designates *epigenesis* – the appearance of organs and organisms neither preformed nor closed one within the other, but formed from something else that does not resemble them: the organ does not arch back to a pre-existing organ, but to a much more general and less differentiated design.[24] Development does not go from smaller to greater things through growth or augmentation, but from the

*The Baroque House (an allegory)*

*Closed private room, decorated with a 'drapery diversified by folds'*

*Common rooms, with 'several small openings' the five senses*

general to the special, through differentiations of an initially undifferentiated field either under the action of exterior surroundings or under the influence of internal forces that are directive, directional, but that remain neither constituitive nor preformative. However, insofar as preformism exceeds simple metric variations, it tends to be aligned with an epigenesis, to the extent that epigenesis is forced to hold to a kind of virtual or potential preformation. The essential is elsewhere; basically, two conceptions share the common trait of conceiving the organism as a fold, an orginary folding or creasing (and biology has never reflected this determination of living matter, as shown nowadays with the fundamental pleating of globular protein). Preformism is the form in which this truth of the 17-century is perceived through the first microscopes. It is hardly surprising that from then on the same problems are found in the sense of epigenesis and preformation.

Thus can all types of folding be called modifications or degrees of developments of a same Animal in itself? Or are there types of irreducible foldings, as Leibniz believes in a preformist perspective and as Cuvier and Baër also contend from an epigenic standpoint? [25] Certainly a great opposition subsists between the two points of view. With epigenesis the organic fold is produced, is unearthed, or is pushed up from a relatively smooth and consistent surface. (How could a redoubling, an invagination or an intubation be prefigured?) Now with preformism an organic fold always ensues from another fold, at least on the inside from a same type of organisation: every fold originates from a fold, *plica ex plica*. If Heideggerian terms can be used, we can say that the fold of epigenesis is an *Einfalt*, or that it is the differentiation of an undifferentiated, but that the fold from preformation is a *Zweifalt*, not a fold in two – since every fold can only be thus – but a 'fold-of-two', an *entre-deux*, something 'between' in the sense that a difference is being differentiated. From this point of view we cannot be sure if preformism does not have a future.

Masses and organisms, masses and living beings thus fill the lower level. Why then is another story needed, since sensitive or animal souls are already there, inseparable from organic bodies? Each soul even seems apt to be localised in its body, this time as 'point' in a droplet, that subsists in a part of the droplet when the latter is divided or diminished in volume: thus, in death the soul remains right where it was, in a part of the body, however reduced it may be. [26] Leibniz states that the point of view is in the body. [27] Surely everything in the body works like a machine, in accordance with plastic forces that are material, but these forces explain everything except for the variable *degrees of unity* to which they bring the masses they are organising (a plant, a worm, a vertebrate. . .) Plastic forces of matter act on masses, but they submit them to real unities that they take for granted. They make an organic synthesis, but assume the soul as the *unity of synthesis*, or as the 'immaterial principle of life'. Only there does an animism find a connection with organicism, from the standpoint of pure unity or of union, independently of all causal action. [28] It remains that organisms would not on their account have the causal power to be folded to infinity, and of

surviving in ashes, without the unity-souls from which they are inseparable, and which break away from Malebranche: not only is there a preformation of bodies, but also a pre-existence of souls in fertile seeds. [29] Life is not only everywhere, but souls are everywhere in matter. Thus, when an organism is called to unfold its own parts, its animal or sensitive soul is opened onto an entire theatre in which it perceives or feels according to its unity, independently of its organism, yet inseparable from it.

But – and here is the whole problem – what happens with bodies, from the time of Adam's seed that envelops them, that are destined to become humans? Juridically, one might say that they carry in a nutshell 'a sort of sealed act' that marks their fate. And when the hour comes for them to unfold their parts, to attain a degree of organic development proper to man, or to form cerebral folds, at the same time their animal soul becomes reasonable by gaining a greater degree of unity (mind): 'The organised body would receive at the same time the disposition of the human body, and its soul would be raised to the stage of a reasonable soul, but I cannot decide here if it occurs through an ordinary process or an extraordinary work of God.' [30] Then in every event this becoming is an elevation, an exaltation: a change of theatre, of rule, of level or of floors. The theatre of matter gives way to that of spirits or of God. In the Baroque the soul entertains a complex relation with the body. Forever indissociable from the body, it discovers a vertiginous animality that gets it tangled in the pleats of matter, but also an organic or cerebral humanity (the degree of development) that allows it to rise up, and that will make it ascend over all other folds.

The reasonable soul is free, like a Cartesian diver, to fall back down at death and to climb up again at the last judgment. As Leibniz notes, the tension is between the collapse and the elevation or ascension that in different spots is breaching the organised masses. We move from funerary figures of the Basilica of Saint Laurence to the figures on the ceiling of Saint Ignatius. It might be claimed that physical gravity and religious elevation are quite different and do not pertain to the same world. However, these are two vectors that are allotted as such in the distinction of the two levels or floors of a single and same world, or of the single and same house. It is because the body and the soul have no point in being inseparable, for they are not in the least really distinct (we have already seen it for

the parts of matter). From this moment on any localisation of the soul in an area of the body, no matter how tiny it may be, amounts rather to a *projection* from the top to the bottom, a projection of the soul focalising on a 'point' of the body, in conformity with Desargues' geometry, that develops from a Baroque perspective. In short, the primary reason for an upper floor is the following: there are souls on the lower floor, some of whom are chosen to become reasonable, thus to change their levels.

Movement, then, cannot be stopped. The reciprocation of the Leibnizian principle holds not only for reasonable souls but also for animal or sensible souls themselves: if two really distinct things can be inseparable, two inseparable things can be really distinct, and belong to two levels, the localisation of the one in the other amounting to a projection upon a point ('I do not think that we can consider souls as being in points, perhaps we might say . . . that they are in a place through a connection'). As degrees of unity, animal souls are already on the other floor, everything being accomplished mechanically in the animal itself at the lower level. Plastic or machinic forces are part of the 'derivative forces' defined only in respect to the matter that they organise. But souls, on the contrary, are 'primitive forces' or immaterial principles of life that are defined only in respect to the inside, in the self, and 'through analogy with the mind'. We can nonetheless remember that these animal souls, with their subjugated organism, exist everywhere in inorganic matter. Thus in its turn inorganic matter reverts to souls whose site is elsewhere, higher up, and that is only projected upon it. In all probability a body – however small– follows a curvilinear trajectory only under the impulsion of the second species of derivative forces, compressive or elastic forces that determine the curve through the mechanical notion of the surrounding bodies on the outside: isolated, the body would follow the straight tangent. But still, mechanical laws or extrinsic determinations (collisions) explain everything except the *unity* of a concrete movement, no matter how irregular or variable it may be. Unity of movement is an affair of the soul, and almost of a conscience, as Bergson will later discover. Just as the totality of matter arches back to a curving that can no longer be determined from the outside, the curvilinear course followed by a given body under the impetus of the outside goes back to a 'higher', internal and individuating, unity on the other floor, that contains the 'law of curvilinearity', the law of folds or changes of direction. [31] The same movement is always determined from the outside, through collisions, insofar as it is related to derivative force, but unified from the inside, to the degree it is related to primitive force. In the first relation, the curve is accidental and derived from the straight line, but in the second it is primary, such that the motive force sometimes is mechanically explained through the action of a subtle surrounding, and sometimes is understood from the inside as the interior of the body, 'the cause of movement that is already in the body', and that only awaits the suppression of an obstacle from the outside.

Hence the need for a second floor is everywhere affirmed to be strictly metaphysical. The soul itself is what constitutes the other floor or the inside up above, where there are no windows to allow entry of influence from without. Even in a physical sense we are moving across outer material pleats to inner animated, spontaneous folds. These are what we must now examine, in their nature and in their development. Everything moves as if the pleats of matter possessed no reason in themselves. It is because the Fold is always between two folds, and because the between-two folds seems to move about everywhere: is it between inorganic bodies and organisms, between organisms and animal souls, between animal souls and reasonable souls, between bodies and souls in general?

*Translation by Tom Conley*

**Notes**

1   *New system of Nature and of the communication of substances*, §7.

2   *Monadologie*, § 61 and *Principles of Nature and of Grace founded in reason*, §13.

3   On Liberty (Foucher de Careil, *New letters and opuscules*).

4   On cryptography as art of inventing a key of something enveloped, fragment *A book on combination* . . . (Couturat, *Opuscules*). And *New Essays on human understanding*, IV, ch17, §8: the folds in Nature and the 'summaries'.

5   *New Essays*, II, ch12, §1. In this book, Leibniz 're-makes' the *Essays* by Locke: the dark room is well invoked by Locke, but not the folds.

6   Cf Wölfflin, *Renaissance and Baroque*, Ed Monfort.

7   *New Essays*, preface.

8   Letter to Des Billettes, December 1696 (Gerhardt, *Philosophy*, VII, p452).

9   *Table of Definitions* (C, p486) and *New Essays*, II, ch 23, §23.

10  Placidus *Philalethi* (C, pp614-615).

11  Letter to Des Billettes, p453.

12  *Protogaea* (Dutens II; and tr . . . fr by Bertrand de Saint-Germain, 1850, Ed English). On the conical veins, ch 8.

13  This theme will be developed by Willard Gibbs. Leibniz supposes that God does not trace 'the first alignments of the tender earth' without producing something 'analogous to the structure of animal or of plants' (*Protogaea*, ch 8).

14  Letter to Des Billettes; and Letter to Bayle, December 1698 (GPh, III, p57) cf Gueroult, *Dynamic and Metaphysical Leibnizians*, The Beautiful Letters, p32: 'How is the spring conserved if one does not suppose that the body is composed, such that it can contract in pursuit of its pores the particles of subtle manner which penetrate it, and in return this more subtle matter can expel from its pores an even more subtle matter etc to infinity?'

15  On elasticity and the detonation, which inspire the concept of reflex in Willis (1621-1675), on the differences of this model with that of Descartes, cf Georges Canguilhem, *The Formation of the Concept of Reflex in the XVII and XVIII Century*, PUF, pp60-67. Malebranche attempts to reconcile the theme of the spring and of relaxation (*loosening*) with Cartesianism, at the same time in the inorganic and in the organism: *Search for Truth*, VI, ch 8 & 9 ('any stiff body which does nothing can spring . . . ').

16  Letter to Lady Masham, July 1705 (GPh, III, p368) and *Considerations on the Principles of Life and on Plastic Nature* (GPh, VI, pp544 & p553): the principles of life are immaterial, but not the 'plastic faculty'. On fossils, cf Protogaea, ch 28.

17  New system of nature, §10. *Monadologie*, §64: 'The tooth of a brass wheel has parts or fragments that to us are no more than something artificial, which have no relation to the machine other than to the use of the destined wheel. But the machines of nature, that is to say living bodies, are again machines in their small parts until infinity'. Letter to Lady Masham, p374: '*The plastic force in the machine*'.

18  On the technological conception of Leibniz, his opposition to that of Descartes and his modernity, cf Michael Serres, *The System of Leibniz*, PUF, II, pp491-510, p621.

19  Letter to Arnauld, April 1687 (GPh, II, p99).

20  New Essays, III, chap 6, §23. It is thus by mistake that Bonnet (*Philosophic palingenesie*) reproaches his teacher Leibniz for having refrained from

variations of cutting.

21  *Monadologie*, §67-70.

22  Cf Serres, I, p371.

23  Letter to Arnauld, September 1687 (p118).

24  In the name of the epigenese, Dalcq may say: 'A caudal appendices could have obtained from a system of action and of reaction . . . or nothing is caudal *a priori*' (*The Egg and its Dynamic Organisation*, Ed Albin Michel, p194).

25  Geoffrey Saint-Hillaire, partisan of *epigenese*, is one of the greatest thinkers on organic folds. He considered different folds as modifications of a sigle animal. One can go from one to the other to fold again (united by a plan of composition), if one folds a vertebrae 'in such a way that the two parts of its spine are brought together, the head near its feet, its pelvis near its nape, and its viscera inside the cephalopodes'. This instigates the opposition by Baër, in the name of the *epigenese*, and already the anger of Cuvier who poses the diversity of axes of development or of plans of organisation (cf Geoffrey, *Principles of Zoological Philosophy*). Despite his monism, however, Geoffrey could call himself leibnizian in other respects: he explains the organism by a material force which does not change the nature of the body, but adds to it in new ways and new relations. It is an impulsive, electric force, or tractive in the manner of Kepler, capable of 're-folding' the elastic fluids and operating at three short distances in the 'world of details' or in the small infinity, no longer by summation of homogeneous parts, but affronted by homologous parts (Synthetic notions and histories of natural philosophy).

26  Letter to Des Bosses, March 1706 (in Christiane Fremont, *The being and the relation*, Ed Vrin) and in a letter to Arnauld, April 1687 (p 100): an insect having been cut into a thousand pieces, its soul stays 'in a certain living part, which will always be smaller than it made to be covered by the action of that which tore him apart. . .'

27  Letter to Lady Masham, June 1704 (p357).

28  *Principles of nature and of Grace*, §4: 'an infinity of degrees' in the souls and *New System of Nature*, §11.

29  *Monadologie*, §74.

30  *God's cause interceded by his justice*, §§81-85 and *Theodicee*, §91, 397.

31  *Clarifications of difficulties that Mr Bayle found in the new system* . . . (GPh, IV, pp544, 558). Gueroult has shown how the external determinism and the internal spontaneity reconcile themselves perfectly, already by account to the physical bodies: pp203-207; and p163 ('the elasticity is now considered as an expression of the first spontaneity, of the primitive active force'.)

Page 32: *Peter Eisenman, Rebstock Park, Frankfurt, view of the model*

ZUKÜNFTIGE
S-BAHN HALTESTELLE

KLEINGARTENANLAGE

UEBERGANG ZUR GEPLANTEN
S-BAHN HALTESTELLE

WIESBADENERSTRASSE

END
HALTESTELLE

MESSEBUS
HALTESTELLE

GARTENHALLENBAD REBSTOCK

SPORTPLATZ

TENNISPLATZ

ZUM REBSTOCKPARK

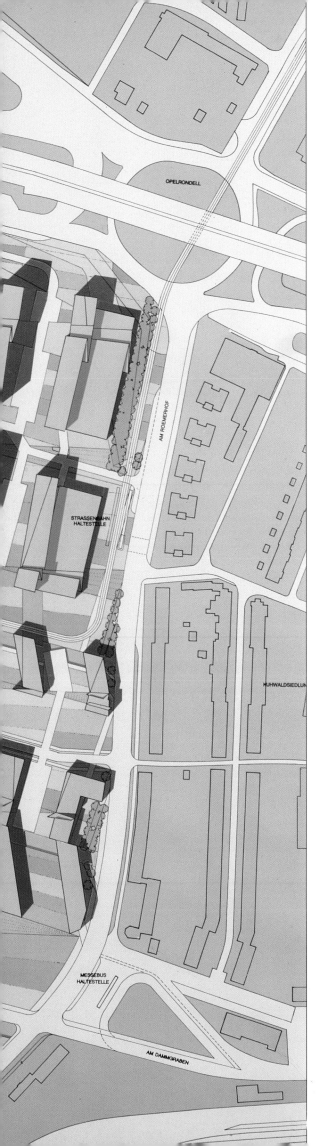

# PETER EISENMAN
## *FOLDING IN TIME*
## *The Singularity of Rebstock*

Modern urbanism, which marked a radical change in urban form, was articulated in three different building types: the high-rise or point block; the piloti or the horizontally extruded slab and the *siedlung*. While all three played a dominant role in the development of the city in the 20th century it was the *siedlung* form which dominated German urbanism in the first half of the century. Nowhere was this evocation more prominent than in the area in and around the city of Frankfurt.

With the advent of the idea of mass production, multiplicity and repetition on the one hand and the need for health and hygiene on the other coupled with the emerging need for mass housing – a new housing industry and with it a new technology of standardisation was born. These new ideas of repetition and standardisation brought about a need to re-think urban form typology and in particular the perimeter block which had been the staple of German housing in the previous centuries. The problem with the perimeter block was twofold: on the one hand it conformed to an outdated urban pattern of streets which made each repetition unique rather than standard; and on the other hand the perimeter block was enclosing and therefore not metaphorically open to the new concerns for health and hygiene.

The *siedlung* form brought a new attitude to urban structure. In the 18th century, urban building was considered traditionally as ground with the void spaces as figure. This changed in the late 19th century when the grand boulevards and avenues cut through not only the existing fabric, but into the open land surrounding the cities where no urban pattern existed. Now the thoroughfares became the ground to figural building which defined its edges. The *siedlung* changed this again and the ground became a neutral datum, while the buildings which were still seen as figural had no relationship to any existing pattern. However, the *siedlung* was not a true figure in the sense of a perimeter block or a freestanding villa. It was a new linear type form that could be extended infinitely in one

direction. However, unlike the horizontal extrusions of Le Corbusier at Algiers and Nemours, it eschewed pattern for its autonomous condition of form. This autonomy brought a new principle to building typology. The *siedlung*, unlike any other previous building type had no back or front. In a sense it was all front since the apartments were entered on both sides of what was a conceptual line; a line which had no hierarchy and no regard for the traditional ideas of place and the public and private realm. In one sense the *siedlung* form with its denial of former patterns of land ownership and privilege was an ideal incarnation for the social ideas of the time. In the world of the *siedlung*, everyone and everywhere was equal. Whether of spatial modulation or individual identity, difference was homogenised in favour of an implacable idea.

Quite naturally such a totalising idealisation would be eventually problematised. This was the case in the immediate postwar years when the devastation of the European city required an urgent solution. Now, while the problem of the mass remained the same, the solution was of necessity to be different. No longer was the cool rationality and autonomy of the *siedlung* form thought to be sufficient to provide for the possibility of a restored urban fabric. In fact, the desolation of the *siedlung* was seen to be as much of a problem to the urban context as was the bombing. In the flight from the grim reality of post-war Germany, the *siedlung* was abandoned and the picturesque nostalgia of the perimeter block returned as an evocation of the past, now projected into the future present.

The argument proposed here is that the idea inherent in the *siedlung* type was not wrong but was rather poorly or inadequately conceptualised, particularly in relationship to the changing ideas of the individual and mechanical repetition. Therefore, it will be argued that it is not a return to the structures of the past that is the solution to urban form today, but is perhaps a reconsideration of the *siedlung* type with respect to ideas of the individual and repetition which may provide a possible context for a solution. This reconsideration of the *siedlung* is the basis for the urban strategy deployed in the Rebstock project.

Basically, this reconsideration deals with two aspects of 20th-century urbanism: space and time on the one hand and repetition and the individual on the other. What the *siedlung* did was to treat the idea of the individual unit within a new idea of the multiple; that is the repetitive unit was treated as if it were the same as the individual unit in the figuration of the perimeter block. In doing so it caused the individual unit to lose its specific identity. Whereas the unit in the perimeter block retained its individuality because of the overall specific character and figuration of the block, in the *siedlung* the block lost its identity and so did the individual unit.

This change in the idea of the individual unit in the *siedlung* can also be seen in the change in the role of individual expression. With the individual unit this change lies partly in the nature of the conception of its repetition. In this context, repetition not only involves space but also time. It will be argued here that the idea of repetition has been greatly altered by the shift from what can be called the mechanical paradigm to the present era of the electronic paradigm. The idea of repetition has changed because the idea of time has changed. Formerly, time in the mechanical paradigm was narrative, linear and sequential.

Now, because of media, time has lost its immediacy. Time can be speeded up or slowed down, replayed or fast-forwarded. The consequence of this change of the condition of time in the electronic media also clearly faces us with the loss of individual expression and response to an *immediate* or present action. This loss cannot be replaced by merely reinstating the old forms of individual expression, because media has brought about a permanent change in the nature of multiplicity and repetition. This difference became important as early as the late 19th century. The change is addressed by Walter Benjamin in his essay *Art in the Age of Mechanical Reproduction* in which he states that a photograph is clearly an original, although a different kind of original from that which, let us say, is crafted by hand. In one sense the art or the craft product, such as a handmade piece of furniture or a handmade book, is different from a book that is made on a mechanical press or a piece of bentwood furniture which is reproduced many times. In another

sense they are both original; the craft product being individual and the bentwood furniture multiple. Now there is a difference between the multiple or repetition in mechanical reproduction and repetition in electronic reproduction: this is the difference between a photograph and a telefax.

The photograph is produced mechanically. It is a product of repetition not a unique handmade artifact – that is, it is not an object of art as craft. The mechanical paradigm dealt with the shift in value from the individual hand (the hand of a painter as an original maker) to the value of the hand as intermediary (as in the developer of raw film); from the creation of an individual to the mediation of the multiple. The photograph can be manipulated by an individual to have more contrast, more texture, more tone. Thus, within the mechanical repetition of a photograph there remains a unique, individual quality; it remains a particular object, even within the idea of the multiple.

In electronic repetition, that is, the telefax, there is less human intervention, a less value-added dimension by the individual. Furthermore, the condition of the original is thrown into question. Whereas one can agree that there is an original negative plate for a photograph and that this plate can be reproduced, there is no negative plate in a telefax. The original that may be on a disk in a computer is no longer an object but rather a series of electronic impulses stored in a matrix. Even the disk original is often modified by corrections and thus a unique original is rarely kept. And in fact now, with telefax, the original may not even ever be sent so as to not confuse its reception with the reception of the telefax.

The question remains how does one make an urbanism in this new media time, a simultaneous time of narration and repetition? For this answer it is possible to introduce two interconnected concepts: the idea of the fold and the idea of singularity – concepts which are both active in the Rebstock project.

For Gilles Deleuze, the fold opens up a new conception of space and time. He argues in *Le Pli* that, 'Leibniz turned his back on Cartesian rationalism, on the notion of effective space and argued that in the labyrinth of the continuous the smallest element is not the point but the fold.' If this idea is taken into architecture it produces the following argument. Traditionally, architecture is conceptualised as Cartesian space, as a series of point grids. Planning envelopes are volumes of Cartesian space which seem to be neutral. Of course these

volumes of Cartesian space, these platonic solids that contain the stylisms and images of not only classical but also modern and post-modern space, are really nothing more than a condition of ideology taken for neutral or natural. Thus, it may be possible to take the notion of the fold – the crossing or an extension from a point – as an *other* kind of neutrality. Deleuze goes on to argue that Leibniz's notion of this extension is the notion of the event: 'Extension is the philosophical movement outward along a plane rather than downward in depth.' He argues that in mathematical studies of variation, the notion of object is change. This new object for Deleuze is no longer concerned with the framing of space, but rather a temporal modulation that implies a continual variation of matter. The continual variation is characterised through the agency of the fold: 'No longer is an object defined by an essential form.' He calls this idea of an object, an 'object event.'

The idea of event is critical to the discussion of singularity. Event proposes a different kind of time which is outside of narrative time or dialectical time. This other time, this outside of time begins to condition the idea of event as well as the idea of singularity. The latter attempts to restore that quality of individuality lost in the *siedlung*, without resorting to the static 19th century idea of individuality. Singularity can be defined as different from either the individual, the specific or the particular. Whereas the particular can always be defined in relation to the general, singularity can not. Singularity is always other, always different. Singularity is an individuality no longer able to belong to the realm of multiple as formerly defined. For singularity does not mean that a thing is simply unique. Singularity refers to the possibility in a repetition or a multiple for one copy to be different from another copy. The difference lies not so much in form, in size or in shape as in the distinction of a *this* thing from any other like thing. Singularity resides in this 'otherness' of the *time* of such a *this* thing; not so much in its form or space.

Place and time when no longer defined by the grid but rather by the fold, will still exist, but not as place and time in its former context, that is, as static, figural space. This other definition of time and place will involve both the simulacrum of time and place as well as the former reality of time and place. Narrative time is consequently altered. From here to there in space involves real time; only in mediated time, that is, the time of film or video, can time be speeded up or collapsed. Today the architecture of the event must deal with both times: its former time and future time of before and after and the media time, the time of the present which must contain the before and the after.

Events correspond to what Deleuze calls a heterogeneous series, which is organised into a system which is neither stable nor unstable; in other words, not in a dialectical either/or relationship but rather endowed with what can be called a potential energy. Potential energy is the energy of the event. Potential energy lies in the pre-present. An event is that which is previous to the present and which also lingers after. It includes the time of nothingness which is prior to and after the present of the event.

These events can never realise the old linear time of a stasis that inhabited those places, because today these very places are overwhelmed with a new mediated time of repetition – with speeding up and slowing down; with 'instant replays' that do not replicate narrative time. Therefore, any condition of place has to be more concerned with this 'other' notion of the particular and the specific which acknowledges this time of repetition. Image must be replaced by mapping, and individuality reconceptualised in the idea of singularity. This raises the possibility of reading the *siedlung* in another frame of reference, one different from the traditional figure-ground.

The *siedlung* form assumed a ground datum as both neutral and ideal. It was a ground that was infinitely extendable and repeatable – there was no specificity of context and thus no realisable edge or boundary, because the ground was neutral. Singularity is not something that emerges from a ground or from a figure form. It is the quality of unfolding in time that allows the possibility of singularity. Thus the fold can never be a neutral datum; it will always be a moment if not a specific object or place in time. As such, it can be an unstable or non-static being in time as well as place. The fold in this sense is neither a frame nor a figure as ground, but contains elements of both. Thus the ground of the Rebstock project must be distinguished from a ground as origin, or a ground as in figure-ground. The ground of Rebstock is no longer a datum or a base condition but rather is, in fact, something which already contains a condition of singularity; that is a groundlessness which can be said to be inherent in the notion of ground. It is a groundless ground. This groundless ground as realised at Rebstock is in the possibility of the fold.

The folded ground of Rebstock inhabits a nether world of a time between the organic and the crystal; between surface and depth. The mediating device between the organism and the crystal is the idea of the membrane, and in the case of Rebstock it is the folded surface. The fold is an aspect of singularity. The fold is never the same, either in space or time. It is a physical condition of difference, of a 'thisness' rather than an 'objectness'. A folded surface maps relationships without recourse to size or distance; it is conceptualised in the difference between a topological and a Euclidean surface. A topological surface is a condition of mapping without the necessary definition of distance. And without the definition of distance there is another kind of time, one of a nomadic relationship of points. These points are no longer fixed by X, Y and Z co-ordinates; they may be called X, Y and Z but they no longer have a fixed, spatial place. In this sense they are without place, they are placeless on the topological ground. Thus, Rebstock uses the fold as an attempt to produce conditions of a singularity of place and time using the *siedlung*. Here the topological event, the dissolution of figure and ground into a continuum, reside physically in the fold; no longer in the point or the grid. The ground surface as a membrane which becomes a topological event/structure is also simultaneously the building form. This topological event/ structure which has a before and after as well as its own present is distinguished from pure media which has only a present. It is the time of art beyond media. If media time is concerned with time in the present – the time of the simulated event – then the time of singularity contains the time before and after within the present of the event itself.

The thought-to-be neutrality of the Cartesian grid or the Platonic solid was seen as a value – a place where order and rationality could begin to create specificity. The Cardos and Decumanus, the earliest articulation of gridded urban space, was if nothing else a specific symbolic point. The fold is a different kind of symbol, it is no longer about image or iconic representation, but rather about index and mapping its own being; a mapping of its thisness in time as an event or a spectacle. As the sublime was to the time of the classical, so too is the spectacle to the time of the fold. Thus, where the specificity of the grid referred to place, the singularity of the fold refers to time. In the movement from grid to fold place no longer remains the dominant spatial condition. In the fold there is a specificity of location but now as a singularity not bound by traditional co-ordinates of space and time.

The use of the fold in Rebstock might reveal other conditions which may always have been immanent or repressed in the urban fabric of Frankfurt: conditions of singularity seen in terms of the ebb and flow of time which could reframe existing structures. The idea of the fold as a time event is neither a call for a radical intervention into the Rebstock area nor a return to the nostalgia of context as a tabula rasa. Rather, it is to see something which extends an existing context into time, producing in this extension the possibility of singularity. Due to the omnipresent simulacra of the electronic paradigm, a time-bound place has lost its placeness. It has moved to a kind of placeless, timeless condition. The fold attempts not to return place and time as they were formerly, but to bring them into the fold.

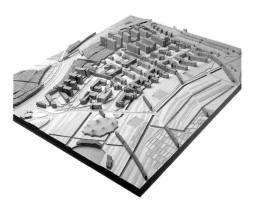

Previous Page: *Competition site plan*; Above: *Views of site*

41

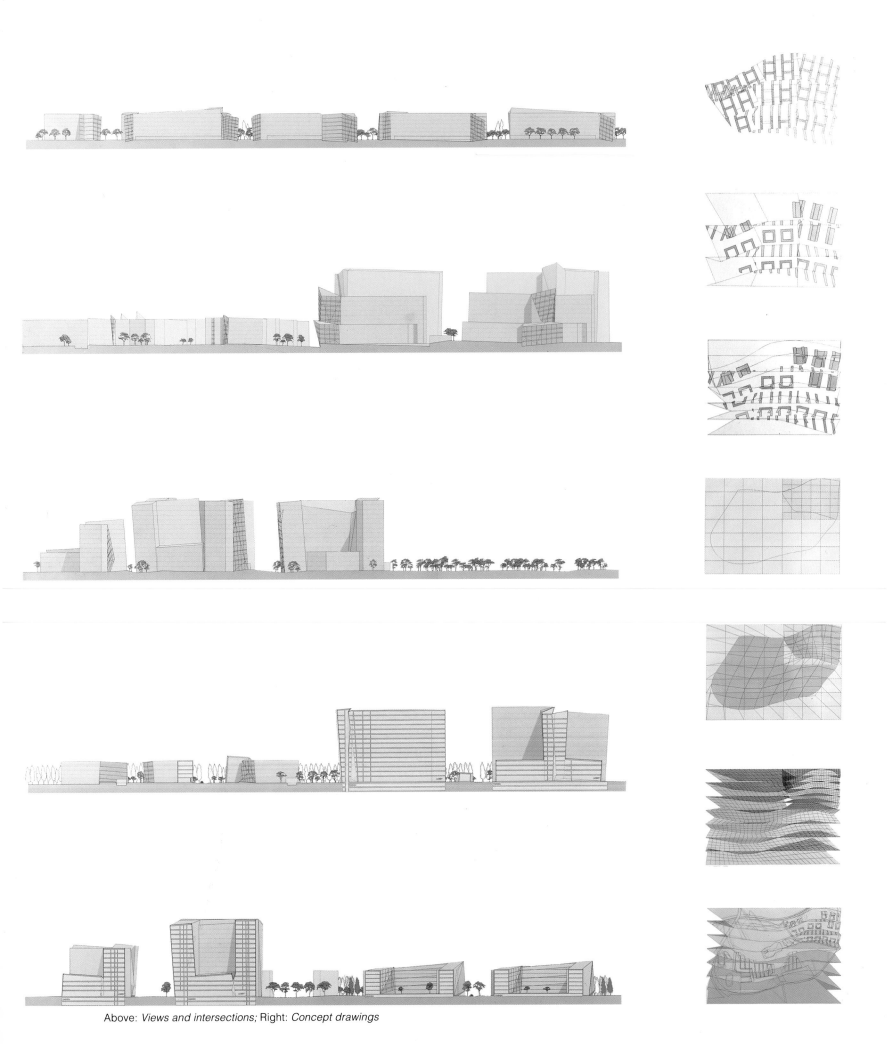

Above: *Views and intersections*; Right: *Concept drawings*

# PETER EISENMAN
## *REBSTOCK PARK MASTERPLAN*
### *Frankfurt, Germany*

In the late 18th and early 19th century the typical perimeter housing and commercial block of German cities defined both the street space and the interior court space as positive. These spaces seemed literally to have been carved out of a solid block of the urban condition. In the mid-19th century with the development of the grand boulevards and allées a new kind of spatial structure appeared. The streets were still positive spaces but were lined with ribbon buildings, so that the rear yards became left over space. This idea led to the development of the German *siedlung* where, since there were no streets adjacent to the buildings, the backs and fronts were now the same. Now all of the open space was in a sense left over; the 'ground' became a wasteland. The object buildings seemed detached, floating on a ground that was no longer active.

Nowhere was this siedlung urbanism more prevalent than in the developing ring around the urban centre of Frankfurt. In the post war era, with the expansion of the autobahn and air travel, a new, more complex task faced urban development. The Rebstock Park masterplan endeavours to reassess the entire idea of a static urbanism, one which deals only with objects rather then events, by taking into account the evolving reality of a media age where dimension of the present becomes an important aspect of the past and the future. This new reading might reveal other conditions which may have always been immanent in the urban fabric allowing for the possibility of new urban structures and for existing structures to be seen in such a way that they too become displaced.

One such displacement possibility can be found in the very history of German thought. Leibniz conceived of matter as explosive and continuous; the smallest element is not the point, but the fold. Framed by a segment of the Mercator Grid, the Rebstock Park masterplan floats within a rectilinear container to obscure the residual position it occupies along Frankfurt's third green belt. By compressing the large grid segment onto the site perimeter and similarly compressing the small scale grid onto the close site, contingent readings emerge as the two site figures fold and unfold, each relative to its expanded position. The idea of the fold gives the traditional idea of edge a dimension. Rather than being seen as an abrupt line, this dimension provides both mediation and a reframing of conditions such as old and new, transport and arrival, commerce and housing. Thus the idea of folding was used on the site to initiate new social organisations of urban space and to reframe existing organisations.

Rebstock Park is a five million square foot housing and commercial development located on the perimeter ring of Frankfurt between the international airport and historic city centre. The project is the winning entry in an international competition. Work on the masterplan guidelines is scheduled for completion in early 1992 with building design slated to begin shortly thereafter.

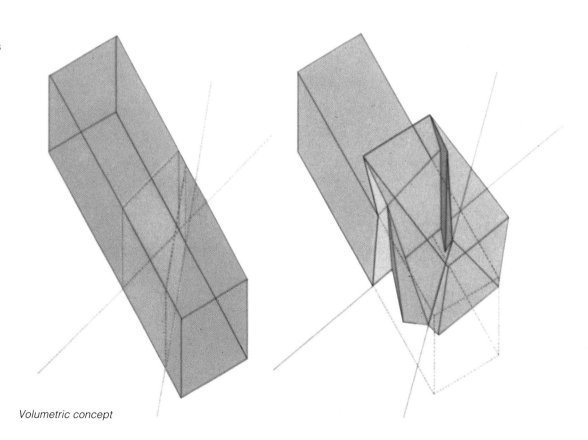

*Volumetric concept*

# PETER EISENMAN
## ALTEKA OFFICE BUILDING
### Tokyo, Japan

Tokyo, a paradigmatic city of accumulation, juxtaposition and compression is an index of contingent, tentative relations and new, complex urban realities. A city enfolded within the evolving reality of a mediated age, each site is a nexus of activity that each building tries to stabilise and repress; a series of discontinuous and 'monumental' episodes they are assumed to be essential and unchangeable .

Our project suggests an-other relationship to the city. For, situated within a condition caught between the traditional city fabric and the *Jigamae* – a new, large avenue (its angular shape the residue of the superposition of many consequent decision frames) – it suggests the notion that an object is no longer defined by an essential form where the idea of standard was one of maintaining an appearance of essence and of imposing a law of constancy, but of our actual situation where the fluctuation of the norm replaces the permanence of law when the object takes place in a continuum by variation. Thus with this other status the object doesn't correspond any more to a spatial mould but to a temporal modulation that implies a continual variation of the matter as much as a perpetual development of the form. This conception is not only temporal but quantitative of the object. The object becomes an event: it is 'eventalised', opening-up, un-folding. It is becoming.

The building's concept is related to this perpetual state of becoming: this evolution/ involution. The typological 'el' frees its own folds from their usual subordination to the finite body, emerging from the context to fold/unfold, contract/dilate, envelope/ develop, envolve/involve, compress/ explode in a matter-fold participation that is a matter-time in which phenomena are like a continuous discharge. In the labyrinth of the continuous, the smallest element is not the point but the fold. The building evades its cartesian definition: not representing an essential form, but a form 'becoming'.

The Alteka project, a mixed use commercial venture in the Shibuya district, combines 30,000 ft $^2$ of retail and office space.

*Typological elevation*

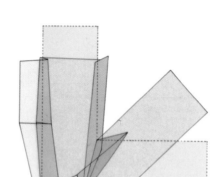

*Infolding*

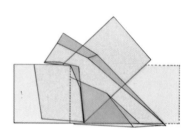

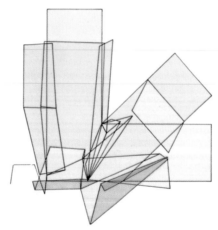

*Unfolding*

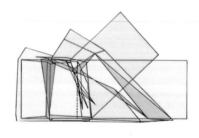

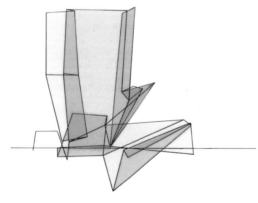

*Envelop(e)*

Above: *Schematic drawings*

44

 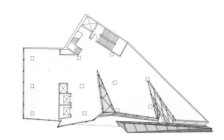 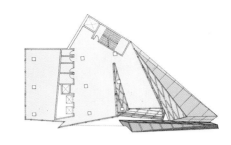

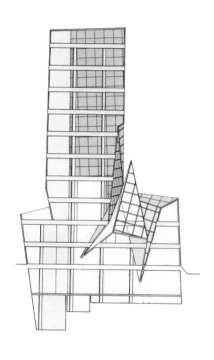 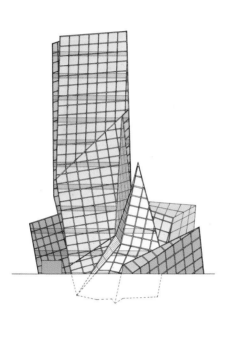 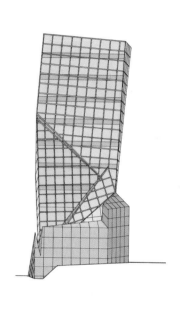

 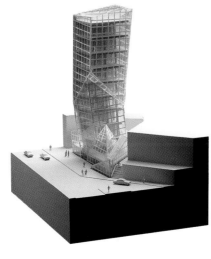 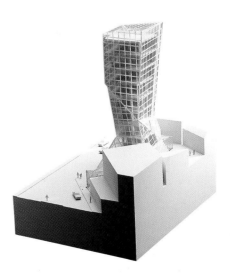

Above: *Basement level plan; second level plan; third level plan;* Centre: *Section to North; south elevation; east elevation;* Below: *Model views*

Background: *Wire frame axonometric*
Above: *Views of model;* Below:
*Elevations*

# PETER EISENMAN
## *CENTER FOR THE ARTS*
### *Emory University, Atlanta*

During the next four years Atlanta will be a unique center. Not only is it the media capital of America, but as host for the 1996 Olympics Atlanta will become the focus of world-wide media attention. Emory's Center for the Arts will be a primary focus of the Cultural Olympiad, unlike any other proposed construction on campus.

The Arts Center will serve two constituencies: the Emory campus and the larger community. Its primary purpose will be to teach and train students in the creative fields of theatre, film, and music. Hundreds of Emory students already take advantage of what the courses offer and the opportunities for performing in a variety of disciplines on campus. In the new Center, students will be able to converge in a single, carefully articulated building devoted to the pursuit of higher standards in the arts studied and practised at Emory. The Center's fertile atmosphere will permit collaboration between different creative enterprises – particularly important at a time when the arts draw increasingly upon each other for inspiration as is the case with performance art, contemporary music and video art.

The Center is located on the edge of the campus, anchoring itself on an existing multiple level garage structure on one side and projecting its main spaces onto a natural knoll. The Center will accommodate four major performing spaces: a music hall, a recital hall, a theatre and a cinema. However, the notion of the event is not confined to these interior spaces alone. The architecture of the building is expressive of and relates to its different environment – topographical, historical and programmatic – to produce a corresponding space. The Center's location at the edge of the campus allows it to serve as a connection between the community and the university through community-oriented performances and through the physical provision of a natural point of entry to the campus. A dual promenade crosses the knoll and passes through the building lobby. It arrives at an open amphitheatre and sculpture garden passing over a main ravine of the campus and leads to the university art museum on the historic, Hornbostel-designed quadrangle.

The historical quadrangle configuration is based on a grid system that is deformed by the topography of the ravine when extended to the Center's site. The initial deformation produced by the ravine approximates a fundamental sine wave, similar in amplitude and frequency to the ravine topography. These fundamental lines and their related harmonic run to the Center, affecting the site and the four 'bars' which constitute the building. The harmonic lines compress and deform the continuous surfaces of the bars, folding them in a multiplicity of different configuration.

The fields of force represented by the harmonic waves inflect the bars in a double way; evidenced by the small-scale and large-scale folds. The two different scales express the multiplicity of reaction to a similar system and compose an ever changing condition. The programme comes to inhabit the folded bars providing a transition west to east from the parking or academical spaces to the lobby, and the main performing spaces; while the performance spaces cross from north to south along a multiple level and lobby.

Currently, the 120,000 square foot, $30 million facility in the design development phase contains a 700 seat Music Hall, a 150 seat Recital Hall, a 150 seat Studio Theatre, a 150 seat Cinema, performance space support and academic space for the department of Theatre and Film Studies and the Department of Music.

*Progressive Architecture Citation, 1993*

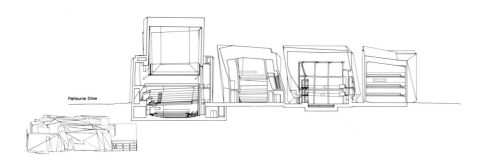

Fishburne Drive

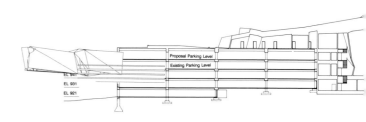

Proposal Parking Level
Existing Parking Level
EL 941
EL 931
EL 921

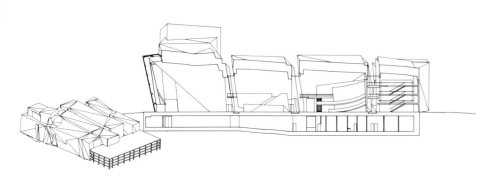

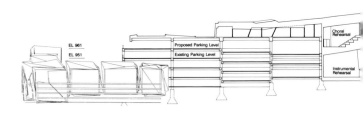

EL 961
EL 951

Proposed Parking Level
Existing Parking Level

Choral Rehearsal

Instrumental Rehearsal

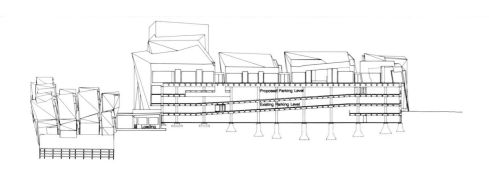

Proposed Parking Level
Existing Parking Level
Loading

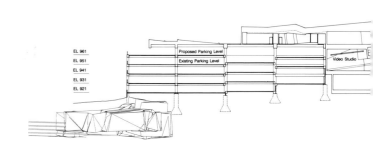

EL 961
EL 951
EL 941
EL 931
EL 921

Proposed Parking Level
Existing Parking Level

Video Studio

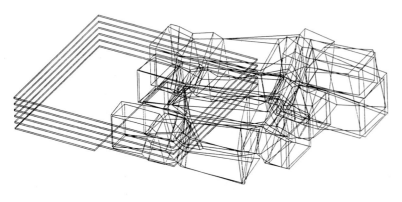

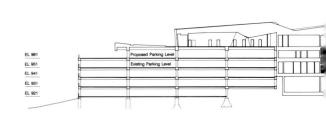

EL 961
EL 951
EL 941
EL 931
EL 921

Proposed Parking Level
Existing Parking Level

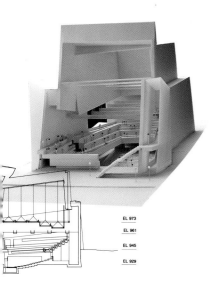

EL 973
EL 961
EL 945
EL 929

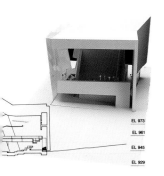

EL 973
EL 961
EL 945
EL 929

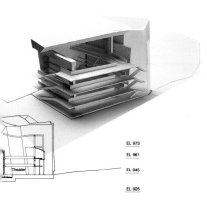

EL 973
EL 961
EL 945
EL 925

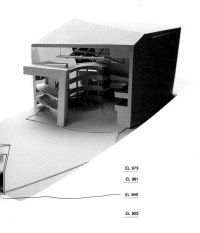

EL 973
EL 961
EL 945
EL 925

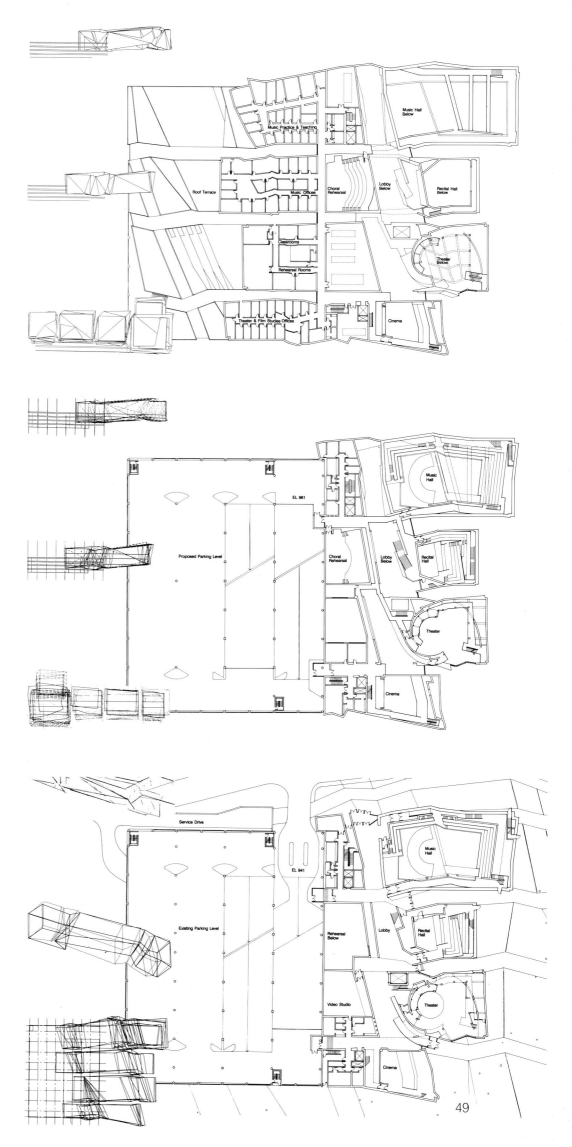

Music Practice & Teaching

Music Hall
Below

Roof Terrace

Music Offices

Choral
Rehearsal

Lobby
Below

Recital Hall
Below

Classrooms

Theater
Below

Rehearsal Rooms

Theater & Film Studies Offices

Cinema

EL 961

Proposed Parking Level

Music
Hall

Choral
Rehearsal

Lobby
Below

Recital
Hall

Theater

Cinema

Service Drive

Music
Hall

EL 941

Existing Parking Level

Rehearsal
Below

Lobby

Recital
Hall

Video Studio

Theater

Cinema

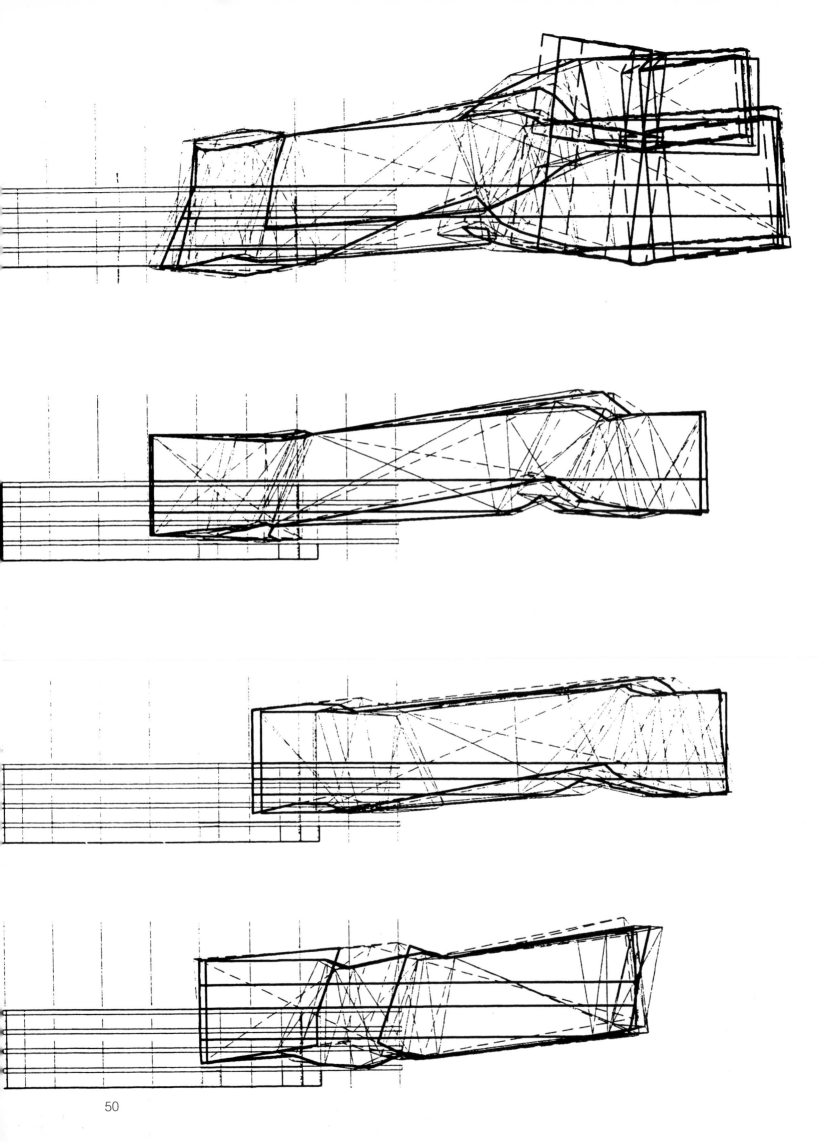

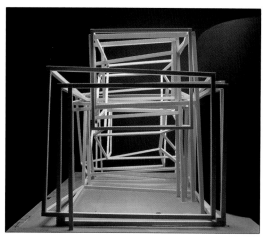

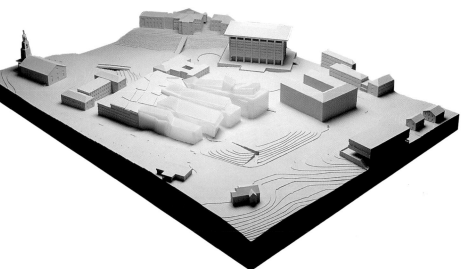

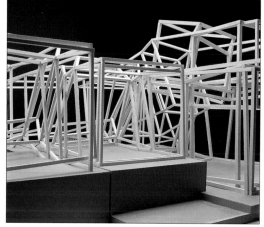

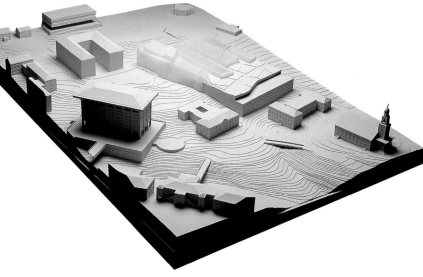

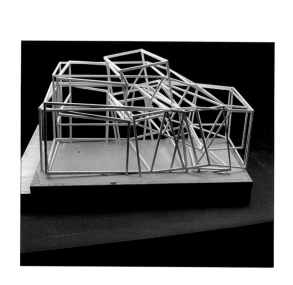

Previous Page Left: *Transverse sections;*
Centre: *Longitudinal sections;* Right: *Roof
terrace plan level; mezzanine plan level;
ground floor plan level;* Left: *Concept line
drawings;* Centre and Above: *Views of concept
and site models*

# FREDERIK STJERNFELT
## *THE POINTS OF SPACE*

For Immanuel Kant, space was a pure intuition a *reine Anschauung*. This seems to be underlined by the fact that we can hardly imagine any human activity of thought except in spatial concepts. Classical physics is famous for proceeding to make even time a purely quantitative parameter, a line, and hence nothing but yet another spatial dimension; but also Quantum mechanics is based on spatial representations, even if in a less straightforward manner – the complementarity between wave and particle derives from the fact that each of these two ways of representing a phenomenon are determined by their own set of spatial pictures, of metaphors: the wave in the water and the grain of sand. It is evident that semiotics, the science of signs, must be implementing spatial metaphors as well; in so far as by its very definition it contains the various spatial imaginations as objects: representations of mind and hence conceivable as signs. It is hardly possible to treat meaning and signs outside a structure which is in itself already an architectonic metaphor (structure, from Latin *struere*, to build) that separates an abstract space into partial spaces which can then be invested with signification (content): black against white, culture against nature etc, featuring characteristic zones of mediation between them in the abstract space of imagination: grey, cultivated etc. All kinds of qualities are probably conceived within such spaces. The possibility of change or development is inscribed therein by means of the routes through space; forcing, for instance, the change between red and green to proceed through yellow, blue or brown via a specific voyage of nuances depending on the route chosen. Thus it is no wonder that our imagination, working in its complicated network of abstract spaces of quality imposed on everyday 3-D space, has to make intense use of metaphors fetched from the most concrete space of experience: architecture.

Architecture is so obviously spatial because its very task is to seek a certain control over the space of living and its design. But all other sciences, too, find their foundations in space – to use a more than central metaphor of architecture: the foundation. Science, fantasy and literature are full of foundations, thresholds, entrances, labyrinths and enlightening views. They articulate themselves immediately 'as if' their subject was an intricate building in which the lover, the scientist, the philosopher is wandering about seeing connections and establishing distinctions. 'As if', we said, and the question is whether what is dealt with here is but a series of metaphors to be seen through, dismantled, deconstructed and so on. Does science have to impose upon itself the task of self liberation from metaphors of architecture? If it is an essential condition of thought to make use of these pictures, then there is no way out (sic!) – one has to merely attempt to control them in relation to the subject that one is seeking to love, to comprehend, to describe. A central 'field' that can hardly be thought without these archi-architectural basic concepts is the subject itself. Already, the body in which it most often finds itself situated is naturally obeying central architectonic relations (up/down, outside/inside, laterality, the body as a building [*Körperbau*]) that seem indispensable when one thinks of the subject as such. The opposition outside/inside can hardly be dispensed with if a soul, a mind, should be thought of as occupant of the building of the body. One only has to cast a glance at the three-storey house of Freud (id/ego/superego) or the Lacanian set of partitions (the 'split subject') to see that these spatial archetypes do not necessarily imply any idealistic metaphysics on behalf of the subject but rather the contrary. The fact that the subject might be a house does not imply that it should mistake itself for a transparent totality, self-controlling, well-arranged. Think of ruins and enormous Piranesian interiors to be convinced that the building does not in this way imply any necessarily organic or metaphysical ideology. On the contrary, if one first conceives oneself exploring, like a building, one is placed at a distance to the immediate consciousness and its self-reflection.

A structure, a subject, a piece of architecture – in each case it is evident that the various kinds of borders in space are crucial to their definition. Perceived from a topological point of view, these borders, walls, partitions and lines drawn in space are singularities; that is, they are sets of points of less probability than the rest of the space – singularities with lower dimension than the space in which they appear. The plane, the line, the point being singularities in 3-D space with decreasing dimension and hence probability. In this purely spatial conception, a piece of architecture would simply mean a structure of connected singularities in space: a composition of walls parting the space and defining it into segments, rooms, yards and so on; or, in the language of the topologists, a manifold, which does not imply any kind of naive pluralism but merely a complex object in several dimensions. In this respect, the less probable singularities, the line and the point, almost become literally on the edge of space: they do not really exist in space – only in so far as a subject is positioned to see, to construct them: when a subject experiences architecture, its body forms a point moving along a line, a route through architectural space. This leads us to two possible notions of this abstract as well as architectural space. Is the space a given continuum, of which the points, lines etc are mere intersections of no real existence; or, is the space itself made up as a mass of singular points, and hence nothing but a compilation of an infinitude of smaller elements? The second view is the one opted for by traditional geometry, but in fact the two points of view go back to two different views of the fundamentals of mathematics. In contrast to the stance taken by ordinary geometry, the French topologist and inventor of the so-called Catastrophe Theory, René Thom, maintains that the only really 'existing' space is 3-D and henceforth the only phenomenology in a given field comprehensible by man is such a space inhabited by 'balls' – connected beings with closed surface: 'atoms', 'elements', 'bodies' 'objects'; in every case small coherent parts of 3-D space. Thus, he posits continuity as superior to discontinuity. On the other hand, geometry makes discontinuity fundamental; thereby conciliating itself with arithmetic and its base, the act of counting. Space is, in this conception, a set of points emerging by virtue of a generative procedure, proceeding from the singular point to larger sets of points. From the latter point of view, the point is a kind of prerequisite to and renunciation of space. From the former, space is the basic and the point only visible therein as a construction. The romantic philosophy of Hegel saw in this antinomy between point and space a veritable dialectics: on the one hand, the point was a negation of space, having in itself no extension; on the other the empty space was the truth of the points, lines and surfaces. This dialectics then found its *Aufhebung* in concrete space, filled with objects defined by precise lines, points and surfaces. Time was then nothing but this very dialectics, this *Werden* working between space and its elements of less dimensions.

This antinomy between point and space, in turn implies certain consequences for architecture. With regard to deconstruction, a possible approach lies in interposing several systems on each other so that the resulting image does not depend on one single system but consists of entangled fragments of several structures; for instance, structures deriving from points, lines, planes respectively. Within this practice the fight waged in our spatial intuition between several possible systems is sought formalised, thereby opening the question of a play between decidability and indecidability. But this question, in turn, throws light back on the very concept of 'metaphysical' architecture. If architecture, by making houses like bodies and thereby giving them all the presuppositions of teleology, of meaning, of fundamentals and so on, is metaphysical – isn't it then already deconstructing itself by the doublesidedness of the singularities of which it consists? The necessary materiality of the singularities, eg, the bricks of a wall, makes possible a zone which is neither inside nor outside, the prerequisite to the uncanniness of houses and their traditional habitation by ghosts and geists which transcend walls and somehow live within them? The simplest singularity of all is the point, dividing the line into two. The next simplest is what René Thom calls a fold,

which makes possible the articulation of a wall: that which is neither inside nor outside. In this way, the fold is an articulation of the indecision already present in architecture: raised in concrete it becomes a monument of formal strength and indecision at the same time; the room under the fold is neither inside nor outside, or is both, depending on the point of view. Here, the subject becomes either spirit or nothing: a ghost. Thus, it is an articulation as well as a questioning of the inside/outside dichotomy: it marks a field of spatial indecision to the subject making its line through it. The fold folds a grid placed on the ground before folding. Now, thanks to gravity, the same effect as contained in Catastrophe Theory appears: it is possible to walk on the fold as well as beneath it, but never on its underside.

By this architecture of indecision, the line is drawn back to the vicissitude of the old *Anhalter Bahnhof* which, after being bombed during the war, was left like a roofless building, a temple (from *templum*, cut out) cutting a section of the sky and making a *coincidentia oppositorum* between inside and outside, sacred and profane. This inherent sacrality of architecture might seem to derive from its metaphysics, from its pretension of being a structure endowed with sense, an aesthetic, unambiguous or functional body. It is quite the contrary: its holiness depends on the fact that it always transcends these determinations. Hence it is in some sense superfluous to aim at architectural deconstruction by emphasising the insistence of points against space – the points are already working within space. This 'dialectics' without *Aufhebung* is contained within the fold; being an unfolding of one single point, a singularity, the point on top of its curvature, the point where the fold starts folding. This is the point that marks the locality as a place.

Now, how does the architectural subject behave? Not only is he a point himself (viewed from the scale of architecture) and a space (the body as a house) but he mediates between point and space by drawing a line – or, as belonging to a mass, covering a surface – in the construction. Attempting to make one's way by constructing an inner map of the surroundings is probably the primordial architectural 'experience', primary to any Heideggerian metaphysics of *Wohnen* (one dwells in a place only in so far as one has already constructed or been given a map thereof). In this walk, in the mind or in reality, several

specific situations occur. Following a path is the most simple: one is simply forced by architecture to choose the route as between two of the small buildings of the grid. Another situation is the dead-end: this is either the (partial) goal, with all the metaphysics of dwelling, function as well as religion, pouring forth; or on the contrary, the fatal sign of having got lost. The third possibility is the crossroads where several choices are possible and one has to choose. These three archi-situations have a common narrative ratio. On his way through architecture, the subject follows the same eternal structure as the prince seeking his princess. And if it is not the case that the fold forms an architectural body giving ends to the subject (like the mega-body of the church), then the fold is rather an orifice, a mouth – one mighty, obscene staring slit, an enormous version of the door with its sensible lips of door frames around it; but like the door, no longer leading anywhere. The fold is a cavern; a simple marking of a place as being neither inside nor outside, making possible the primitive cult or dwelling – and thence it marks the subject seeking its way within it and between the various small buildings on the grid folded up through it. Creeping inside as far as possible and becoming the ghost in the machine; or wandering onto the top of the fold and becoming a god lifted over the indecision of the fold, the subject is left to itself by being given all the narrative possibilities. Here, no entrance or system of passages is forcing or securing the roads, only the pure and indecisive distinction between inside or outside. Grasped as a totality the fold is easily imagined and controlled. As an object for a diversity of routes or being a mere punctiform orifice on the earth's surface, it depends on the infinitude of points in space – hence its *unheimlich* character.

The narrative that defines the subject by leading it through space can never be totally determined; the points being the ends as well as the beginnings of space. The interplay between point and space never ceases to create effects of sacrality and delusion because they are folded together in our Kantian imagination. The battle between point and space need not be dramatised as a battle between systems. It is waged within every system due to the very character of a system: an ordered set of points in space. Thus the fold might be the most simple and crude expression because any architecture, from a topological point of view, consists of many folds.

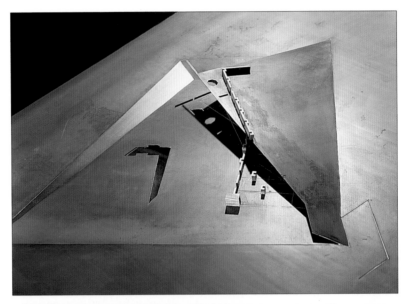

# CARSTEN JUEL- CHRISTIANSEN
## *THE ANHALTER FOLDING*

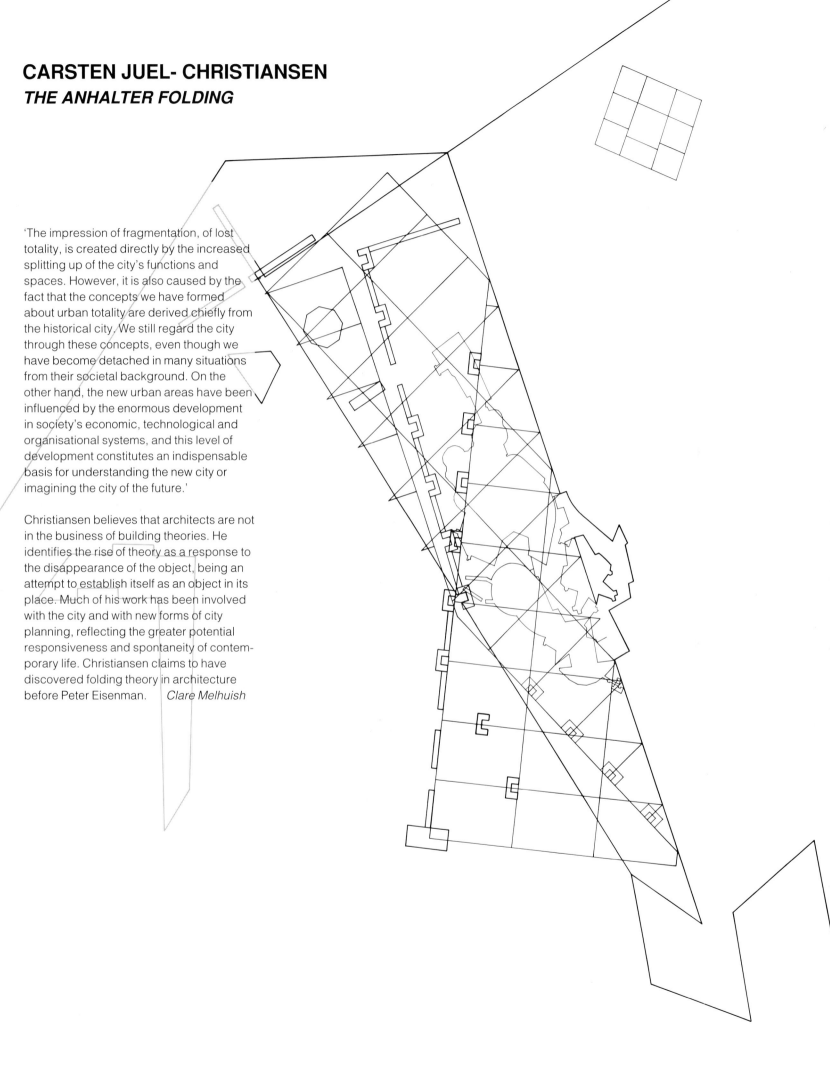

'The impression of fragmentation, of lost totality, is created directly by the increased splitting up of the city's functions and spaces. However, it is also caused by the fact that the concepts we have formed about urban totality are derived chiefly from the historical city. We still regard the city through these concepts, even though we have become detached in many situations from their societal background. On the other hand, the new urban areas have been influenced by the enormous development in society's economic, technological and organisational systems, and this level of development constitutes an indispensable basis for understanding the new city or imagining the city of the future.'

Christiansen believes that architects are not in the business of building theories. He identifies the rise of theory as a response to the disappearance of the object, being an attempt to establish itself as an object in its place. Much of his work has been involved with the city and with new forms of city planning, reflecting the greater potential responsiveness and spontaneity of contemporary life. Christiansen claims to have discovered folding theory in architecture before Peter Eisenman. *Clare Melhuish*

# JEFFREY KIPNIS
## *TOWARDS A NEW ARCHITECTURE*

'Well, I stand up next to a mountain,
and I chop it down with the edge of my
hand.
Then I pick up all the pieces and make an
island,
might even make a little sand.' *Jimi Hendrix*

Over the last few years, a few projects by a
handful of architects have broached
discussions of a New Architecture. The
themes of this discussion are only now
coming into sufficient focus to allow for the
preliminary efforts to articulate some of
them in this volume. Before we turn our
attention to that specific task, however, let
us consider for a moment what is at stake in
the endeavour.

'A New Architecture'. Today one whispers this phrase with trepidation and
embarrassment, perhaps for good reason.
True enough, most New Architectures are
so ill-conceived that they are stillborn or die
a merciful death early in infancy. But the
prognosis is poor even for those with the
strength to survive their hatching, for the
majority of these are killed by a well co-
ordinated, two-pronged attack.

There are several variations, but the
general schema of this attack is well-
known: first, critics from the right decry the
destabilising anarchism of the New Architecture and the empty egotism of its
architects; then, critics from the left rail
against the architecture as irresponsible
and immoral and the architects as corrupt
collaborationists. Sapped by this on-
slaught, the eviscerated remainders are
quickly mopped up by historians, with their
uncanny ability to convince us that the
supposed New Architecture is actually not
new at all and that it was in fact explored
with greater depth and authenticity in
Europe some time ago.[1]

Today, historians and critics alike
proselytise upon the creed that there is
nothing new that is worthwhile in architecture, particularly no new form. Their doxol-
ogy is relentless, 'praise the past, from
which all blessings flow.' Thus, we retreat
from the new and have become ashamed to
look for it. I have colleagues who comb

drafts of their work before publication in
order to replace the word 'new' as often as
possible; I have done it myself. As a result,
PoMo, whose guiding first principle is its
unabashed and accurate claim to offer
nothing new, has become the only architecture to mature over the last 20 years.

'Nonsense!' It will be argued. 'During the
same period a flourishing revival of the
avant-garde has developed' and fingers
will point to MOMA's Decon exhibition and
to the buildings of Eisenman, Gehry,
Libeskind, Tschumi, Koolhaas, Hadid and
others. Yet, upon closer examination, it is
not more accurate to say that these works
have been executed under the auspices of
an implicit contract of disavowal. In other
words, is it not the case that these designs
are celebrated as auratic, signature
buildings of interest only for their
irreproducible singularity, rather than as
sources of new principles for a general
architectural practice. In that sense, the
discipline of architecture has recognised
them as exotic, precisely so as to suppress
their contribution to a New Architecture.

Yet within these disparate works are
insights that might well contribute to
formulating a framework for a New Architecture: one that promises both formal
vitality and political relevance. Consider the
work of Daniel Libeskind, for example. From
his *Chamber Works* to his recent projects in
Germany and elsewhere, one finds a
sustained, penetrating critique of the axis
and its constellation of linear organisations.
Considering the political, social and spatial
history of the axis in architecture and
urbanism, this is no minor issue. Yet, very
little on this subject can be found in the
critical literature treating these projects.
Instead, Libeskind is configured as an
avatar of the esoteric and the status and
power of the axis in quotidian architectural
practice, so thoroughly re-thought in his
projects, is left unquestioned.

On the surface, our retreat from the New
seems both historically and theoretically
well-informed. Towards its utopian aspirations, architectural Modernism sought to
overthrow obsolete spatial hierarchies and

establish a new and more democratic,
homogeneous space. However well-
meaning this goal was, insofar as its search
for the New was implicated in an Enlighten-
ment-derived, progressivist project, it was
also implicated in the tragedies that
resulted. The instrumental logic of architectural Modernism's project of the new
necessarily calls for erasure and replacement, of Old Paris by Le Corbusier, for
example.

In the name of heterogeneity, post-
modern discourse has mounted a critique
of the project of the new along several
fronts. It has demonstrated both the
impossibility of invention *tabula rasa* and
the necessity to celebrate the very differences Modernism sought to erase. Its own
version of the search for the New, a giddy
logic of play, of reiteration and recombination, of collage and montage, supplants
Modernism's sober, self-serious search for
the Brave New. In Post-Modernism's play,
history regains renewed respect, though on
different terms. Rejected as the linear,
teleological process that underwrites its
own erasure and replacement, history is
now understood as the shapeless well of
recombinatorial material; always deep,
always full, always open to the public.

In Post-Modernism's most virulent
practices, those that use reiteration and
recombination to insinuate themselves into
and undermine received systems of power,
a relationship to the New is maintained that
is optimistic and even progressive, albeit
not teleologically directed. In such post-
modern practices as deconstruction, the
project of the new is rejected. New intellectual, aesthetic and institutional forms, as
well as new forms of social arrangements,
are generated not by proposition but by
constantly destabilising existing forms.
New forms result as temporary
restabilisations, which are then
destabilised. Accelerated evolution
replaces revolution, the mechanisms of
empowerment are disseminated,
heterogeneous spaces that do not support
established categorical hierarchies are
sought, a respect for diversity and differ-

ence is encouraged. Far from being nihilistic, Post-Modernism in this conception is broadly affirmative.

Unfortunately, however, Post-Modernism's critique of the politics of erasure/replacement and emphasis on recombination have also led to its greatest abuse, for it has enabled a reactionary discourse that re-establishes traditional hierarchies and supports received systems of power, such as the discourse of the nothing new employed by Ronald Reagan and Margaret Thatcher for their political ends and by Prince Charles, Roger Scruton and even Charles Jencks to prop up PoMo.

I believe, therefore, that it is not Post-Modernism itself, but another, more insidious pathology, a kind of cultural *progeria*, that underlies our current withdrawal from the New. The symptoms of this disorder were first diagnosed by Nietzsche and have been thoroughly analysed more recently by Roberto Unger.[2] Briefly, it manifests itself as a rationale which holds that the catalogue of possible forms (in every sense of the word form: institutional, social, political and aesthetic) is virtually complete and well-known. We may debate the relative merits of this form or that, but we will no longer discover nor invent any new forms. This position is far from the suppositions of post-modern combinatorics.

Is it possible that 'Westernity' as a cultural experiment is finished and, put simply, that we are old? Only in that context could our current, excessive veneration for the received catalogue of forms be valid. Frankly, I cannot believe that in the short span of our history we have experimented with and exhausted the possibilities of form. It seems to me that every indication today is to the contrary; whether one considers the political transformations in Eastern Europe or the technological transformations that characterise today's society. The building of the catalogue of available forms, aesthetic forms, institutional forms and of forms of social arrangement, has only just begun.

I have already indicated some of the broader criteria for a New Architecture. If it is not to repeat the mistakes of Modernism, it must continue to avoid the logic of erasure and replacement by participating in recombinations. As far as possible, it must seek to engender a heterogeneity that resists settling into fixed hierarchies. Furthermore, it must be an architecture, ie, a proposal of principles (though not prescriptions) for design. Finally, it must experiment with and project new forms.

The first two of these criteria, already belong to architectural Post-Modernism, However, the last two criteria – the call for principles and the projection of new forms – detach fundamentally the theorisation of a New Architecture from Post-Modernism proper, however much it draws upon the resources of the latter.

Indicative of that detachment is the degree to which some New Architecture theorists, notably Sanford Kwinter and Greg Lynn, have shifted their attention from post-structural semiotics to a consideration of recent developments in geometry, science and the transformations of political space, a shift that is often marked as a move from a Derridian towards a Deleuzian discourse.[3]

In these writings, the Deleuzian cast is reinforced with references to Catastrophe Theory – the geometry of event-space transformations – and to the new Biology. Not only are geometry and science traditional sources par excellence of principles and form for architecture, but, more importantly, the paramount concern of each of these areas of study is morphogenesis, the generation of new form. However provocative and invaluable as resources these studies in philosophy or science are, it must be said that neither provide the impetus for a New Architecture, nor the particulars of its terms and conditions. Rather, these have grown entirely out of architectural projects and developments within the discipline of architecture itself.

One contributing factor to the search for a New Architecture is the exhaustion of collage as the prevailing paradigm of architectural heterogeneity. In order to oppose Modernism's destituting proclivity for erasure and replacement, Post-Modernism emphasised grafting as the recombinatorial instrument of choice. The constellation of collage, in all its variations,[4] offered the most effective model of grafting strategies. From Rowe to Venturi to Eisenman,[5] from PoMo to the deconstructivists, collage has served as the dominant mode of the architectural graft. There are indications, however, to suggest that collage is not able to sustain the heterogeneity architecture aspires to achieve. In lieu of the meticulous study necessary to support this claim, allow the suggestion of two of its themes, the first, historical, and the second, theoretical. First, post-modern collage is an extensive practice wholly dependent on effecting incoherent contradictions within and against a dominant frame. As it becomes the prevailing institutional practice, it loses both its contradictory force and its affirma-

tive incoherence. Rather then destabilising an existing context, it operates more and more to inscribe its own institutional space. The only form collage produces, therefore, is the form of collage.

Secondly, and perhaps more importantly, collage is limited to a particular order of semiotic recombinations. Each element in a collage, even in the aleatoric process-collages of dada, must be known and rosterable in its own right. Thus, although collage may engender new compositions as well as shifts, slips, accidents and other chimeral effects, the long-term effect of collage is to valorise a finite catalogue of elements and/or processes.

Collage is only able to renew itself by constantly identifying and tapping into previously unrostered material. Thus, collage can never be projective. The exhaustion of collage derives from the conclusion that the desire to engender a broadly empowering political space in respect of diversity and difference cannot be accomplished by a detailed cataloguing and specific enfranchisement of each of the species of differentiation that operate within a space. The process is not only economically and politically implausible, it is theoretically impossible.[6] If collage is exhausted as a recombinatorial strategy – a matter still debated[7] – then the problem becomes one of identifying grafts other than collages. The key distinction from collage would be that such grafts would seek to produce heterogeneity within an intensive cohesion rather than out of extensive incoherence and contradiction.[8]

In a lecture delivered in 1990 to the ANYONE conference in Los Angeles, the neo-modern social theorist Roberto Mangeiberra Unger took issue with current post-modern practices in architecture, primarily in terms of what he saw as the 'ironic distancing' effected by both PoMo and Deconstructivist architecture. At the conclusion of his lecture, he outlined five criteria that any New Architecture seeking to contribute to a non-hierarchical, heterogeneous political space must meet.

According to Unger, such an architecture must be *vast* and *blank*, it must *point* and be *incongruous* and *incoherent*.[9] It is not clear from the lecture how Unger intended his criteria to be interpreted, but I was struck by the degree to which, with one exception, they lent themselves to a discourse on grafting alternatives to collage. Particularly interesting to me was how well these criteria read as generalisations of the spacial/formal project of

Modernism outlined in Le Corbusier's points. Where Le Corbusier's points are directed towards producing a broadly democratic space by achieving homogeneity, Unger's are directed towards a similar political goal by achieving a spatial heterogeneity that does not settle into stable alignments or hierarchies. I interpret and modify Unger's criteria as follows: (i) Vastness – negotiates a middle-ground between the homogeneity of infinite or universal space and the fixed hierarchies of closely articulated space. Recognising the necessity of finitude for heterogeneity, vastness seeks sufficient spatial extension to preclude the inscription of traditional, hierarchical spatial patterns. Design implication: generalisation of free-plan to include disjunction and discontinuity; extension of free plan to 'free-section'; emphasis on residual and interstitial spaces. (ii) Blankness – extrapolates the Modernist project of formal abstraction understood as the suppression of quotation or reference through the erasure of decoration and ornament to include canonic form and type. By avoiding formal or figural reference, architecture can engage in unexpected formal and semiotic affiliations without entering into fixed alignments. Design implication: generalisation of free-facade to free-massing. (iii) Pointing – architecture must be projective, ie, it must point to the emergence of new social arrangements and to the construction of new institutional forms. In order to accomplish this, the building must have a point, ie, project a transformation of a prevailing political context. The notion of pointing should not be confused with signifying, and in fact is a challenge to the determined structure of the signifier/signified, whether monosemic or polysemic. The indeterminacy of pointing shifts the emphasis from the formation of stable alignments and/or allegiances to the formation of provisional affiliations. (iv) Incongruity – a requirement to maintain yet subvert received data, including, for example, the existing site as a given condition and/or the programme brief. Maintenance and subversion are equally important; either alone leads inexorably to spatial hypostatisation. Design implication: a repeal of the architectural postulates of harmony and proportion, structural perspicuity and system co-ordination (eg, among plan, section and facade, or between detail and formal organisation). (v) Intensive Coherence – in fact, Unger stresses the necessity for incoherence, understood as a repeal of the architectural postulate of unity or wholeness. However, because incoherence is the hallmark of post-modern collage, I suggest as an alternative, a coherence forged out of incongruity. Intensive coherence implies that the properties of certain monolithic arrangements enable the architecture to enter into multiple and even contradictory relationships. It should not be confused with Venturi's notion of the 'difficult whole', in which a collage of multiplicity is then unified compositionally.

At the beginning of this essay, I noted that a handful of recent projects offer specific terms and conditions for a New Architecture. While, in general, these projects show a shift away from a concern for semiotics towards a concern for geometry, topology, space and events, in my view, they subdivide broadly into two camps, which I term DeFormation and InFormation. DeFormation, the subject of this volume, seeks to engender shifting affiliations that nevertheless resist entering into stable alignments. It does so by grafting abstract topologies that cannot be decomposed into simple, planar components nor analysed by the received language of architectural formalism.

The strategy of InFormation, of which Koolhaas' Karlsruhe and Tschumi's Le Fresnoy are exemplary cases, is to form a collecting graft, usually by encasing disparate formal and programmatic elements within a neutral, modernist monolith. The resultant incongruous, residual spaces are then activated with visual layering, programmatic innovation, technological effects and events.

Although both evolve from the same problem, the architectures of DeFormation and InFormation are by no means simply collaborative. In general, both agree on certain architectural tactics that can be understood in terms of Unger's criteria (as modified). Both, for example, rely on such devices as box-within-box sections with an emphasis on interstitial and residual spaces (vast, incongruous); also, both deploy monolithic forms and avoid any obvious applied ornament or figurative reference (blank, intensive cohesion).

Yet the tensions between them are pronounced. While DeFormation emphasises the role of new aesthetic form and therefore the visual in the engenderment of new spaces, InFormation de-emphasises the role of aesthetic form in favour of new institutional form, and therefore of programme and events. The event-spaces of new geometries tend to drive the former, while the event-spaces of new technologies occupy the latter.

One of the pervasive characteristics of InFormation is its unapologetic use of the orthogonal language of Modernism. When post-modernist architecture first emerged, the formal language of Modernism was simply condemned as oppressive and monotonous – recall Venturi's 'Less is a bore'. Subsequently, that critique was deepened as architects and theorists demonstrated that, far from being essentialist, the language of Modernism constituted a sign-system. Once the demonstration that architecture was irreducibly semiotic was complete, the essentialist justification for the austere language of Modernism dissolved and the door opened to the use of any and all architectural signs in any and every arrangement.

InFormation posits that the exhaustion of collage is tantamount to a rendering that is irrelevant of all aesthetic gestures.[10] The architectural contribution to the production of new forms and the inflection of political space therefore can no longer be accomplished by transformations of style. Furthermore, InFormation argues that the collective architectural effect of the orthogonal forms of Modernism is such that it persists in being Blank; often stressing that blankness by using the forms as screens for projected images. Pointing is accomplished by transformations of institutional programmes and events. For, DeFormation, on the other hand, architecture's most important contribution to the production of new forms and to the inflection of political space continues to be aesthetic. Far from being Blank, DeFormation perceives the modernist language of InFormation as nothing less than historical reference and the use of projected images no more than applied ornament. Instead, DeFormation searches for Blankness by extending Modernism's exploration of monolithic form, while rejecting essentialist appeal to Platonic/Euclidean/Cartesian geometries. Pointing is accomplished in the aesthetics; the forms transform their context by entering into undisciplined and incongruous formal relationships. InFormation sees the gestured geometries of DeFormation as predominantly a matter of ornament style.

To examine the design consequences of these issues, let us look at a brief comparison of Tschumi's InFormation at Le Fresnoy with Shirdel's DeFormation at Nara. The National Center for Contemporary Arts at Le Fresnoy offered a perfect circumstance in which to reconsider the graft. In his description of the problem, Tschumi was specific in outlining the various possibilities. Since many of the existing structures were in disrepair, a return to an erase-and-replace approach was perfectly plausible. On the other hand, the quality of the historical forms and spaces at Le Fresnoy also suggested a renovation/restoration approach à la Collage. Tschumi eschews both, however, and envelops the entire complex within a partially enclosed modernist roof to create a cohesive graft. The graft does not produce a collage; rather than creating compositionally resolved collection of fragments, the roof reorganises and redefines each of the elements into a blank, monolithic unity whose incongruity is internalised. Tschumi sutures together the broad array of resulting spaces with a system of catwalks and stairs, visually interlacing them with cuts, partial enclosures, ribbon windows and broad transparencies. Wherever one is in the complex, one sees partial, disjointed views of several zones from inside to outside at the same time.

Like the visual effects, the role of programming in this project concerns the production of space as much, if not more than, the accommodation of function. As far as possible, Tschumi programmes all the resultant spaces, even treating the tile roofs of the old building as a mezzanine. Where direct programming is not possible, he elaborates the differential activation in material/events. In the structural trusses of the new roof, he projects videos as an architectural material in order to activate those residual spaces with events.

The result is a project which promises a spatial heterogeneity that defies any simple hierarchy: a collection of differentiated spaces capable of supporting a wide variety of social encounters without privileging or subordinating any. Le Fresnoy undermines the classical architectural/political dialectic between hierarchical heterogeneity and homogeneity and points to a potentially new institutional/architectural form.

Like Tschumi at Le Fresnoy,Shirdel also uses a collecting-graft to unify an incongruous, box-in-box section in his project for the Nara Convention Center. Unlike Tschumi, however, he shapes the form and internal structure of the graft by folding a three-bar parti with two complex regulating line geometries. The first geometry involutes the exterior of the building into an abstract, non-referential monolith whose form flows into the landscaping of the site. The second

geometry has a similar effect on the major structural piers that hold the three theatres (each one a box whose form is determined simply by exigent functional requirements) suspended in section.

The internal and external geometries connect in such a way that 'major' space of the complex is entirely residual, an alley, so to speak, rived in the provisional links between two invaginated geometries. The residual-space effect is reinforced by the fact that all of the explicit programme of the building is concentrated in the theatres and lobbies that float as objects above and away from the main space. In a sense, Shirdel's attitude towards programme is the opposite of Tschumi's. Although the building functions according to its brief, there is no architectural programme other than the function, no informing choreography nor any use of technology to activate spaces. Shirdel's computer renderings of Japanese dancers performing in eerie isolation in the emptied, residual space underline the point. The entire issue of spatial heterogeneity rests in the aesthetics of the form and in the opposition between unprogrammed event and function. In passing, it is worth noting that the risk of proposing that the dominant (and most expensive) space of a building be nothing other than residual space should not be underestimated.

I pursue the development of DeFormation in greater detail below and will have occasion to return to the Shirdel Nara project. However, I believe that the brief comparison above, is sufficient to indicate both the similarities and divergences in the routes that are being mapped by InFormation and DeFormation towards a New Architecture.

## DeFormation[11]

As is always the case in architectural design theory, Deformation is an artifact, a construction of principles that have emerged after the fact from projects by diverse architects that were originally forged with different intentions and under different terms and conditions. Thus, strictly speaking, there are no DeFormationist architects (yet), just as there were no Mannerist or Baroque architects. It is a minor point, perhaps too obvious to belabour; yet as we move towards a development of principles and a technical language with which to articulate them, we must be cautious not to allow these prematurely to circumscribe and regulate a motion in design whose fertility derives as

much from its lack of discipline as from its obedience to policy. If there is a DeFormation, it has only just begun.

Much has been written and no doubt more will be written that consigns the work of DeFormation (and InFormation) to this or that contemporary philosopher, particularly Gilles Deleuze. It cannot be denied that a powerful consonance exists between the field of effects sought by these architectures and various formulations of Deleuze and Guattari in A Thousand Plateaus or by Deleuze in Le Pli. The sheer number of terms that the architectural literature has borrowed from the Deleuzian discourse (affiliation, pliancy, smooth and striated space, etc) not to mention such fortuities as the shared thematisation of folding, testify to the value of this correspondence. However, for all of the profitability of this dialogue there are costs to which we should be attentive. In general, obligating any architecture to a philosophy or theory maintains a powerful but suspect tradition in which architecture is understood as an applied practice. In that tradition, the measure of architectural design is the degree to which it exemplifies a theory or philosophy, rather than the degree to which it continuously produces new architectural effects; as a consequence, the generative force of design effects in their own right are subordinated to the limited capacity of architecture to produce philosophical (or theoretical) effects.

In his reading of Leibniz in Le Pli, Deleuze stages his meditation on the fold in part on an interpretation of the space of Baroque architecture, thus it might be assumed that Baroque architecture stands as a paradigm of the architectural effects of the fold. Such an assumption, however careless, would be fair and would underwrite the configuration of DeFormation as nothing more than a neo-Baroque.

Now, though Deleuze's reading of Baroque architecture is adequate to exemplify his thought on the fold, it is by no means an adequate reading of the architectural effects of the Baroque. Baroque architecture is no more able to realise the contemporary architectural effects of the fold than Leibniz's philosophy is able to realise the contemporary philosophical effects of Deleuze's thought. In other words, Deleuze's philosophy is no more (merely) neo-Leibnizian than DeFormation is (merely) neo-Baroque.

However much Deleuze's philosophy profits from the generative effects of Leibniz's texts, its payoff, ie, what it has new to say, does not rest on the accuracy of its scholarly recapitulation of Leibniz's philosophy; rather, it rests primarily on the differences between what Deleuze writes and what Leibniz writes. On this point, I believe Deleuze (and Leibniz!) would agree. In the same way, the interest of DeFormation does not rest on its recapitulation of Baroque themes, but primarily on the differences it effects with the Baroque and its other predecessors.

But perhaps, the dearest cost to which we must be attentive is the degree to which formulating DeFormation in terms of a Deleuzian language belies the independent development of the (consonant ideas within) architecture. No doubt this development, more a genealogy than a history, lacks the grace and pedigree that it would obtain from architecture conceived as applied philosophy. Yet, the halting, circuitous pathways of DeFormation's evolution – here lighting on cloth folds depicted in a painting by Michelangelo, there on train-tracks, here a desperate attempt to win a competition, there a last-minute effort to satisfy a nervous client, and always drawing upon the previous work of others – not only bears a dignity all its own, but also materially augments the substance of the philosophy.

Allow me then, to retrace some of these paths, collecting my effects along the way. Neither arbitrarily nor decisively, I begin with three contemporaneous projects: Shirdel and Zago's Alexandria Library Competition entry, Eisenman's Columbus Convention Center and Gehry's Vitra Museum.[12]

For a number of years beginning in the early 1980s, Bahram Shirdel, in association with Andrew Zago, pursued an architecture which he termed black-stuff. Ironic as the term may first appear, black-stuff is quite an accurate name for the effects Shirdel sought to achieve. Rejecting the deconstructivist themes of fragments, signs, assemblages and accreted space, Shirdel pursued a new, abstract monolithicity that would broach neither reference nor resemblance. Shirdel was interested in generating disciplined architectural forms that were not easily decomposable into the dynamics of point/line/plane/volume of modern formalism. We will come to refer to these forms in terms of anexact geometries and non-developable surfaces, but Shirdel's black-stuff set the stage for the Deformationist principle of non-referential, monolithic abstraction we have already discussed.

To generate these forms, Shirdel developed a technique in which he would begin with one or more recognisable figure(s) whose underlying organisation possessed the desired internal complexity. Then, in a series of steps, he mapped the architectural geometry of these figures in meticulous detail, carefully abstracting or erasing in each progressive step aspects of the original figure that caused it to be referential or recognisable – a process I termed disciplined relaxation at the time. Similar processes appear in the discussion of the Gehry and Eisenman projects to follow.

The culmination of the black-stuff investigations was the Shirdel/Zago entry premiated in the Alexandria Library competition, a design that evolved from a disciplined relaxation of a painting of folded cloth by Michelangelo. In that figure of the fold, Shirdel found precisely the formal qualities he sought. Although the final form shows no obvious traces of the original painting, relationships among surface, form and space are captured in the architecture.

Shortly after the Alexandria competition, Peter Eisenman entered a limited competition against Holt, Henshaw, Pfau and Jones, and Michael Graves[13] to design a convention centre for Columbus, Ohio. Because the City of Columbus framed the opening of the centre in terms of its quintcentennial celebration of Christopher Columbus' first voyage, Eisenman's initial strategy was to design a collage project based on the nautical architecture of the Santa Maria. With only three weeks remaining in the 12-week competition period, Eisenman learned that Graves, too, was basing his design on a nautical theme. Anxious to win the competition, (he had only just opened his own office) Eisenman took the extreme risk of abandoning nine weeks of work and shifting to an entirely different scheme, taking a moment to send Graves a postcard of a sinking ship en passant.

The new scheme was based on the notion of 'weak form' Eisenman had only just begun to formulate.[14,15] Working from two oddly similar diagrams, one of a fibre-optics cable cross-section and the other of the train-track switching system that once occupied the site in Columbus, Eisenman produced the winning design: a monolithic box knitted out of vermiform tendrils. The likeness shared by the two diagrams is important to note, for in that weak resemblance, Eisenman first saw the potential of weak form.

Although similar in many respects, the Eisenman weak-form projects are different

from Shirdel's black-stuff in one aspect that is of fundamental significance to the principles of DeFormation. Eisenman also attempts to achieve an abstract monolith free of explicit reference. But while the black-stuff projects were intended to be radically other, Eisenman's notion of weakness requires the form to retain a hint of resemblance, so that it might enter into unexpected relationships, like the one that connects the two diagrams.

True enough, once alerted, one is quite able to read both the train-truck and fibre optic diagrams in the convention centre form. However, the most surprising weak link occurs when the scheme is placed on the site. As is to be expected, the design addressed many traditional architectural relationships to the site; such as reinforcing the street edge and negotiating a severe scale transition. On the other hand, almost as if it had been planned from the beginning, the braided forms of Eisenman's project connected the mundane three-storey commercial buildings across to street from centre to the complex highway system interchange behind it. Though entirely unplanned, this connection has the effect of transforming the prevailing architectural logic of the site.

Borrowing from Deleuze, DeFormation refers to these tentative formal links with contingent influences as affiliations, and engendering affiliations is the foremost mechanism by which DeFormation attempts to Point. Affiliations are distinct from traditional site relations in that they are not pre-determined relationships that are built into the design, but effects that flow from the intrinsic formal, topological or spatial character of the design.

Typically, one identifies important site influences such as manifest or latent typological/morphological diagrams, prevailing architectural language, material, detailing or the like, and incorporates some or all of these influences into a design, often by collage. Such relationships are not affiliations, but alignments and serve to reinforce the dominant architectural modes governing a context.

Affiliations, on the other hand, are provisional, ad hoc links that are made with secondary contingencies that exist within the site or extended context. Rather than reinforcing the dominant modes of the site, therefore, affiliations amplify suppressed or minor organisations that also operate within the site, thereby re-configuring the context into a new coherence. Because they link disjoint, stratified organisations into a coherent heterogeneity, the effect of such affiliations is termed 'smoothing.'[16,17]

In order to complete our initial survey of affiliative effects, we must pick up a few threads from Frank Gehry at Vitra. Gehry's design process, not unrelated to Shirdel's disciplined relaxation and Eisenman's weakening, involves incessant modelling and remodelling an initial figure or set of figures. Though he distorts and deforms the figures towards architectural abstraction, Gehry is even more concerned than Eisenman to preserve a representational heritage in the design.

Gehry's Vitra commission called for a site masterplan, a chair assembly factory, and a museum for the furniture collection. In the preliminary design, Gehry simply aligned the new factory with the factory buildings previously on the site, while his Museum, a geometer's Medusa, stood in stark contrast. Though Gehry reduced the difference to some extent by surfacing the Museum in white plaster, so as to relate to the factory buildings; nevertheless, as a graft on the site, the form of the Museum installed the familiar disjunctive incoherence I have associated with collage. The client, fearful of employees' complaints that all of the design attention was being invested in the Museum and none in the workplace, asked Gehry as an afterthought to enliven the new factory building. In response, Gehry appended some circulation elements that reiterated the stretched and twisted tentacles of the museum to the two corners of the new factory nearest the Museum.

The architectural effect was dramatic, for like the Eisenman Convention Center, the additions knit affiliative links between the factory buildings and the museum, smoothing the site into a heterogeneous, but cohesive whole. However, unlike the Convention Centre, the staircases entered the site as a field rather than as an object – pointing to the possibility of intensive coherence generating a smoothing effect at an urban scale. From this perspective, the circulation additions contribute as much to the architecture of DeFormation as the Museum itself.

Because other genealogies tracing through other projects can also be drawn, it cannot be said that DeFormation is born from these three projects, two of the key principles of DeFormation are in place. In summary, these are: (i) an emphasis on abstract, monolithic architectural form that broaches minimal direct references or resemblance and that is alien to the dominant architectural modes of a given site; (ii)

the development of smoothing affiliations with minor organisations operating within a context that are engendered by the intrinsic geometric, topological and/or spatial qualities of the form. However, before we examine the discussions that have developed around these issues, the evolution of one last principle must be traced.

As Bahram Shirdel and I analysed these and related projects, we noticed that, for all of their other movements, they tend to leave the classical congruity between massing and section largely intact. As a result, the skin of the building continues to be partitioned into the familiar programme-driven hierarchies of major, minor and service spaces implied by the massing. The issue, as we saw it, was to avoid both the continuous, homogenous space of the free plan and the finite, hierarchical space of more traditional sectional strategies.

Several projects suggested different ways to approach the problem of section. Among the more influential of these were Eisenman's Carnegie Mellon research institute, the Nouvel/Starck entry for the Tokyo Opera House competition and Koolhaas' Bibliothèque de France. In the Eisenman scheme, essentially a chain of pods, a large sculptural object whose form was congruent with the pod, floated concentrically within each pod; in effect rendering the primary space of the building interstitial. The striking Nouvel/Starck Opera House was noteworthy for the way its theatre was embedded as in incongruent object into the urban object massing. In his competition entry for the Bibliotheque de France, a seminal example of Information, Koolhaas achieved an extreme detachment of sectional space from the massing. Bahram Shirdel, Andrew Zago and I formed a partnership in order to continue to develop methods for generating affiliative, monolithic forms and, as well, to develop these sectional ideas. Our Event-Structure entry for the Place Jacques Cartier-Montreal competition, for example, called for a large DeFormed envelope within which three independently DeFormed theatres floated as sectional objects. As in InFormation, every surface, including the outside and inside of both the exterior envelope and the floating theatres was programmed. Our goal was to render all of the spaces in the building interstitial and/or residual and to activate them into a non-hierarchical differential structure. However, the formal similarity between the two systems, the envelope and the sectional object-theatres, resulted in spaces that

were less interstitial than homogeneous.[18]

Our subsequent design for the Scottish National Museum competition produced somewhat more interesting results. The typical section of such museums partitions the space into well-defined compartments determined by the categories of the different collections. In order to counter this alignment between form and programme, we devised a section and circulation system in which elements of differing collections would enter into various and shifting associations as one moved through the museum. The effect of encouraging provisional, weak-links among the items in the collection was further augmented with a series of windows calculated to frame objects in the urban setting as if they were objects within the collection. Finally, two of the major lobes of the building itself stood as objects within the basement galleries.

The section/circulation system was embedded within a three-lobed, articulated monolith. Though conspicuously alien to the classical language and other dominant architectural influences of the site, the geometry of the massing took good advantage of several subordinate organisations within both Edinburgh and the larger context of Scotland to extend the production of affiliative effects. A catalogue of over two-dozen of these relationships generated by Doug Graf, an architectural theorist specialising in formal relations, was included with the competition submission.[19] As we and others worked on similar problems, the two major sectional themes of DeFormation began to emerge. First, as far as possible, the section space of the building should not be congruent with the internal space implied by the monolith. Secondly, wherever possible, residual, interstitial and other artifactual spaces should be emphasised over primary spaces. Because the box-within-box section is effective at producing both of these effects, it is often the tactic of choice, though by no means the only one possible. The impetus to programmatic saturation so central to InFormation plays a much less significant role in DeFormation.

With these sectional themes, the last of the preliminary principles of DeFormation is in place. Yet, we should not prematurely draw the conclusion that DeFormation is complete and that a prescription for its architecture written. Indeed, though paradigmatic building projects such as Eisenman's Max Reinhardthaus[20] or Shirdel's Nara Convention Hall can be identified, the internal debates among these and other related projects assure us that there are principles and projects to follow. The most interesting of these debates revolve around design techniques for producing smoothing affiliations.[21] Because such affiliations require that loose links be made among dominant and contingent organisations operating within a context, some architects work by identifying examples of both types of organisation and then drive the design towards their connection, while others rely entirely on the intrinsic contextual affiliations engendered by the Eisenman Convention Center or the Shirdel, Zago, Kipnis Scottish National Museum are examples of the latter; in each case, most of the links were unplanned and occurred only after grafting the project to the site.

Shoei Yoh's Odawara Sports Complex, on the other hand, is a conspicuous case of the former. Shoei Yoh designed the complex's roof by mapping a detailed study of a variety of contingent forces confronting the roof such as snow loads into a structural diagram. He fine-tuned the mapping by abandoning the coarse, triangulated structural geometries that generalise force diagrams, choosing instead to use computer-generated structural analysis that resolves force differentials at an ultra-sensitive scale. The unusual undulating form of the roof resulted. This process, enables Shoei Yoh to avoid the pitfalls of stylistic necessities of the project. As computer aided manufacturing techniques proliferate, such approaches which maximise efficient use of material will no doubt enjoy favour.

Undoubtedly, such an approach to contingency is attractive; yet, questions arise. At the very least, these processes threaten to turn DeFormation into a single theme architecture based on a search for contingent influences, much as Arnold Schoenberg's dodecaphonic theories of atonal music composition resulted in a decade during which serious music composers devoted all of their attention to finding new tone rows. As Greg Lynn quipped, 'soon we'll be designing form based on the air turbulence generated by pedestrians walking near the building.' More significant, however, is the degree to which such processes are actually aligning, rather than affiliative. It seems to me that by predetermining the contingent influences to be addressed, the process simply redefines the dominant architectural influences on the site. The test of whether or not the results are DeFormative, therefore, will not

depend on the success of the project in embodying responses to those influences, but on the other contingent effects it continuously generates.

If embodying effects into the design a priori is problematic, then the central issue for DeFormation design technique becomes the elucidation of methods that generate monolithic, non-representational forms that lend themselves well to affiliative relationships a posteriori. If all that were required was gesture and articulation, then the problem would pose no particular difficulty and could be saved by employing familiar expressionist techniques. Yet, the DeFormationist principle of minimal representation also prohibits explicit reference to Expressionist architecture, much as it criticises InFormation for its explicit reference to formalist Modernism. I have already mentioned a group of related techniques that start with a complex figure or set of figures and then move these towards non-representational abstraction while preserving the intrinsic complexity. These techniques have stimulated investigations into a variety of methods for accomplishing that movement towards non-representation; for example, including the study of camouflage methods, experimenting with computer 'morphing' programmes that smoothly transform one figure into another, or employing topological meshing techniques such as splines, NURBS, etc, that join the surfaces delimited by the perimeters of disjoint two-dimensional figures into a smoothed solid. Because these methods often yield anexact geometries and non-developable surfaces, other architects have turned their attention to these areas of study. Anexact geometry is the study of non-analytic forms (ie, forms that are not describable by an algebraic expression) yet that show a high degree of internal self-consistency. Non-developable surfaces cannot be flattened into a plane.

As far as I am concerned, it is in the context of the development of architectural technique rather than as applied philosophy that the issue of the fold in DeFormation is best understood. Clearly, the initial figure and transforming process in any DeForming technique does not in itself guarantee the results, nevertheless, both of these mainly contribute to the effective properties of the results. It has occurred to many architects that the fold as a figure and folding as a transformative process offered many advantages, long before any of these persons ever heard of Le Pli or paid any attention to the diagrammatic folds found in

Lacan or René Thom's Catastrophe Theory.

Neither pure figure nor pure organisation, folds link the two; they are monolithic and often non-representational, replete with interstitial and residual spaces, and intrinsic to non-developable surfaces. As a process exercised in a matrix such as urban site, folding holds out the possibility of generating field organisations that negotiate between the infinite homogeneity of the grid and the hierarchical heterogeneity of finite geometric patterns, an effect which Peter Eisenman employs in his housing and office park in Rebstock, Germany.[22] Finally, when exercised as a process on two or more organisations simultaneously, folding is a potential smoothing strategy.

All of these aspects of the fold are related to architectural effects. Although they may be attracted to the underlying work, none of the architects who make use of Thom's fold diagrams, for example, make any claim, as far as I know, to inscribing the four-dimensional event space that the diagrams depict for mathematicians in the resultant architecture; any more than any architect claims to be inscribing the effects of Descartes' philosophy when they employ a cartesian grid. And, fortunately, there do not seem to be too many persons suffering from a radical mind/body split walking around mid-town Manhattan. In both cases, architects employ these diagrams for the architectural effects they engender.

As is typical of Eisenman, both the Rebstock Park and the Alteka Tower are driven more by folding as a process than by any particular fold as a diagram or spatial organisation. In the former, Eisenman inscribes an initial parti derived from the modern housing schemes of Ernst May on the site. Then, operating strictly in the representational field of drawing, he projects the both extended site and the parti into the respective figures formed by the boundaries of these two sites. The resulting drawings create the representational illusion that these two organisations have been folded. This drawing, neither axonometric, nor perspective or fold, is than massed as the project. Through this process, he attempts to transform the modern, axonometric space characteristic of the original scheme into a visual space that hovers between an axonometric and a perspectival space with multiple vanishing points. The figure of the fold, a quotation of sections cut through a Thomian diagram, appears on the tops of the building to effect the weak, cross-disciplinary links of which

Eisenman is so fond.[23] Similarly, the Alteka tower begins with the high-rise type and folds it in a process reminiscent of *origami* in order to deform the type and to produce multiple residual spaces.

Many diagrams such as those depicting Lacan's 'mirror state' or parabolic umbilic fold and the hyperbolic umbilic fold associated with Thom's Catastrophe Theory, have attracted architectural interest for several reasons. In order to avoid the pitfalls of expressionist processes, such diagrams offer a level of discipline to the work. Using these diagrams as a source of regulating lines, so to speak, allows the architect to design with greater rigour. As Le Corbusier writes, 'The regulating line is a guarantee against wilfulness.' Moreover, as stated, such diagrams are neither purely figural nor purely abstract. They therefore hold the potential to generate weak, resemblance effects. Finally, the multiple and disjoint formal organisations that compose these compound diagrams themselves have many of the desired spatial characteristics described previously on sections.

A more sophisticated use of these diagrams as regulating lines can be found in Shirdel's Nara Convention Center. To better understand the role of the diagrams in this project, it is necessary to examine its design process in greater detail. Rather than beginning with a typological or formal parti, Shirdel initiated the design for the Hall by grafting a carefully excerpted portion of the Scottish National Museum project to the site. He chose a portion of the museum where two independent lobes of the museum joined obliquely and were subtending a constricted, interstitial space. Transferred to Nara, this graft had the advantage of already being incongruent but coherent, an after-effect of excerpting the connection between the two disjoint lobes. Shirdel reinforced this effect by using the resultant interstitial space as the main entry-way into the new building.

Studying the famous Todai-ji temple in Nara, Shirdel found the temple space dominated by three figures: a giant central Buddha and two smaller flanking attendant figures. Stimulated by this analysis, Shirdel decided to encase each of the Hall's three theatres in objects that would float in the section. The forms of these theatre-objects were determined simply by functional exigencies. Other than their patinated copper cladding, chosen to link the sectional objects to the figures in the temple, the theatres were entirely undesigned.

Visitors to the Todai-ji temple encounter the Buddha figures frontally; a classical arrangement that emphasises the subject/object relationship between the two. Shirdel, on the other hand, arranged his three sectional objects axially. Visitors entering the Convention Hall confront nothing but empty space – the enormous mass of the three theatres hovering off to the side. In order to design the envelope of the Hall and to configure the main entry as residual space, Shirdel uses two folds. First, he reconfigured the massing of the original graft with a Thomian diagram of a hyperbolic umbilic fold, extending this fold into the surrounding landscape so as to smooth the connection of the building with its immediate site. Then, he shaped the concrete piers holding up the three theatres and the lobby of the small music theatre according to the parabolic umbilic fold. As a result, the main space of the Hall is the residual space between the topology of these two folds, an effect that the constricted entry-way again reinforces. Shirdel's scheme introduces into Nara an entirely new form in both the architectural and institutional sense. More interestingly, it effects its affiliations spatially as well as formally. At the level of a building, it accomplishes the effects that the preliminary principles of DeFormation seek to engender. I also believe that it meets the five criteria for a New Architecture, ie, that it Points, that it is Blank, Vast, Incongruent and Intensively Coherent.

Whether or not DeFormation and /or InFormation mature into a New Architecture, remains to be seen. Certainly, the rate of realisation for DeFormation is not yet as promising as it is for InFormation and not sufficient for either to develop or evolve. Yet, I believe it can be said with some confidence that at least these architectures have broached the problem of the New and thus offer a measure of optimism. But, the critics and historians have not begun to circle them in earnest. Yet.

## Notes

1   Historians may note similarities in the work included in this volume to the spatial character of Baroque architecture and/or to the formal character of German Expressionism. I predict their observations will conclude that none of the architects or theorists working in this area are aware of these similarities. Because the writings and projects are not salted with analyses of Borromini, Guarini and Bernini or references to Finsterlin, the Tauts, Polzig, Haring, Mendelsohn, Scharoun, Steiner, etc, it will be assumed the work is conducted in blissful ignorance of these similarities.

This first conclusion is necessary to support the second, namely that the similarities are far more important than the differences. Thus, recalling Marx, they will argue that the second instance is but a parody of the tragic profundity of the first; a tautological argument, since the first instance establishes the terms and conditions of similarity. By coincidence, this argument also happens to support the capitalisation of their professional activities). However interesting and worthy of study the similarities are, greater stakes are found in the differences: historians will again miss the point.

2   Cf, Unger, RM, *Knowledge and Politics*, Free Press, New York, 1979; Unger, RM, *Social Theory*, Cambridge University Press, 1987.

3   Other post-structural architectural theorists, notably Jennifer Bloomer and Robert Somol, have appealed to the writings of Deleuze and Guattari, though to different ends.

4   'Collage' is used here as a convenient, if coarse umbrella term for an entire constellation of practices, eg bricolage, assemblage and a history of collage with many important distinctions and developments. This argument is strengthened by a study of the architectural translations of the various models of collage and its associated practices. As we proceed further into the discussion of affiliative effects below, one might be inclined to argue that surrealist collage, with its emphasis on smoothing the seams of the graft, might provide an apt model. Though there is merit in this position, it seems to me that so-called seamlessness of surrealist collage, like all collages, acts actually to emphasise by irony the distinct nature of the elements of the collage and therefore the incoherent disjunctions at work.

A better model might be Jasper John's cross-hatch paintings, prints and drawings. Though these works certainly employ many techniques associated with collage, their effect is quite different. In them non-ideal, grid-like organisations are materialised by grafting elements whose form is disjoint from the overall organisation. Moreover, in some of these works, other cloud-like shapes entirely outside of the dominant formal/tonal language are built up of the medium itself and camouflaged within the work. For me, these paintings are good examples of a cohesive heterogeneity engendered out of an intensive coherence in the elements themselves.

5   For example the Wexner Center for the Visual Arts and his 'scaling' projects eg, 'Romeo and Juliet.'

6   Clearly, the economic and political difficulties that result from a model of heterogeneity based on rostering definable species of difference I have associated with collage have broad implications across many institutional frontiers. In the recent US presidential election, for example, a key issue in the election was the widely felt frustration over the number of officially recognised special interest groups (now numbering in the thousands) seeking

to influence decisions by federal government. However cynical one may be about this situation, it is an inevitable consequence of a social arrangement that attempts to negotiate the classical conflict between individual and community and to achieve a democracy by offering the right to adequate voice and recognition of differences, ie, democracy through extensive incoherence. Models of heterogeneity achieved through intensive coherence would need not only to rethink the individual/community conflict, but ultimately to rethink the entire notion of a democracy achieved by systems of rights.

7    Cf, Robert Somol, 'Speciating Sites', in *Anywhere*, Davidson, ed, Rizzoli, 1992.

8    To be sure, we have already seen possibilities for such grafts, eg, in the work of Hejduck or Rossi. It is entirely unpersuasive to account with the logic of collage for the effects of Aldo Rossi's incongruous grafts of received institutions with his catalogue of autonomous architectural forms or for the effects of Hejduk's mytho-poetic, scenographic urban grafts.

9    See Unger, 'The Better Futures of Architecture', in *Anyone* Davidson, ed, Rizzoli, 1991.

10   Rem Koolhaas stresses this point in his short programme for the recent Shinkenchiku Housing competition, entitled, 'No Style'. cf JA 7.

11   Many of the ideas introduced in the second part of this text grew out of discussions I have enjoyed with Greg Lynn and Sanford Kwinter as well as from their writings. That I do not cite these writings in particular in this text is merely a testimony to how thoroughly it is suffused with their influence. Cf, Greg Lynn, 'Inorganic Bodies', *Assemblage 19*, or Sanford Kwinter in the *Journal of Philosophy and the Visual Arts*, Vol 2, Benjamin, ed. For related issues, see *Incorporations*, Crary and Kwinter, eds, UrZone Press, New York, 1992.

12   In order to achieve some focus, in this account I stress DeFormation primarily as a matter of building design and touch on urban issues only as they arise in that context. Several projects have attempted to extend the themes I here identify with DeFormation to urban design, such as Eisenman's office and housing park in Rebstock and the Shirdel, Zago, Kipnis project for the central business district of Montreal. There are also projects incorporating the themes of InFormation such as Koolhaas' Lille and La Defense or Tshcumi's Chartres. I will attempt a treatment of these works in another setting.

13   For a discussion of these three projects, see my 'Freudian slippers, or what were we to make of the Fetish', in *The Fetish*, Lynn, Mitchell and Whiting, Princeton Architectural Press, Princeton, 1992.

14   For a discussion of Eisenman's weak form projects, see my 'A Matter of Respect', in the *A+U* special edition on Eisenman, January, 1990.

15   One of the most fascinating aspects of Peter Eisenman's design career is his uncanny ability to derive an entire architectural design thesis from a key word or phrase happened upon in his reading of criticism or philosophy. While not underestimating the significance of this eventual arrival at some understanding of the source of the term in question, the fact of the matter is that Eisenman's design inventions virtually always evolve from his intial reaction to what he sees as the architectural implication of the term or phrase, loosened from its original discursive context. Whether it was Chomsky's 'deep structure', Derrida's 'trace', Mandelbrot's 'fractal scaling', or Vattimo's 'weak', Eisenman's architectural derivations have much more to do with his stimulated intuition of potential architectural effects than with embodying the original philosophical effect in question. Eisenman's 'deep structure', 'trace', 'scaling' and 'weak form' therefore have little to do with the philosophy, but much to do with architecture. This comment is by no means meant to disparage. Indeed, to the contrary – insofar as Eisenman's work has at one and the same time maintained a dialogue with philosophical discourse while loosening the domain of architectural effects from and exemplifying/embodying obligation to philosophical effects may be its most important contribution. The conspicuous absence of this issue from the critical literature on Eisenman's work – including my own – testifies to an institutional need for critical literature to maintain a metaphysic of embodiment at any cost, even at the cost of paying attention to the architecture.

16   Camouflage is often cited as a paradigm of affiliations that smooth. Effective camouflage such as 'dazzle painting' is often entirely different from the prevailing influences of the operative context and almost always outside of the dominant modes of the primary discipline (ie, of clothing design or the surface treatment of ships or planes). Yet the effect of camouflage is to smooth the disjoint relationship between site and interloper into another context.

17   Though the discussion of affiliation to this point emphasises form-to-form effects, a meditation on the weak-links of affiliative effects also undermines the most pre-eminent of strongly aligned relations in architecture: the correlation between form and programme. 'Form follows function', is, of course, the declaration par excellence of an alignment between architectural design and programme. Yet, does a close attention to the history of architecture actually sustain that position? I believe a careful reading of that history would require a negative answer to the question.

Throughout its history, the relationship between form and programme has been far more affiliative than aligned, a fact to which the endless numbers of reprogrammings more than testify (houses to museums, fascist headquarters to state treasury facilities, fire stations to Ghostbuster's offices ad infinitum). This is not to say that there is no relationship between form and function, but that the relationship is in its essence weak. It is the affiliative character of the form/programme relationship that allows Rossi to produce his typological grafts and Tschumi to theorise about dis-cross and trans-programming. After all, has the design of any building significant to architectural history ever achieved its status due to how well it functioned? But the most glaring case of form/programme affiliation is to be found in the house, for no one ever lives in a house according to its architectural programme. Can a theory of strong alignment between form and programme account for reading in the bathroom or eating in the livingroom, or for the particular pleasures of having sex anywhere but the bedroom? No doubt it was out of a frustration over the failure of affiliations to congeal into alignments that drove Mies van der Rohe to nail down the furniture. The affiliative nature of the relationship between form and programme accounts in the large part for DeFormation's relative complacency vis a vis InFormation on the issue of programme.

18   For additional discussion of the Shirdel, Zago, Kipnis Place Jacques Event Structure project, see *L'Arca*, December 1991, no 55.

19   For additional discussion of the Shirdel, Zago Kipnis project for the Scottish National Museum, see *ANYWHERE*, Rizzoli, 1992.

20   A mixed-use office tower in Berlin. Though unavailable for publication at this time, the Max Reinhardthaus project is scheduled to be published in *ANYWHERE*.

21   To state that the most interesting discussions in architecture revolve around design technique, is, to me, virtually a tautology. The most interesting aspect of any and every study of architecture – historical, theoretical or otherwise – is its consequence for current design technique.

22   For more on the Rebstock project see R Somol, 'Accidents Will Happen', *A+U* September 1991 and John Rajchman, 'Perplications', the catalogue essay for the *Unfolding Frankfurt* exhibition, Aedis Gallery, Ernst & Sohn, Verlag, 1991. For Eisenman on folding see 'Visions Unfolding', *Incorporations*, Crary and Kwinter, eds, UrZone Books, 1992. An earlier version is in *Domus*, June 1992.

23   In his studio at the Ohio State University, Eisenman and his students began to develop the implications of the initial Rebstock folding for the building sections and to study its capacity to interlace disjoint organisations. I intend to treat this work and further developments of the scheme in more detail in my forthcoming treatment on InFormation and DeFormation urban design.

The illustrations with this article are of the *Briey Intervention,* a project by Jeffrey Kipnis in consultation with Philip Johnson.
Project Architect: Matt Geiser; Producers: Don Bates, Ken Rabin; Construction Supervisor: Greg Skogland; Computer drawings: *Modelling on the Form Z*

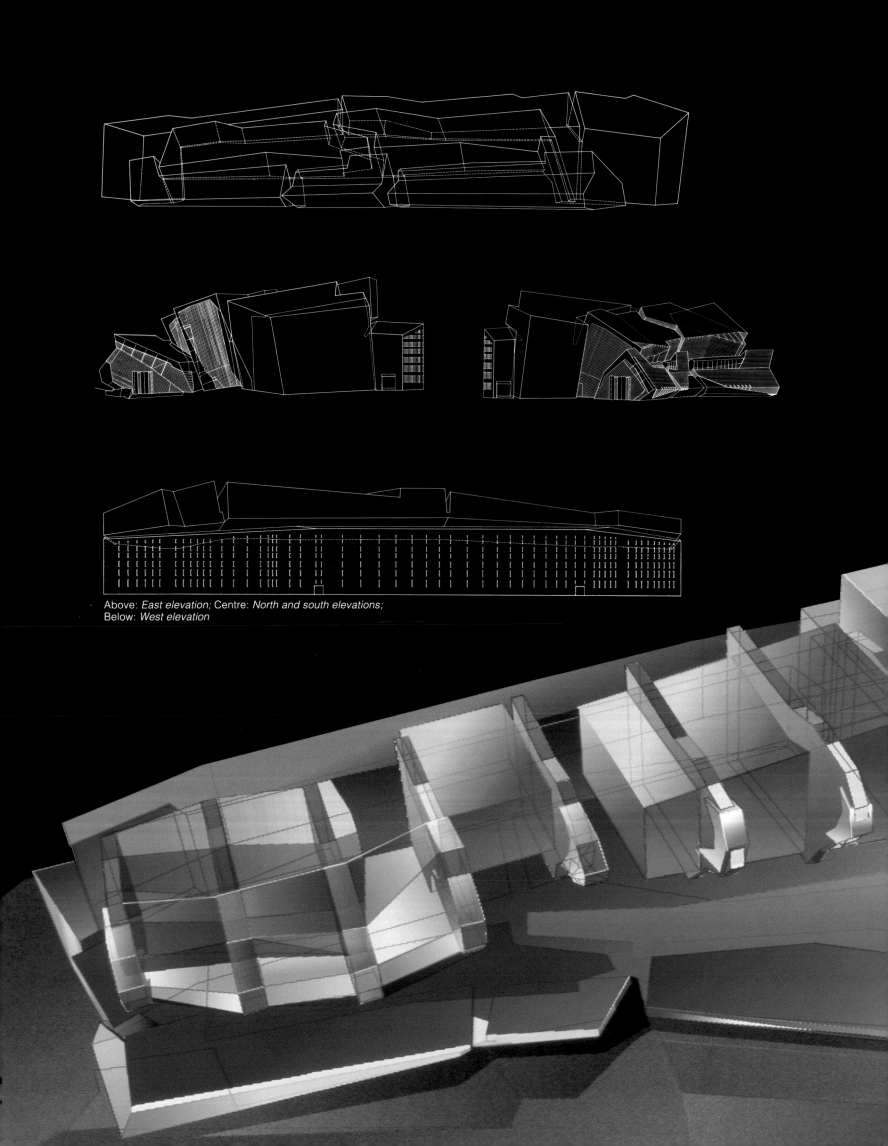

Above: *East elevation;* Centre: *North and south elevations;*
Below: *West elevation*

# BAHRAM SHIRDEL
## *NARA CONVENTION HALL*

Our goal for the Nara Convention Centre is to weave the three principal functions of a major civic building - the aesthetic/symbolic relationship to cultural context, the relationship to the immediate site, and the programmatic experience – into a complex spatial unity guided by the theme of the symbiosis of history and the future. To accomplish this, we have employed the space and the geometry of the FOLD. The spatial structure of the Fold establishes the architectural space of symbiosis; that is, a collaborative relationship between two distinct spaces. The geometry of the Fold lies between the pure abstract geometry of Modernism and the representational figure of Historicism. However, the Fold is not the simple synthesis of geometry and figure; rather, it is the situation in which the geo-metric and the figurative collaborate without dominating. Using the Fold enabled us to attempt to realise the difficult goal of a symbiosis of history and the future.

The City of Nara is a distinct, anomalous entity participating in a symbiotic relationship with the dominant cultural tradition of Japan. To capture the feeling in the Convention Centre of one space operating collaboratively within another, explicit representational reference has been avoided. A more abstract language is employed to realise the spatial aspirations of the project. While the form of the building suggests both the traditional and modern aesthetics of context it is, on the other hand, entirely unique and mimics neither. The form relates to Nara as Nara relates to Japan.

In order to capture and experience the space of the Fold in the interior of the Convention Centre, the spatial structure echoes that of the Todai-ji Daibutsu-den which is entered on a frontal axis with the great Buddha. The Daibutsu and the two accompanying figures hover in the space of the Temple enclosure, which is thus confiscated by scale, mass and spiritual presence, creating a memorable spatial experience for resident and visitor alike.

The Convention Centre reveals how we have adapted the transverse section of the Temple and floated the three great masses of the theatres within a single envelope. The relationship of the theatres to the figures of the Todai-ji Temple is echoed further in the choice of material. While the Temple figures are alive in the spiritual sense, the theatres of the Convention Centre are alive in the programmatic sense. However, in a distinct way from the frontal axis of the Daibutsu-den, we have oriented tangentially the relationship of the floating theatre forms to the visitor, to create a modern, secular axis and a striking vista. The visitor is compressed between the folded skin of the envelope and the presence of the theatres. Hence, he at once feels both the historical/spiritual memory of the space of the Daibutsu-den as well as the contemporary space of modernity. From the Space of the Fold, the visitor proceeds to the Geometry of the Fold. Having assembled in the main space, he moves to the theatres by way of escalators located within the piers. The organisation and form of the piers articulate the structural geometry of the Fold. The visitor lands on a mezzanine/lobby from where the entire space and form of the Centre can be viewed dramatically.

The massing of the building symbolises the transition from the permanence of ideal form to unpredictable changes of the earth. Offices and auxiliary services are located in a modern bar on the west side of the site. The movement from ideal form to the articulated form of the Fold can be discerned as the building proceeds from west to east. This bi-directional movement is symbolic of the movements of History and Culture; alternating between the Ideal and the Real, the East and the West. The Fold continues from the building into the Urban Park and landscape, creating a unity of form and site.

In order to unify the spatial effects further, the Y-diagram of the building is to be found in both section (as the Fold) and in plan. In the latter, the diagram frames the relationship between the Centre and Rail Station; capturing and unifying space of the main processional.

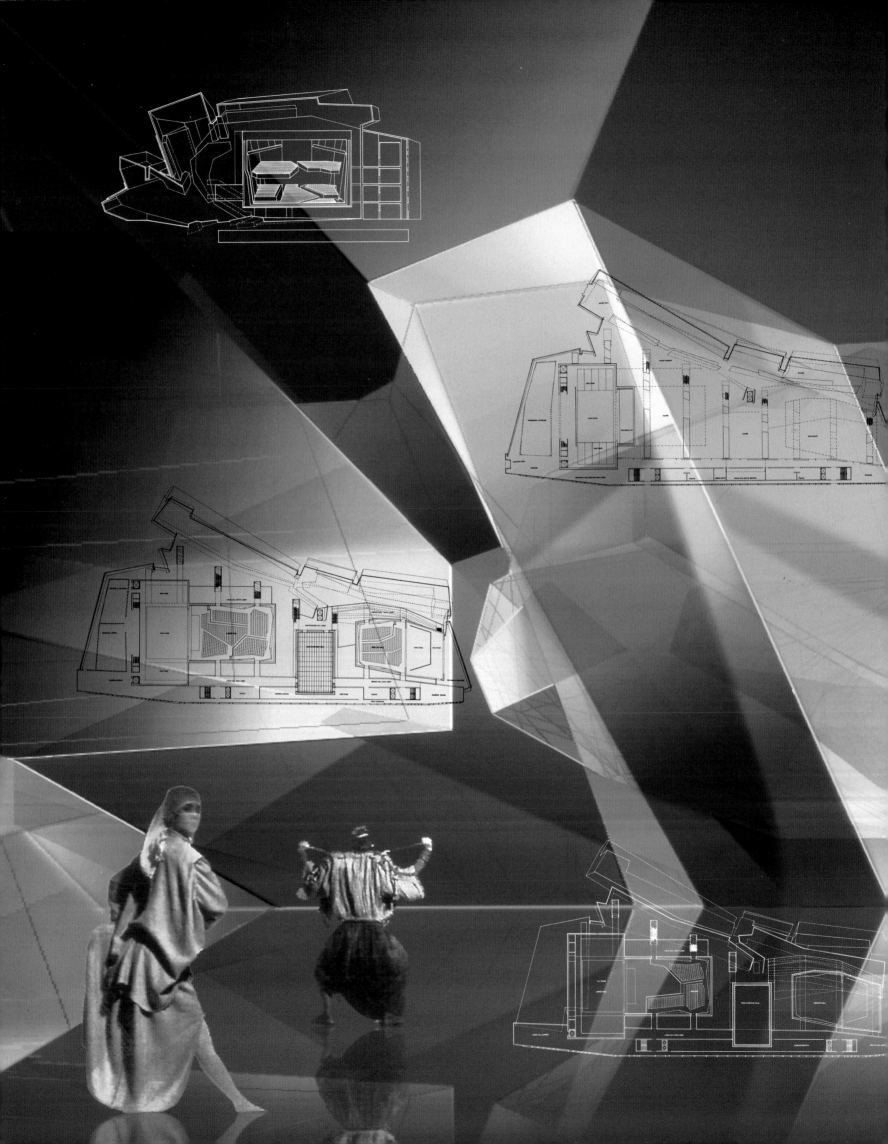

Opposite, From Above: *Transverse section; ground floor plan; second floor plan; first floor plan;* Left: *Axonometric massing;* Centre: *Folded space grid;* Below: *Folded axonometric massing*

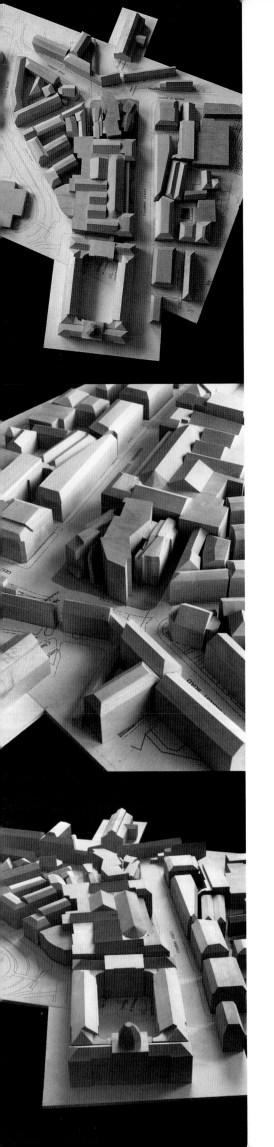

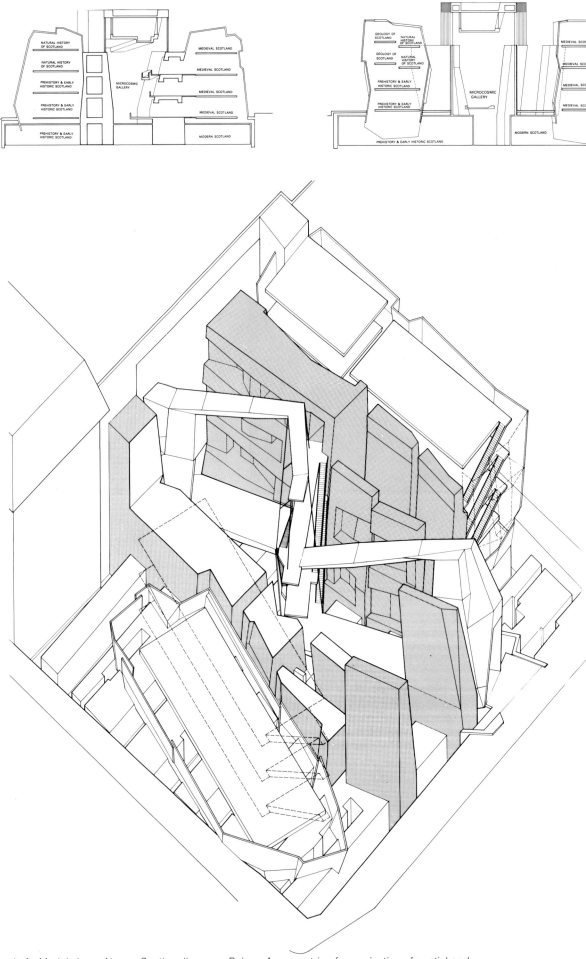

Left: *Model views*; Above: *Section diagrams*; Below: *Axonometric of organisation of spatial and circulation elements*

# BAHRAM SHIRDEL
## *SCOTTISH NATIONAL HERITAGE*
### *A Living Museum*

Our design concept for the Scottish National Museum is directed towards a Living Museum. The traditional role of the museum is enhanced as a place for objective contemplation of the past by expanding the presence of the museum in the intellectual, political and spiritual texture of everyday life.

The presence of the Living Museum is asserted through a careful consideration of the symbolic character of the building. Topography and landscape are deeply rooted in the heritage of Scotland and we have drawn therefore both from Scotland's natural history and her architectural history to achieve the appropriate image. While the organisation of the plan alludes to that of the existing museum, the footprint of the building suggests the three regions of the country. The general massing echoes features such as the Great Glen, the Grampian Mountains, the Caledonian trend and the ancient and mysterious Standing Stones. The spatial organisation is derived from a synthesis of the complex geometries of the Broch with the vernacular architecture of Edinburgh, such as its bridges and feus. Through such gestures we seek to embody a unique component of Scottish Heritage in form and in space.

As well as appealing to the urban history of Edinburgh, close attention has been given to integrating the museum into the city's urban fabric. A 'breathing space' has been preserved on the street as an amenity for pedestrians; rather than confronting Lindsay Place with a massive wall. The geometry of the building highlights notable features local to the context such as the theatre and Greyfriars Church. Dramatically framed views draw the city into the museum as if it were part of the collection.

An important innovation found in the Living Museum is the Microcosmic Gallery. This occupies the circulation bridges organising the amphitheatre-like Great Hall. Here, significant examples from the collection of each department are located and views into the main galleries can be seen, along with changing glimpses of the city. Thus, the visitor progressing through the gallery surveys a microcosm of the entire heritage of Scotland in an ever-changing matrix of relationships.

The Microcosmic Gallery is conceived as an environment that stages complex and changing interactions between viewers and items in the collection. While respecting the traditional role of the collection, the space encourages a questioning of the identity of objects in a manner resonant with Hume's epistemology. This serves to elevate the status of the collection beyond the chronological and the categorical, in exploring its transformative capabilities.

Another innovation is the Rays of Thought. Each ray is dedicated to a great thinker of Scotland such as Hume, Maxwell, Smith or Adam. The rays create a network of form and light suffusing the museum. They interact with and transform the perception of the collection, rendering physical expression to the world-shaping force of Scotland's intellectual heritage.
*Project designed with Andrew Zago and Jeffrey Kipnis*

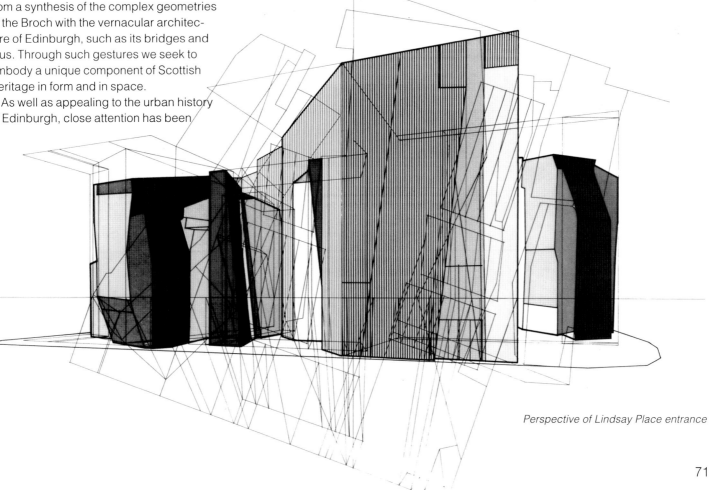

*Perspective of Lindsay Place entrance*

Left: *Expanding geodesic domes*; Above: *Iris Dome*
*Interior partially retracted*

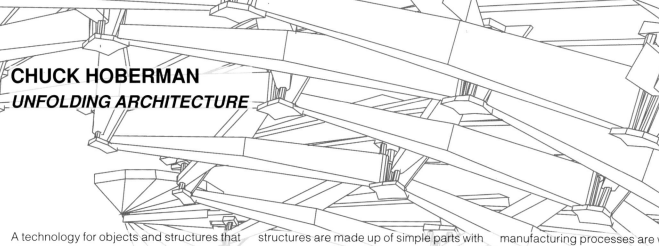

# CHUCK HOBERMAN
## *UNFOLDING ARCHITECTURE*

A technology for objects and structures that change their size and shape is being developed. Its potential lies in making new products, new spectacles and experiences, a new kinetic architecture. Transformation is at the heart of this technology: a metamorphosis akin to natural processes of growth and change, it is complete, fully three dimensional, fluid and continuous. Designs, prototypes and full-scale structures have been built which demonstrate the capabilities of unfolding architecture. Applications currently under development range from consumer products to architectural-scale projects.

With the emphasis placed directly on the transformation process itself, a new type of object is created. By the application of force at one or more points, it transforms in a fluid and controlled manner. Despite such ease of transformation, these structures are stable, strong and durable. Thus, unfolding architecture exhibits the seemingly contradictory qualities of strength and fluidity.

### Underlying Principles

Unfolding architecture posits an object that is identically a structure and a mechanism. The pieces connect to form a working structural network that can span distances, support loads and provide shelter. Yet they also function simultaneously as the links of a mechanism, transferring forces and motion in a controlled manner. The integration of structural and mechanical functions ensures that these structures are able to operate without secondary structural supports or external mechanical devices for controlling motion.

Underlying these unities of structure/mechanism and fluidity/strength are unique mathematical principles. The elegance and economy exhibited by unfolding architecture derive from this mathematical and geometric basis. The basis of each folding structural system, is embodied in a minimum number of representative connected parts. When such a linkage is manipulated, its edge or border exhibits key properties that allow it to maintain a mechanical connection to other similar units. Unfolding structures are made up of simple parts with simple connections between them. A rich transformation arises from the accumulation of incremental movements between adjacent parts. The result is synergistic: the behaviour of the system unpredicted by its parts. A systematic methodology has been developed for designing and building transforming structures based on these principles. Given a set of physical and functional requirements, designs may be synthesised on the basis of an extensive vocabulary of folding forms.

### Unfolding Surface Structures

A basic category of unfolding architecture is formed by those structures comprised of a single surface or sheet. This surface may be as simple as a sheet of paper. Pleats are inscribed along unique tiling patterns – space-filling patterns that can fold or develop. When folded along these pleat lines, such surface structures can transform smoothly between an extended structural configuration and a compact bundle. The sheet's third dimension, its thickness, is incorporated into surface structure design. By adjusting geometric parameters, thick structural materials may be used.

Thus, unfolding surface structures behave as rigid plates connected by hinges rather than as simple coverings. The structure's kinetic and fluid action arises because the surface functions as a mechanism – a matrix of interconnected linkages. When surface structures are supported consistently around the perimeter they gain a structural integrity similar to unitary shell structures. This stability is enhanced by an effective surface thickness that is related to the depth of the folds as well as the material thickness.

A structure made from a single sheet has inherent economies. Living hinge technology, where a single sheet of material is treated to form durable folding units is well established. Stamping cardboard and melting hinges into plastics are simple and effective techniques. For larger structures, a fabric and frame construction may be used. In general, materials, tooling and manufacturing processes are well suited to low production costs. Various products are currently under development, including toys, tents and folding luggage.

### Unfolding Truss Structures

Unfolding architecture's second basic category is that of the structural linkage or truss. These structures function as complete and integrated shapes. They are examples of form-resistant structures, where strength derives from shape. Unfolding truss structures are made up of rigid links connected by simple pivots. Expanding structures of any form may be built. Such structures will fluidly transform in size, while their overall shape remains constant. The largest unfolding structure built to date is a geodesic dome spanning six m when open. It expands from a compact duster that is 1.5 m in diameter. In all positions, the structure is stable and rigid, maintaining its shape and geodesic configuration. The dome rests on five roller supports. By simply pulling outwards on these points the dome fluidly expands. The client is the Liberty Science Center.

A second type of unfolding truss structure is a dome with a centre that retracts, even while the perimeter remains stable and fixed. In this way, the smooth motion of this structure is like the iris of an eye. It has been developed into a retractable roof for covering an arena or stadium. A working scale model of this Iris Dome has been built. In configuration it is a lamella dome with a geometry of interlocking spirals. When released, it retracts without resistance to a compact ring, maintaining a constant and stable perimeter.

Rigid panels may be attached directly to the Iris Dome to provide a weather-tight covering in its extended position. The panels slide over one another and nest compactly when the dome is retracted. The oculus in the Iris Dome appears in dynamic form. When the structure starts to retract, a circular opening appears at the apex of the dome. As the roof opens, the oculus expands – transforming continuously the space from indoors to outdoors.

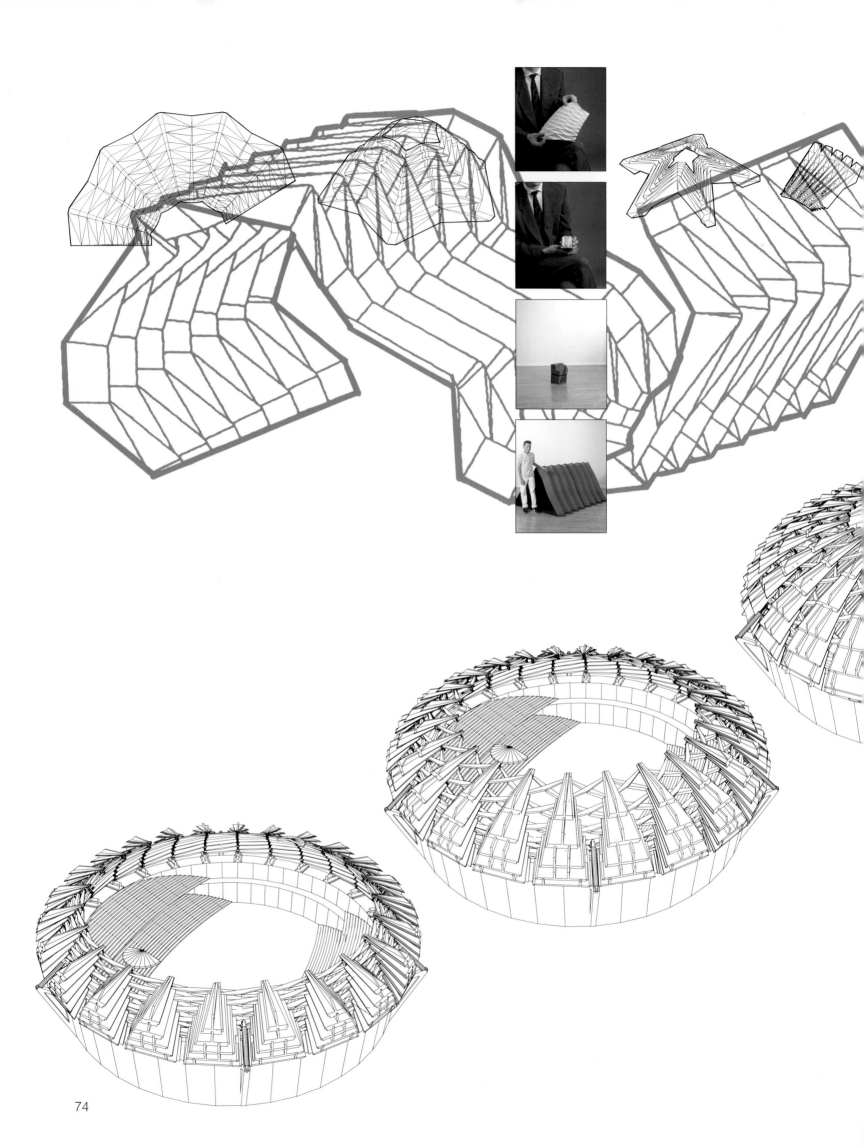

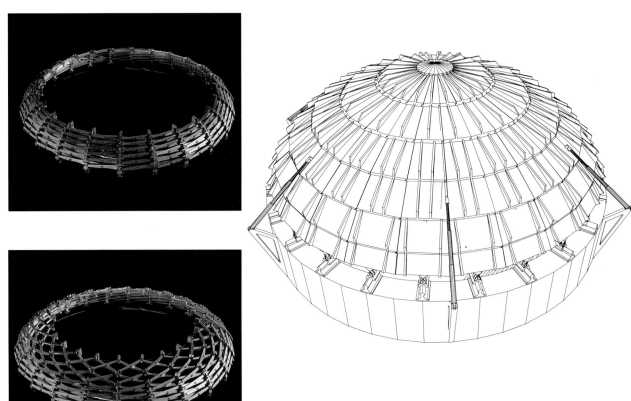

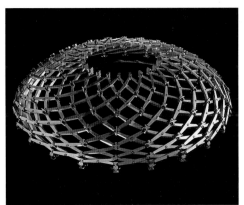

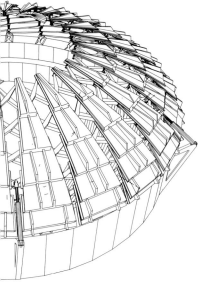

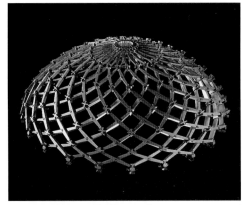

Opposite Above: *Folding surface structures and folding polypropylene tent;* Left and Above: *Iris Dome structural models fully expanded and contracted, drawings indicate covering panels*

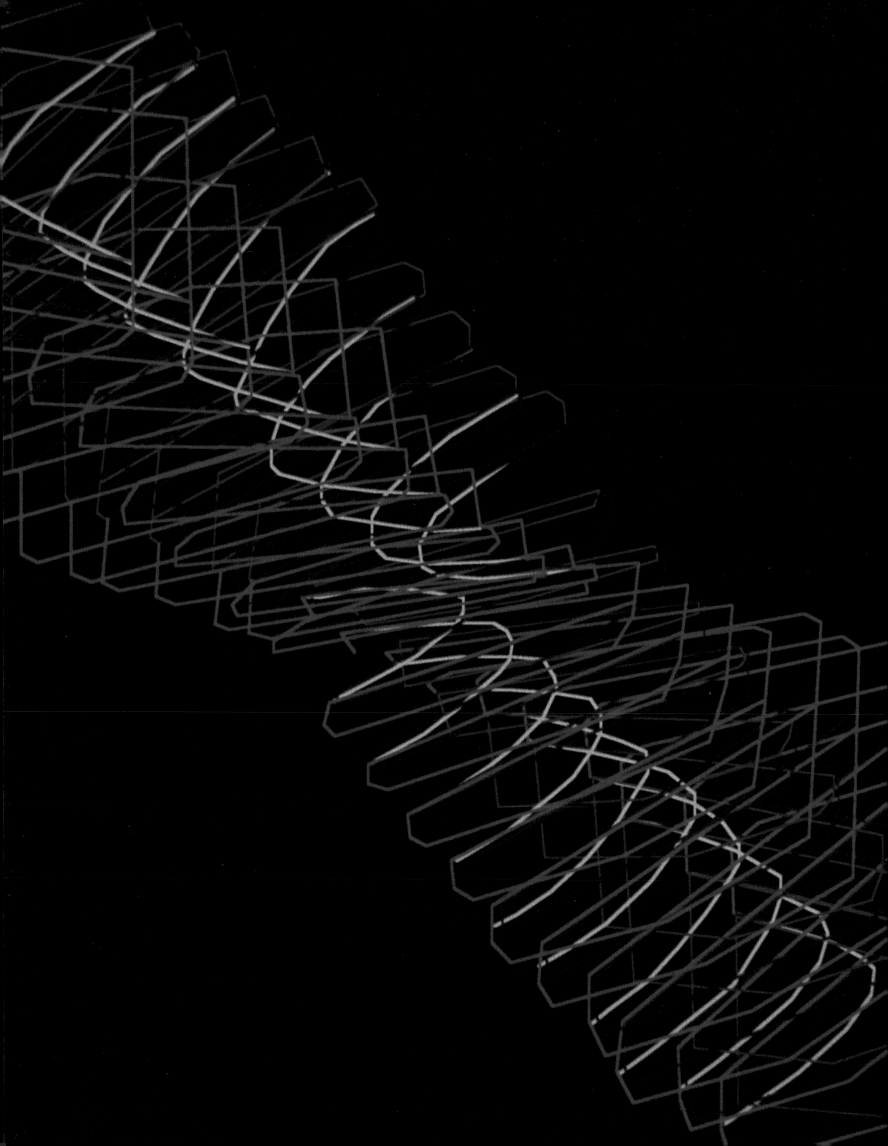

# JOHN RAJCHMAN
## *OUT OF THE FOLD*

What might architecture and urbanism make of the concept of the fold today – to what new places might they still take it?

The concept is a very old one. And yet, one cannot say that it is a concept traditional to philosophy, even though as an etymological matter it is parent, in European languages, of many concepts that are: 'explication' and 'implication', 'perplexity' and 'complexity', for example, derive from it. As such, it has a long history. The Greek root, to do with weaving, recurs in the *symploke* or weaving-together of discourse that Plato describes in the *Sophist*; but it is through Latin that words like 'implicate', 'explicate' and 'replicate' enter French, and in a slightly different way, English. Already we find Plotinus speaking of a great 'Complicatio' of the One in all that is. Much later, rather independently, we find references to the fold in Heidegger and, of course, in Mallarmé.

Perhaps the most intricate and extensive contemporary treatment of the concept is to be found in Gilles Deleuze's book, *Le Pli* (The Fold) that advances a new perspective on Leibniz and the Baroque. But then, Deleuze has a special view of what philosophical concepts are: they are *monsters*. They *show* (*montre*) things which, since they can't yet be said, appear incongruous or untimely. Deleuze wishes to restore to concepts in philosophy a dimension, not of logical possibility or necessity, but of logical *force* – the manner in which such concepts expose new 'enfoldings' or 'implications' that are yet to be 'unfolded' or 'explicated'; the manner in which they instigate new unanticipated possibilities in the midst of things, without predetermining or prefiguring the outcome; the manner in which they thus take a given conceptual space elsewhere, out from itself.

In fact, one may read Deleuze as offering an original image of conceptual space itself as something 'pliable' or ever susceptible of being folded, unfolded and refolded anew. Thus he writes of the bifurcations, the openings and closings, the surfaces, intervals, heights and depths of conceptual space, and of the manner in which thought 'orients' itself within that space. He thereby offers a different image of conceptual space from Frege (a philosophical concept is not a function mapping a range onto a domain) and from the austere Wittgenstein, whose image of the purity and simplicity of elements Adolf Loos found so appealing.

For Deleuze, conceptual space is not divided up by sets of discrete elements, nor given through a Unity or Totality of parts; and its aim is not to 'represent' or 'depict' the world by ordered combinations of such elements, any more than it is to 'express' the unity of such parts. Indeed, the world itself is not 'all that is the case' (as Wittgenstein took it to be) for it includes an undepictable anterior element out of which new kinds of things can happen, new concepts emerge – the space where unforeseen things 'take place'.

Conceptual space is thus neither timeless nor time-bound, but implies a peculiar type of temporality that Deleuze tries to unfold from 19th-century thought: from Proust's notion of a 'complicated time' (that still is connected to the Cathedral); from Bergson's notion of 'virtuality' (in which we can in retrospect see a relation to 'motion pictures'); and especially from Nietzsche's notion of the 'untimely' (which Deleuze sees Foucault as introducing into the archival study of history). At the end of the century, Frege had focused on the problem of numbers and sets. However, with the concept of the fold, Deleuze's philosophical imagination is drawn rather to mathematicians like René Thom and Benoît Mandelbrot, whose topographies suggest resonances with other domains, other spaces.

Fold-words – words with *plic-* and *plex-* – do of course also enjoy a prominent role in the discourses of architecture and of urbanism. Perhaps there is no word used more frequently than 'complexity'; and for Wolf Prix of Coop Himmelblau, architecture is a key art of the 90s because it must deal at once with social, economic and formal complexities. But 'complexity' has not always been so central a concept, and an important date for its emergence is pro-vided by a work that for many marked a turning-point in architecture and architectural discourse: *Complexity and Contradiction in Architecture* of 1966. In this book, Robert Venturi drew on a vocabulary that had been elaborated by the Anglo-American New Critics, and was unaware that during the same years Deleuze was elaborating in France a different kind of vocabulary, a logic of 'difference and repetition', on which he would later draw in his own discussion of Mannerism and the Baroque in *Le Pli*. This other logic would be taken up some years later in architecture: For example, in his *Manhattan Transcripts* Bernard Tschumi would appropriate from Deleuze the notion of 'disjunctive synthesis', that in turn would lead to Derrida's reference to the fold in his essay on 'Maintaining Architecture'. However, out of the fold there may yet arise other possibilities, other ramifications; and some implications and complications of the concept may be traced along these four lines: multiplicity, chance, orientations and manners.

### Multiplicity

The *pli*-word of which Deleuze is fond of above all others, and through whose eyes he sees all others is the word 'multiple'. On the first page of his book he declares: 'The multiple is not only what has many parts, but what is folded in many ways'. In Deleuze's philosophy, the multiple comes first before the One. States of affairs are never unities or totalities but are rather, 'multiplicities' in which there have arisen foci of unification or centres of totalisation. In such 'multiplicities' what counts is not the elements or the terms but what is in between them, their intervals or 'disparities'. Multiplicity thus involves a peculiar sort of complexity – a complexity in divergence – where it is not a matter of finding the unity of a manifold but, on the contrary, of seeing unity as a holding-together of a prior virtual dispersion. This sort of complexity does not consist in the One that is said in many ways, but rather in the fact that each thing may always diverge onto others, as in the ever-forking paths in Borges' fabled garden. A 'multiple' fabric is therefore one that can never be completely unfolded or definitively explicated, since to unfold or explicate it is only to fold or complicate it anew. Thus the multiple is not fragments or ruins of a lost or absent Whole, but the potentiality for divergence within any given unity. In this manner, the concept of complexity is freed from the logic of contradiction or opposition and connected instead to a logic of intervals: it becomes a matter of a 'free' differentiation (not subordinated to fixed analogies or categorical identities) and a 'complex' repetition (not restricted to the imitation of a pre-given model, origin or end).

Such a notion of 'complexity in divergence' differs from Venturi's notion of a contradictory or 'difficult' whole, just as it involves a strange, invisible, groundless depth; unlike the 'ground' in Colin Rowe's picture of Cubist collage and Gestaltist perception. For, Venturi would reduce complexity to a given totality and simplicity of compositional elements, and Rowe would reduce depth to the simultaneity of figure and ground. In this way they would eliminate just that which makes complexity multiple and divergent, and just what makes depth intensive and ungrounded. For them, architectural or urban vision remains fundamentally a matter of discovering an imperceptible unity in a perceptible diversity of elements. Deleuze suggests another kind of vision: one that tries to find the 'signs' of an imperceptible 'disparation' in what presents itself as a perceptual totality – the vision of an intensive 'multiplexity' in the midst of things.

## Chance

For Deleuze, there is thus a folding of things that is prior to design or principle and that subsists as a potential complication in them. As such, the fold is connected to a notion of chance and necessity, which Deleuze formulates in his study of Nietzsche by saying: 'Nietzsche identifies chance with multiplicity . . . What Nietzsche calls *necessity* (destiny) is thus never the abolition but rather the combination of chance itself.'

Such views belong to a more general 'erosion of determinism' in which a Laplacian image of the universe as a sort of clock wound up by God opens onto a stochastic, unpredictable universe, where the laws of complex forms are not determined by those of simpler ones, but come into existence as those complex forms are created in the history of the universe: the universe as a great casting of the dice, the

patterns of which, upon falling, would assume a kind of necessity. For Peirce, as for Nietzsche, this new territory of chance opened up new sorts of philosophical questions. For, as Ian Hacking has argued, these two philosophers help to distinguish a 'bifurcation' in the new territory, dividing along the lines of two concepts of chance; one 'tamed', the other 'untamed'. In this way, we see how statiticians and dadaists came to populate the same conceptual and social world.

In Deleuze, we find a similar distinction between 'sedentary' and 'nomadic' views of chance. Pascal, in his wager, exemplifies the first, since he plays the game of chance according to pre-existent categorical rules that define probabilities which allow one to calculate gains and losses. But Nietzsche and Mallarmé play the game in another way: the table itself bursts open and becomes part of a larger, more complex game that always includes the possibility of new rules, so that in making each move one must affirm all of chance at once. And as the game of 'nomadic' distributions replaces the game of categorical ones, chance ceases to be tamed or hypothetical, and becomes free and imperative.

For Deleuze, the fold therefore involves the subsistence of a virtual space of chance in the organisation of design and of programme. And perhaps one might argue that this nomadic or untamed kind of chance was something that a certain heroic ambition in architecture and urbanism, and a certain image of the architect or the planner as a sort of master-builder, tried unsuccessfully to eliminate: the spaces of 'envelopment' in development, the spaces of virtual 'diagrammatisation' in plans and plannings. The question then arises of how and where such spaces might be discovered in another way than through the sense of omnipotence (and dejection) that comes from the desire to eliminate them.

## Orientations

Heights and depths, ups and downs – these belong to what Deleuze terms the 'ascensional psychism' that Plato helped introduce into philosophy with his proverbial stories of the soul con-verting, reorienting itself out of the cave towards the light. What Socrates' suicide shows, he suggests, is the depressive side of such celestial orientation along a vertical axis. Deleuze wants to propose a different way of orienting oneself in thought: it would not be a matter of turning or looking up to the heights above things, any more than of

delving down into the formless *bas* beneath them, but of looking along the surfaces, in their intervals and midsts for what yet may happen, coming thus to see that 'the most profound is the skin'. *The Logic of Sense* offers many perspectives on this place where sense and non-sense would meet and where new, unforeseen things might happen. And, for Deleuze, this 'mid-place', this '*mi-lieu*', is precisely where folding occurs: 'Things and thoughts grow or grow up through the midst (*milieu*), and it is there that one has to be, it is always there that things are folded (*que ça se plie*).'

Through his notion of the *milieu*, Deleuze would deliver us from a 'linear' picture of time, proceeding from beginnings to endings as in a story or *histoire*. The midst is rather where beginnings are recast and new endings opened up in our stories; a *milieu* always interrupts the calm narrative of things, exposing a prior complexity and complication in them. And conversely, in the intervals in the midst of things there always subsists the chance for the sort of free self-complication of a space that instigates without prefiguring.

For Deleuze, events never happen out of a tabula rasa, but come out of complications, out of the fold; and time occupies a 'complicated' rather than a linear or circular space: it lies at the intersection of multiple lines that can never be disentangled in a single transparent plane given to a fixed external eye.

Thus Deleuze sees Leibniz as introducing a new 'regime of light', different from the Cartesian regime of the clear and the distinct: a baroque regime where things can be continuous even though they are distinct, and where what is clear or clarified is only a region within a larger obscurity, as when figures emerge from the 'dark background' in the paintings of Tintoretto or El Greco. For Leibniz's 'windowless monads' illuminate or clarify only singular districts in the dark complexities of the world that is expressed in them; and Leibniz becomes a perspectivist philosopher where things themselves are points of view on the world they express. Yet Leibniz retains the meta-principle that God selects this world as best, and that everything that happens is thus 'compossible' in that world. Deleuze considers Nietzsche to take things further: whereas for Leibniz, things are points of view on the same city, for Nietzsche, each point of view is a different city, resonating through its divergences with others, such that *his* principle was 'always another city in the city'.

## Manners

We ourselves are folded beings, for there is a sense in which we never stop folding, unfolding, refolding our lives; and we are 'complicated' beings before we are logical ones, following out our 'life plans' within the spaces in which they can be expected to occur. When Deleuze says we are each of us plural or multiple, he doesn't mean that we are many things or have many egos, but that we are 'folded' in many entangled, irregular ways, none the same, and that this 'multiplicity' goes beyond what we can predict or be aware of: we are 'folded' in body and soul in many ways and many times over, prior to our being as 'subjects', as masters and possessors of what happens to us in our lives. Each of us is thus 'multiplicitous'; but not because we divide into distinct persons or personalities looking for a unity, lost or supposed, and not because our brains are programmed by several helpfully interacting cognitive 'modules'. It is rather that our modes of being are 'complicated' and 'unfold' in such a way that we can never be sure just what manners our being will yet assume.

Sartre saw the being of the other, of *autrui*, as this ungraspable gaze that captures and involves one in a violent struggle for recognition. But Deleuze, who admired Sartre, thought we should see *autrui* rather as the 'expression' of enfolded or implicated possibilities that don't yet exist outside the expression, but that may be unfolded or explicated through those 'encounters' that release them; and it is thus that they determine the points from which one can 'look' and be 'looked at', or the terrains in which struggles of gazes can transpire. 'The other' is thus not a subject any more than it is an object for one; it is rather the existence of multiple unrealised possibilities that go beyond the subject and that come to be expressed through what Deleuze called 'signs', in his study of Proust. In this book, Deleuze underscores that at least in the Proustian universe such involuntary 'signs' of enfolded possibilities are far richer in love and jealousy than they are in the friendship and goodwill that attracted those ancient Greek philosophers, who tried to make 'recognition among subjects' seem more important to our manners of being than 'encounters' among different worlds of possible complication. Conversely, to put 'encounters' before 'recognitions' is to see that there is something of which the body is yet capable, just as there are always states of the soul or mind that go beyond what one may be

conscious of: that is, using Spinoza's word, what Deleuze calls *affects*. Our enfoldings and unfoldings 'affect' us before we re-collect them in the planned spaces of our purposeful undertakings. And if we can today re-read Spinoza and Leibniz as 'expressionist' philosophers, it is because, unlike Descartes' view of the mechanical or robotic body, they thought of body and soul as 'expressions' of the same thing: of entangled, enfolded manners or modes of our being, themselves as splendidly impersonal as the 'it' in 'it's raining'. Thus they thought that the soul is not 'in' the body, any more than it is 'above' it, but that it is rather 'with' it, accompanying it along the bifurcating paths of its distinctive manners of being.

It is this 'expressionist' construal of the philosophical theme of 'manners' or 'modes' of being that Deleuze connects, in *Le Pli*, to 'Mannerism' and the Baroque, and so reads the interior and exterior of Baroque architecture in terms of the Leibnizian theme of the windowless monad, and the harmonies of body and soul. And yet, Deleuze thinks, our own moment of complication requires another kind of expression. For we no longer have use for a principle of pre-established harmony; we have passed from the notion of the best compossible world to the possibility of a 'chaosmotic' one, in which our 'manners' ever diverge into new complications.

For Deleuze, the fold thus involves an 'affective' space from which the diverging manners of our being come and go, of which one may ask whether it will discover an architectural expression. The modernist 'machines for living' sought to express a clean efficient space for the new mechanical body; but who will invent a way to express the affective space for this other multiplicitous one?

What then might architecture make of this contemporary philosophy of the fold? Perhaps it is too soon to say, for it is a matter of new connections and of the creation of spaces in which such connections might acquire their vitality. It is a matter of the *force* of the concept in its encounter with architects.

*Axonometric view of the René Thom Catastrophe Section drawn by Jeffrey Kipnis*

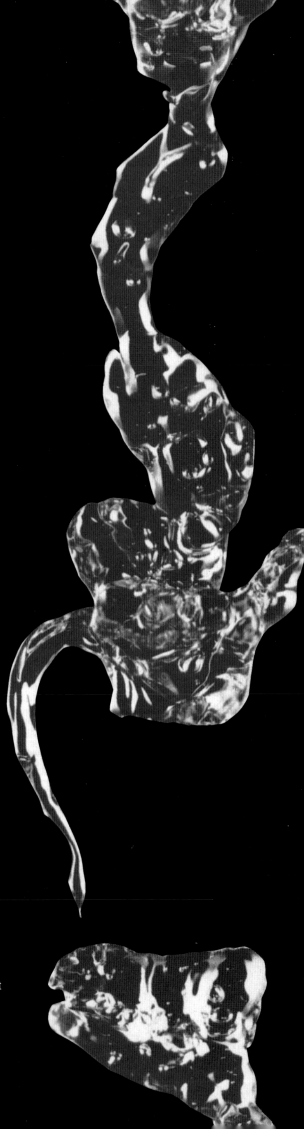

# CLAIRE ROBINSON
## THE MATERIAL FOLD
### Towards a Variable Narrative of Anomalous Topologies

The fold, the fringe, the dovetail, the butterfly, the ombillic hyperbolic, the elliptic ombillic, the parabolic umbillic: René Thom's Catastrophe Theory invites the discontinuous, the topological into architecture. Topology becomes a geometry of reconciliation between building and ground, logos and noise. Inherent in his work of identifying and naming mathematically singular discontinuities is a concern for the phenomenological otherness inherent in the resultant geometries.[1] This otherness has a materiality. To take the fold as solely formal gesture is the same as allowing its materiality to be evacuated.

If one is content to uphold the extrapolated image of Thom's 'remarkable section' as an invitation to create a 'new form'; the fold's spatial potential is suppressed in favour of a reiterated platonism. Although the mathematical impetus of the Catastrophe Theory may have been Platonic in origin, the age-old query of how to explain the relation between a pyramid and a dodecahedron, a tetrahedron and a cube, a cube and an icosahedron . . . seems to give way. Another potential cosmology emerges from Thom's work; one with tremendous ramifications for architects and other proto-workers of space. 'The chosen model is a fluid one, it is no longer a crystal, nor the five regular polyhedrons that are the solids of the Timaeus; it is flow.'[2]

Venus her(e) folds.

Chora, Her, Space: a continually folding, constantly evolving, perpetually holding and loosing ephemeral place. Chora should not receive but allow itself to borrow, or receive only in order to give away, to possess nothing and to be in and of itself nothing other than the process which inscribes itself on it. Chora is neither subject or support; is giving way and not giving place, more situating than situated. Chora is inaccessible, impassable, amorphous? Chora is virginity resistant to anthropomorphism.

Seaweed.

Applying the lessons of the turbulent dance of seaweed (a continually folding entity) to architecture, one is faced with that existing outside the idea of the 'flat', outside of the impetus of perfect horizontal and perfect vertical. Locally, seaweed's ease of movement is rendered possible by a crucial absence of material, a series of perforations along crease lines. The holes throughout the seaweed are not faults but necessary interruptions – perpetual thresholds for water's passage. A chora work, seaweed's global structure allows it to be malleable and permeable to its surroundings. Unharmed by, 'maritime turbulence, turbantibus aequora ventis . . . in th(is) theoretical text the reference to individual bodies is again only related to fluids: imbris utiguttae . . . certainly a question of weight, of gravity, but never of solids.'[3]

René Thom, speaking of the constructive and the destructive aspects of the catastrophe, names the following archetypal morphologies: to finish, to begin, to unify, to separate, to become, to capture, to emit, to fault, to suicide, to agitate, to cross, to give, to take, to send, to link, to cut.[4] With respect to the fold's topological properties, the act of architecture is one of embodying the rupture which is also the link between physically discontinuous realms of space.

Unable to resist, (s)he caught the seaweed, pulled it out of the flow, and set it upon the rock – glistening. The space between the undersurface of the seaweed and the surface of the rock fused to form an admirable, if ephemeral, model for a crenellated building envelope.

The fold – this catastrophe $V=x3$, the border, the end, the beginning, is not static geometry but one of spatial, temporal, material flux.

From fluid to solid, an architectural interest in 'the fold' is commensurate with an obsession for cyclical processes. One may embrace the fold as a design choreography of discontinuity, a design process in which the 'architecture' is not primarily upheld as an immutable object. One in which the building is not thought of as autonomous, as hermetically sealed without interstices or breaks; not idealised as a perfect uninterrupted connection of parts.

Around the graaf follicle, the swollen

ovarian lining folds to form a pocket. On the verge of rupture and ready to flow across the breach into the uterine oviduct, it is an entity maintained in position by continuity with the uterus. In ordinary conditions, the uterine tube is held between leaves of the large ligament, however, during pregnancy, it becomes very mobile.

Back on the rock, the water shed quickly from the surface of the translucent seaweed; moisture steadily evaporating. In the dazzling sunlight the glistening object did not survive in immutable form but collapsed suddenly onto the surface of the rock. After this point the seaweed's process of desiccation continued quietly, introducing further complicated folds.

Leibniz's law of continuity (germ of catastrophe theory) sustains a fold 'where there is continuity between data such that one case continually approaches and at length loses itself in another, there will be corresponding continuity in results or properties.'

'What noise did the classical age muffle, to which sounds did it close its ears in order to invent our rationalism? It is necessary to have the audacity to uncover ichnography - that which one always carries around with oneself, in the dark and as if secret, in a set back alcove, or under a veil.'[5]

Venus her(e) folds.
Her architecture would be thus a local emergence within a saturated landscape. Questions situated deeply within, yet extending to the exterior surface . . . of the discipline. The folds of mons veneris. The fringe of History. The dove(tail) whispers: 'butterfly goddess, ombillic hyperbolic concavity, elliptic hyperbolic placenta, parabolic ombillic convexity.' The architecture of the fold is one of becoming; one of a specific gestational process. If the task is to define or theorise the fold as a place in architecture, this must certainly be within place(entation). If not . . . 'language will reproduce with you in the folds of skin, this endless version of your body from now on unalterable'.[6]

For some architects, the earth's crust may be understood as placental; for others, the strata of the 'site' are seen as bulk, the architectural intervention as penetration (without possible unfolding): violation, transgression. 'The three membranes of the uterus tie themselves together by means of the cotyledons . . . just as fingers of the hand are interwoven, one in the interval of the other . . . so these fleshy rosettes interlock and are attached as burrs do among each other. The cotyledons have

male and female parts. You will now note whether the male or female remains attached to the uterus or not.'[7]

The place(nta) is formed of a series of folds; within these pliant swells, are gently interfering waves: the Herme-Aphrodite architect. At the place where the foot touches the ground, the movement is downward toward the roots of building. The building becomes porous to chthonic presences, to dreams to oracles, traditionally located beneath the earth's crust.

Within the fold, certain navigational horizons are inscribed. The placental wall – a translucent barrier characterised by the dynamics of the concave and the convex – is a receptacle within a receptacle. What of architecture as a culmination of a cycle within cycles: the incredible presence of the red rooms, the utter sophistication of the uterine wall, villa of the mysteries, delicate translucent veils externalised in paintings of her? In placental logic, the weather/whether of architectural design emerges: within the welcoming, ever changing section of the wall one finds local conditions of heterogeneous spatial varieties. The wall locally becomes an intelligent and responsive membrane with innate capacities to direct the flow of space; the separation and connection between discreet places. The Herme-Aphrodite is working on both sides of the fold: on one side losing the clear edges of plane geometry to find the feminine lurking somewhere in the centre; on the other embracing the 'grid' as overlay of order.

Despite the Jeffersonian effort, the chaotic paths of tumbleweeds, grains of dust, constantly shifting waves of low flying turbulence continue to ripple over the earth's surface. Reverse this fold: 'reason has triumphed over myth. Euclidean space has repressed a barbarous topology . . . Myth is effaced in its original function, the new space is universal. As is reason of the ratio that it sustains, only because within it there are no more encounters.'[8]

Question 1 – Lucretius and the Architecture Firm: If the hermaphrodite architect made a perfect, platonic solid – and threw it into a bog where the ground is unstable, wet, porous, topological in nature – how would these two entities fold together? With respect to the Blue Sea, or the Mer Bleue Bog; if there is an architecture nascent here it does not emerge from solid ground. It is not necessarily hard and dry. This fold of architecture may not be limited to orthogonal projective geometries and building systems.

Question 2 – The Hesiodic Earth: If the hermaphrodite architect seeks a place of projection, how might the folds of the earth's surface be assimilated into the 'deadly flat' of the drafting table?

With every step on to the Blue Sea Bog, the earth bears a compressive collapse which is audible. This noise is associated with the giddy earth and with that which is folded into and hidden within the ground. Churning within the buoyant mass of peat are plants and seed which have blown in from the outskirts of the bog for thousands of years.

The top side, in evidence, in print, written (and built). The other side, of an intimate yet unrealised immediacy, whispers. She offers a new understanding of 'section'. 'Immediately Mrs Ramsay seemed to fold herself together, one petal closed in another, the whole fabric folding in exhaustion upon itself . . . like the pulse of a spring which has expanded to its full width and now gently ceases to beat, the rapture of successful creation.'[9]

You hold the book, the room you read in holds you; one pocket of thick contracting wall. The hermaphrodite architect: on one side '(s)he is the worker of a single space, the space of measure and transport. The Euclidean space of every possible displacement without changes of state. On the other side, (s)he is the worker of proliferating multiplicities, of unlinked morphologies.'[10]

The material fold.

## Notes

1  Refer to René Thom, *Morphogenese et l'imaginaire*.
2  Michael Serres, *Hermes: Literature, Science, Philosophy*.
3  Ibid.
4  Refer to René Thom, *Mathematical Models of Morphogenesis*.
5  *Genese*, M Serres: 'Quelle noise L'age classique refoule-t-il, à quel bruit ferme-t-il ses oreilles, pour inventer notre rationalisme? . . . il faut avoir l'audace d'évoiler l'ichnographie, parfois, celle qu'on porte toujours avec soi, dans le noir, et comme au secret, dans une alcôve retiré, sous un voile.
6  Nicola Brossard, *Picture Theory*.
7  Refer to description in Leonardo da Vinci's Notebooks.
8  Michael Serres, *Hermes: Literature, Science, Philosophy*.
9  Virginia Woolf, *To the Lighthouse*.
10  Michael Serres, *Hermes: Literature, Science, Philosophy*.

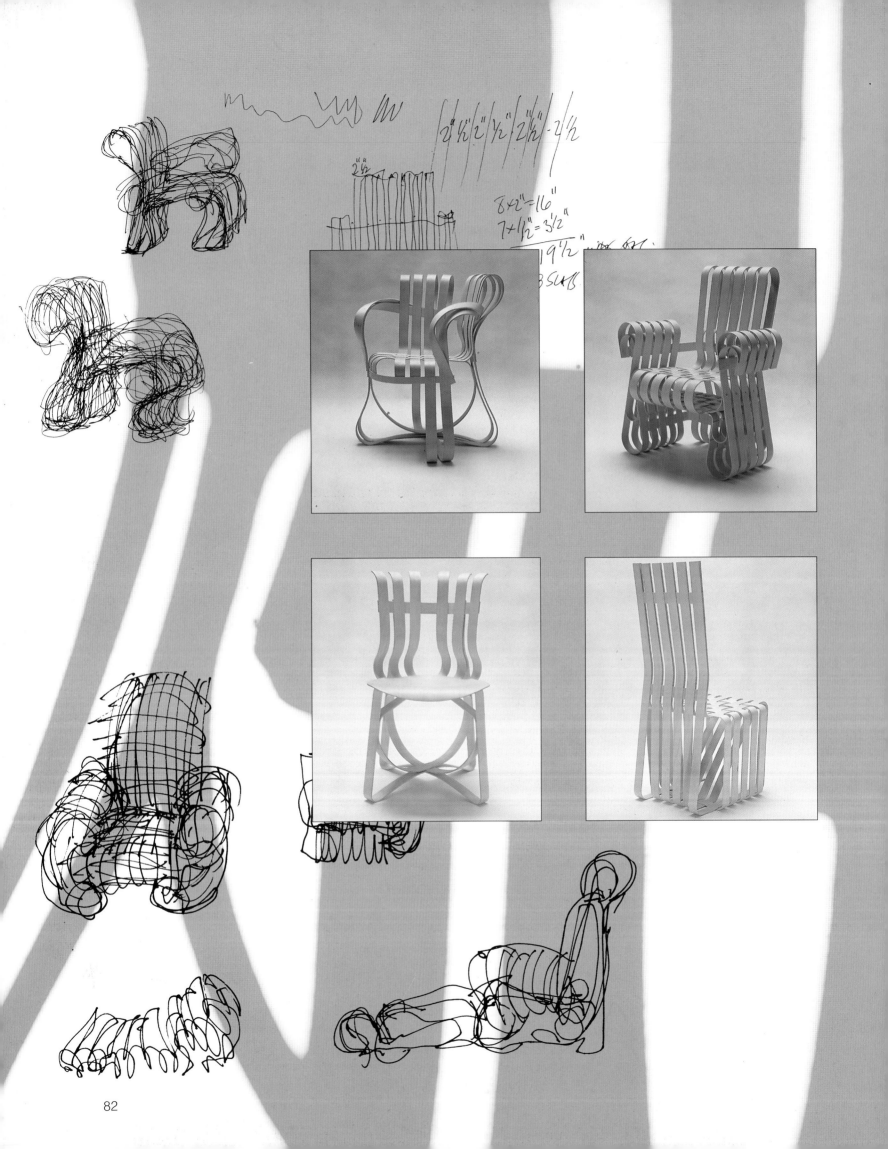

# FRANK GEHRY
## *BENTWOOD FURNITURE*

I've always been interested in furniture, probably because my dad had a little furniture company in Toronto for a while. Architecture takes so long to make . . . that's why furniture is always so interesting to me. It's instant gratification. My experience as an architect selecting furniture for a client has been very disappointing. You go into the market and always find the same thing: a Mies chair. It's especially difficult for low-budget projects. I would always wind up designing furniture.

I became interested in paper furniture when I was designing for department stores and had to invent display furniture that nobody really had to sit on, and which could then be easily disposed of. It led to the *Easy Edges* furniture, which evolved in a shop in my studio. I would draw and my assistants and I would then make them. I never expected to sell these things until someone from Bloomingdales saw them and suggested I develop them. I got some investors, and in short order the chairs got a big play. But I felt very insecure . . . I was not then well known as an architect, yet there I was talking furniture sales with Marvin Traub. That was not how I wanted to be seen, so I stopped.

The strange thing with these new bentwood chairs is that everyone always

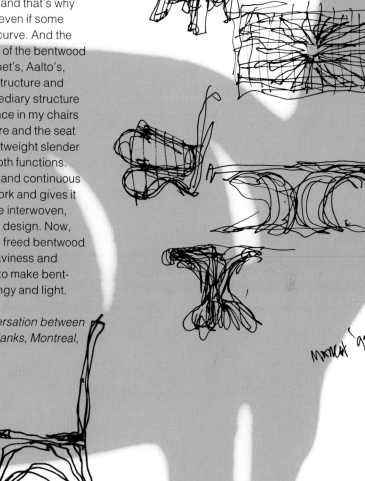

likes the straight models. When they think of Gehry they think of neo-modern. Then they look at the *Cross Check* chair and they say, 'Horrors! It looks 'decorative'. But I am not interested in making 'decorative' things. The swirls and curves of my chairs are structural and they grow out of necessity. If you look at Thonet chairs you see that all those curves are structural and that's why Thonet structures work . . . even if some extra twirls are added to a curve. And the same is true in my chair. All of the bentwood furniture to this point – Thonet's, Aalto's, Eames' – had a heavy substructure and then webbing, or an intermediary structure for the seating. The difference in my chairs is that the (support) structure and the seat are formed of the same lightweight slender wood strips, which serve both functions. The material forms a single and continuous idea. What makes this all work and gives it extraordinary strength is the interwoven, basket-like character of the design. Now, structure and material have freed bentwood furniture from its former heaviness and rigidity. It really is possible to make bentwood furniture pliable, springy and light.

*Excerpt from a taped conversation between Frank Gehry and David A Hanks, Montreal, May 24, 1991*

# FRANK GEHRY AND PHILIP JOHNSON
## *LEWIS RESIDENCE*
### *Cleveland, Ohio*

The Lewis Residence to be built on a hilltop in Lyndhurst, a suburb of Cleveland is a 22,000 square foot house for Peter Lewis, an insurance executive. Functioning as a mix of semi-public areas for entertaining and private areas for residents, the complex includes a main house with living room, dining room, two master bedroom suites, hall/gallery, library, exercise area and an enclosed lap pool. There are also three guest houses and a six car garage.

The house is a collaborative effort between Frank Gehry and Philip Johnson. Gehry's sweeping sail-like forms of the main house are in contrast to the euclidean geometries of the guest suites by Johnson.

The design of the house is conceived of as a composition of complex curved elements that will be constructed from a variety of materials including stone, metal and glass. The participation of trades and artisans in the process is integral to the form-making envisioned. 3-D computer modelling can provide the means on this project for reintegrating the architects with the trades.

The residence is organised around a main court that is cut into the hilltop. The court can be tented for lavish affairs and compliments the main hall and gallery.

Opposite: *Detail of model*; Left: *Site plan*; Above: *Model*; Below: *Site model*

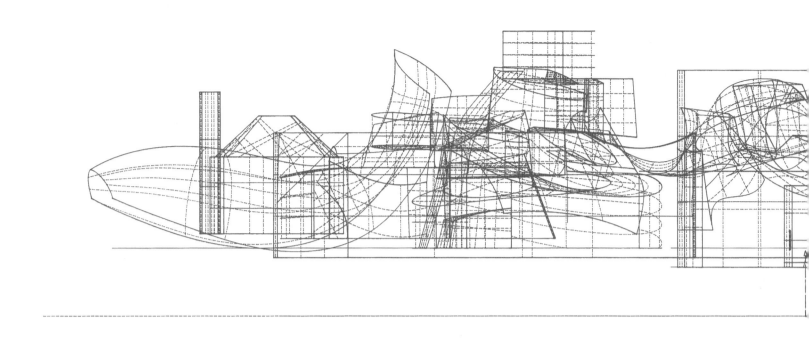

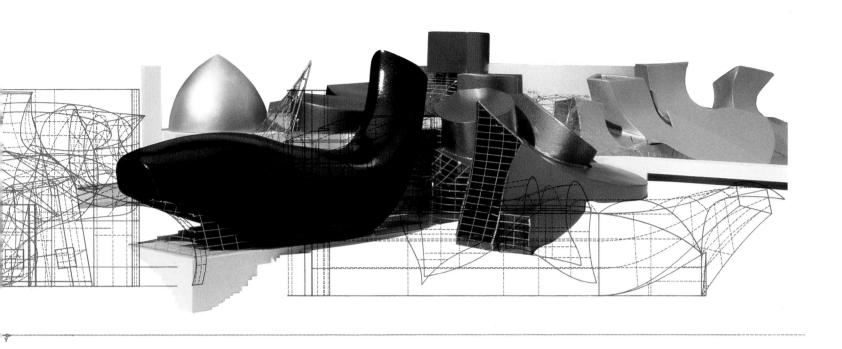

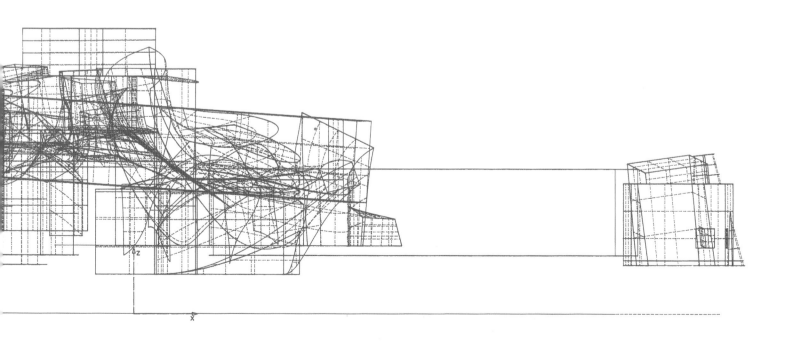

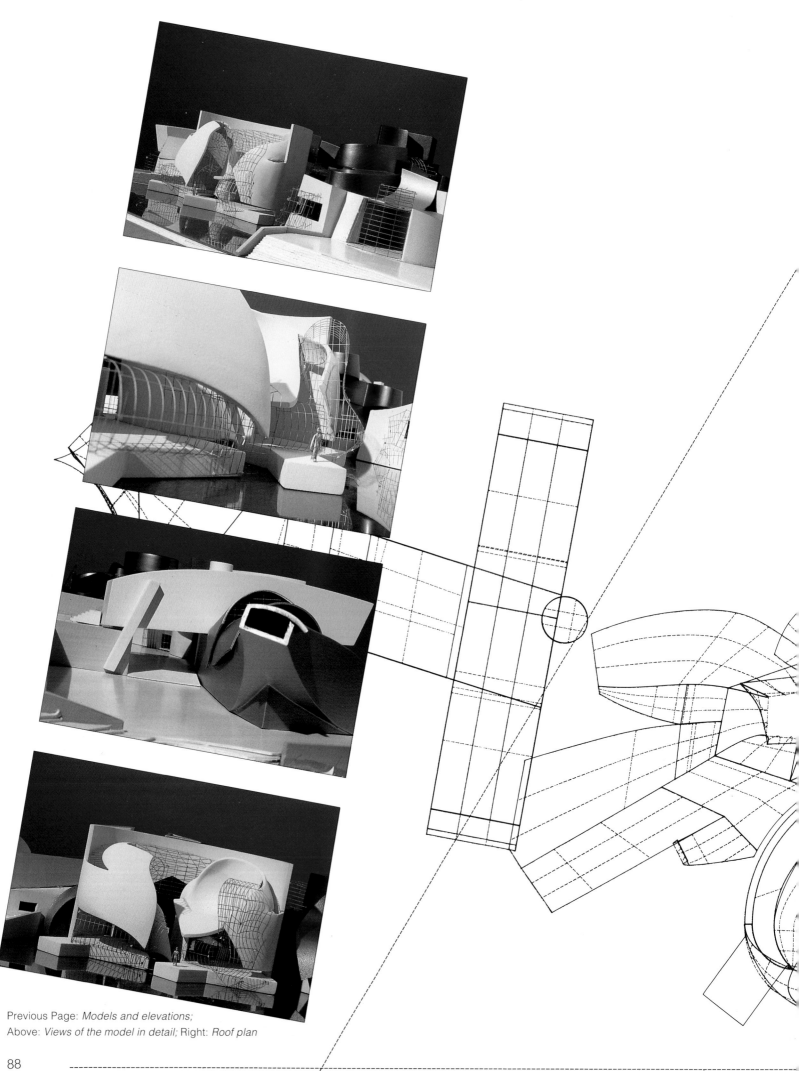

Previous Page: *Models and elevations;*
Above: *Views of the model in detail;* Right: *Roof plan*

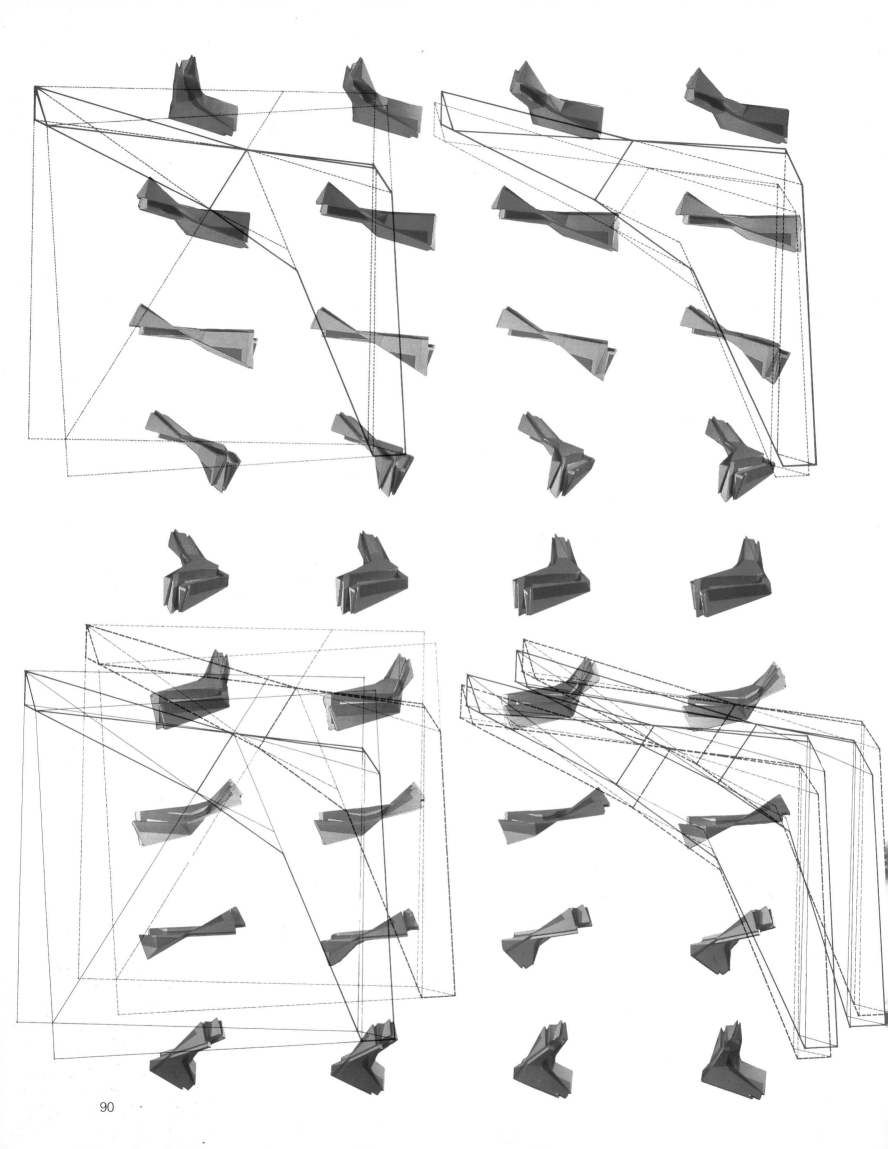

# THOMAS LEESER
## *IN VER(re*)T.EGO*

Medieval scholars of optical sciences were aware that they could not anticipate the future applications of their most advanced principles and theories. Among the most sophisticated of these theories was that of image-formation in a concave spherical mirror, wherein an erect and virtual image appears behind the mirror while the image in front of the mirror appears inverted and real. Lacan describes the diagram in his discussions of the mirror stage:

> Virtual images in some instances behave like objects, and real images can be made into virtual objects . . . Here the imaginary space and the real space fuse, nonetheless, they have to be conceived of as different.

The very same principle of mirror is evident in what could be described as the most powerful and promising eye of the 20th century: the Hubble Telescope floating in outer space. Only now, through a flaw in the mirror's curvature, the inverted and real image that is being produced is also distorted. We are blinded, disrupted in our desire to make the real image coincide with the imaginary. This 'loss of perceptual co-ordinates in the post-modern world, its hallucinogenic hyperreality, an undifferentiated vision of the world in the present', as Jaqueline Rose puts it, is that 'which deprives the subject of the ability to locate her/himself in either space or time'.

This project is based on inversion, difference, 'loss of perceptional coordinates' and immaterialisation in the post-modern world. The inversion diagram serves as a reference; a structure set up as a starting point. Each end of the structure represents an inverse of the other. Any point of the two ends projected forms a line and any line will eventually form two points which define the extent of the line described previously. The images inverted in this way, undergo a similar transition from a real to a virtual condition. What is upside-down can be seen as the real; therefore, what is right-side-up becomes the image of the virtual:

> For there to be an optics, for each given point in real space, there must be a corresponding point in the virtual, the imaginary space. *Lacan*

Thus, a line is not perceived in the tradition of Western thinking as a linear continuum, but rather as a constantly changing condition of inversion. In optics, this process of translation is known as the circle of confusion: through variations in the polished surfaces of a single lens, two spatially and directional distinct focal lines are produced simultaneously by the same projection. In psychoanalytical discourse this diagram is used to illustrate the splitting of the Ur-ich from the external world of difference.

The diagram's interest for this project lies in its potential to manifest spatially the liquidity of processes rather than the stases of iconic imagery. Fusing the con-fusion of difference and the understanding of the folding-in and onto itself of reality and virtuality makes it possible to allude to issues of gender, sexuality and desire, electronic and television environments, biological and non-perspective space without having to resort to a display of their respective images. Traditional politics and power relations are undercut by a complete loss of hierarchy through an ever present simultaneity. One thing is always also the other. This loss of traditional power is made manifest through what could be described as a 'zero-space': a space of no dimension – precisely the point where the inversion or translation takes place; a space of no depth; a line and two points. All parts of any image through which space is produced will eventually have to pass through this 'zero-space' of translation and will generate a distorted and inverted reflection of themselves: the virtualisation of space.

Through this process the twin inhabitants occupying opposite ends of the space, at any given time each standing on the same plane that forms the others ceiling, are entwined irrevocably with one another even though they are physically apart. The inhabitants' twin-ness is thus inscribed spatially in the structure, creating a condition of inseparability in absentia: one is caught within the liquid mirror.

The introduction of the double twists the

experience of the other. Suddenly, one is not only confronted with one's own virtual reality but con-fused further with yet another mirroring. 'For each given point in virtual, imaginary space, there must be a corresponding point in real space' wrote Lacan. 'Objects in some instances behave like virtual images, and virtual images can be made into real objects.' This manifest heterotopia allows for a deliberate false recognition between the doubles: the virtual reality of one projection is seen as the inverted reality of its double. But now, this structure has been turned upside down. Consequently, one can read simultaneously two inverted images as well as one erect image on one side, and two erect images and one inverted on the other. In reading B as the invert of A and A' as its double, one finds that the relationship has suddenly switched over and a direct correlation cannot be established: B is now found as the invert of A' rather than A.

Misreading the virtual reality of one projection as the inverted reality of the other allows one to see the process only as a complex folding back and forth and inside out, rather than a single and linear event. The continuous process of 'copying' introduces mutations, like a xerox machine, that open the door for further impurities. Function, arbitrary and interchangeable – left in its traditional familiarity only to reveal its alienated and estranged reality – is radically seen as an impurity, a perfect accident, contradicting traditional methodology of design. Another impurity is introduced through shifting the focal line of each projection out of its alignment: one up and consequently the other one down. On top of the doubling, a blurring is produced that further undermines the possibility of reference and enforces the immaterialisation of image.

Misrecognition and total invisibility are significant to the war machinery this century. Deception is a condition of immaterialisation; whether present in electronic noise or today's radar evading, stealth aeroplanes, or in the dazzle paintings of battle ships in the First World War before electronic surveillance was available. The desired state of confusion was not, it was discovered quickly, achieved through invisibility alone but through deliberate conspicuousness. A fundamental loss of (self) referentiality can be seen in this dislocation of images and their respective objects, the 'indeterminacy of the visual sign' (Rose). Reconfiguration of image and identity is enforced by the introduction of delamination and subsequent slippage of structure and skin. The surface is dislocated from the body underneath and its edges displaced by slipping slightly out of register without actually reshaping the volume itself. Here, opacity turns into transparency and allows the occurrence of literal cracks in its shell. The multiple pieces, like the reconfigured elements of a broken jar, no longer fit properly together and enable one to enter the entire structure in a critical manner.

Previous Page Left: *360° Rotation in 10° intervals of solid model; diagrams of doubling and blurring;* Previous Page Right: *Image formation in a concave spherical mirror;* Right: *Site plan; plans and elevations*

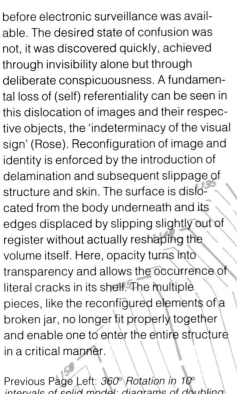

BM #2
R.R. SPIKE IN 24"TREE
1'ABOVE GROUND LEVEL
ELEV= 1120.03 (ASSUMED BASIS)

POSSIBLE
BUILDING
SITE

WOODED
AREA

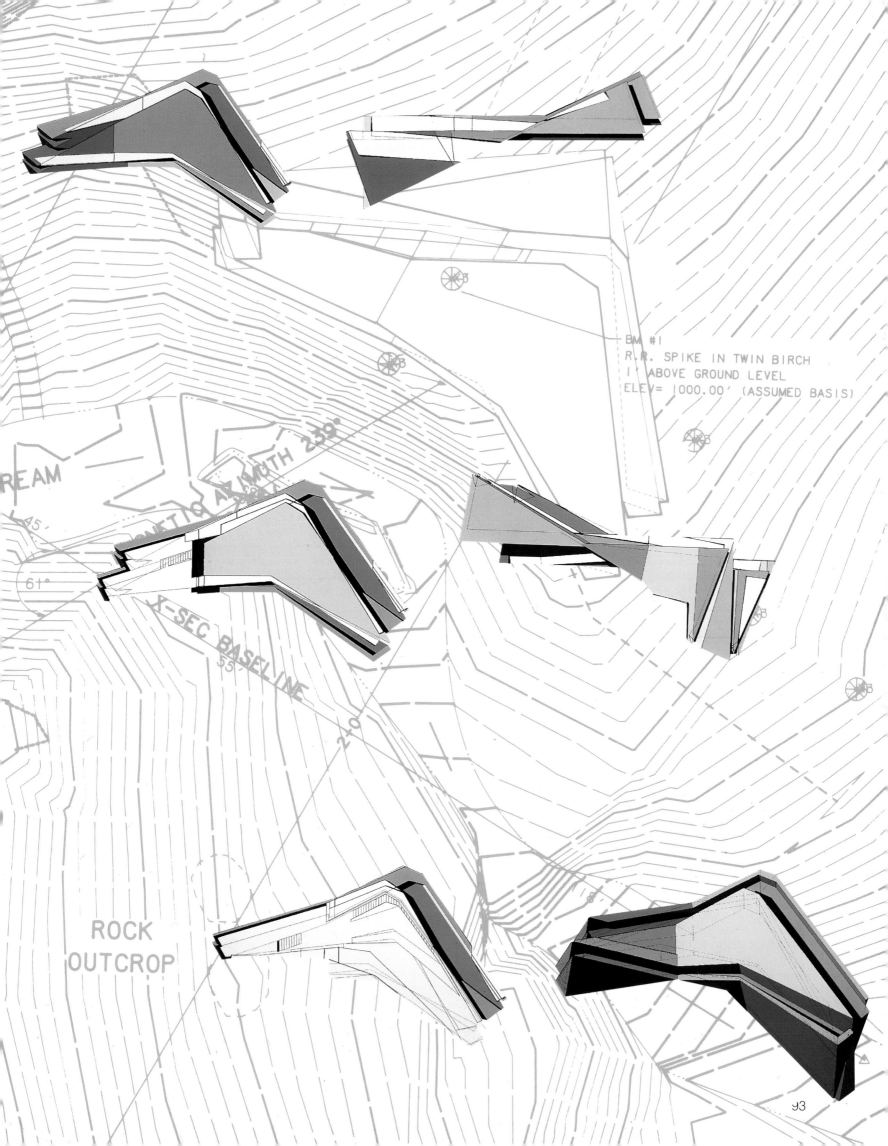

REAM

ROCK
OUTCROP

BM #1
R.R. SPIKE IN TWIN BIRCH
I' ABOVE GROUND LEVEL
ELEV= 1000.00' (ASSUMED BASIS)

93

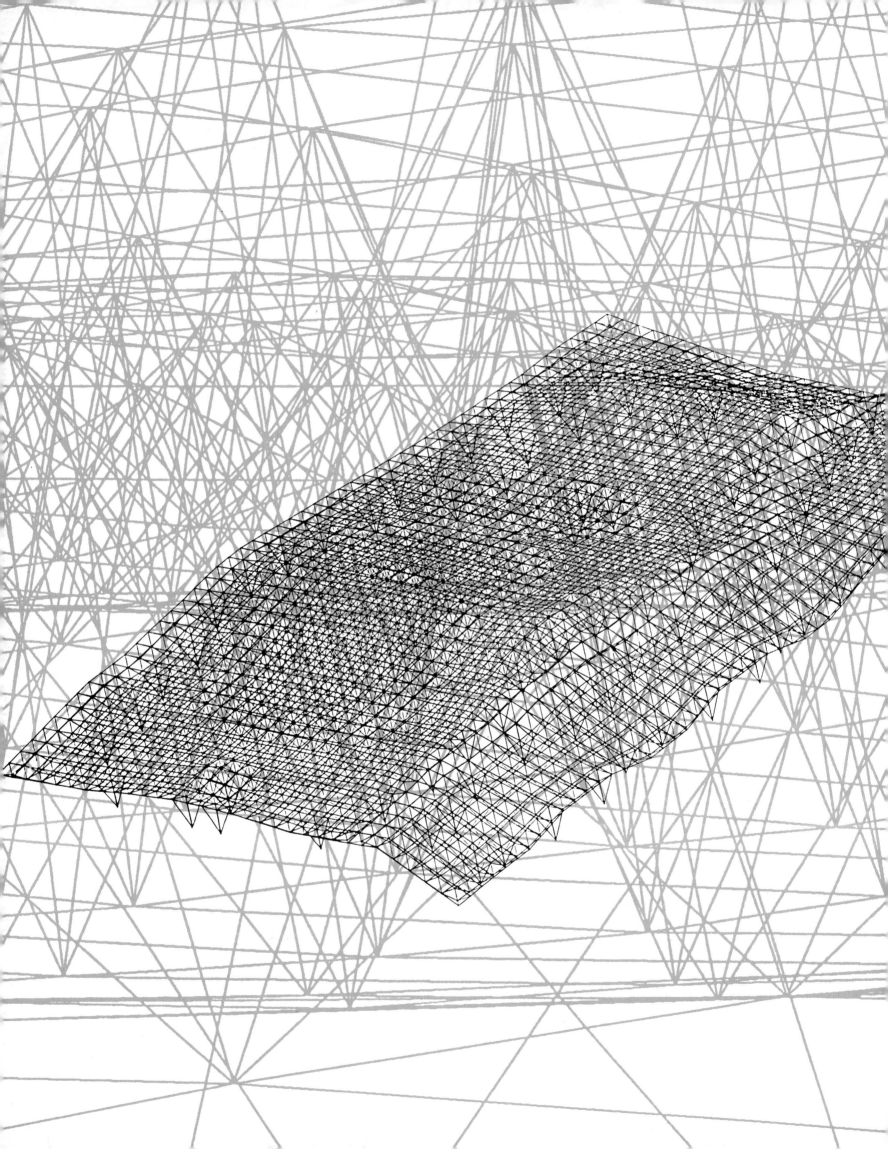

# SHOEI YOH
## *PREFECTURA GYMNASIUM*

Shoei Yoh describes his Prefectura Gymnasium and Odawara Complex buildings as examples of aquatic architecture. Along with Kisho Kurokawa's logic of symbiosis, this project contributes to a movement towards more fluid and open systems of aqueous urban space, presently being formulated in Japan. Like Kurokawa, Yoh proposes unpredicted connections between programmatic, structural and cultural contingencies and form. Such a logic of *viscosity* develops stability by exploiting differential and fluctuating forces. The relations of spaces are extremely complex, rigorous and precise, yet irreducible to any single or holistic organisation. This complex resistance to reduction either to unity or contradiction distinguishes Yoh's sensibility from either the universal spaces of Modernism or the arrested formal conflict of Deconstruction. This irreducible complexity is engendered by the supple transformations of *an exact yet rigorous geometry* of the Prefectura Gymnasium roof structure.

The structural members cannot be reduced to any single uniform dimension. Their particular lengths and contours present an image which is seemingly between geometric exactitude and arbitrary figuration. This simultaneity of both figure and structure differs from a more familiar contradiction between decoration and structure. The roof of Yoh's project employs a particularised, 'diffcomorphic' and supple topological surface capable of fluid transformations. The precision and clarity of the continuous yet heterogeneous roof system should be distinguished from the reducible homogeneity of Mies van der Rohe's Berlin National Gallery. Similarly, this project is not merely driven by structural necessity but becomes involved with a multiplicity of subsystems including lighting, acoustics, programme and aesthetics. The roof structure employs affiliations between disparate programmatic, structural and mechanical systems; a supple rather than rigid geometry which is capable of sustaining the differences which result from unpredicted connections; and finally a resistance to arresting these complex relations in either fixed points of resolution or contradiction. Although Yoh, along with several others, could be inscribed within an expressionist style of curved forms, the specific and specialised roof structure responds to the smooth and intensive internalisation of outside forces. This differentiated smoothness results from an adherence to the pragmatic contingencies of structure, programme and cost.

Surprisingly, the plexing roof form spans a more or less straightforward grid of programme. The athletic fields determine specific span lengths and ceiling heights. A uniform snow load establishes the variable beam depths and roof heights. Finally, the internal surface is adjusted for lighting and acoustical concerns. Rather than averaging these requirements as a single mean dimension, their differences are maintained. These disparate forces become involved with this flexible system without revision to the global organisation. Yet, the entire organisation fluctuates subtly with every local adjustment. The savings on material costs, through this sustained precision and particularisation, outweighed the fabrication costs of the various structural members. These developments are now possible given the new technologies which can sustain multiplicity and complexity through the computerisation of the design, construction and fabrication process.

It is the discontinuity between part and whole and the smooth fluidity with which external forces are compliantly involved with internal requirements which gives Yoh's project its complex character. Both the structure and figure of the roof are generated through the unpredicted connections between a multiplicity of plexing and pliant subsystems. In this sense, the form of the roof is constructed by vicissitude. The roof structure proposes a pliant architecture of surface and field relations. Yoh's aqueous paradigm results in an involved and intense system of connections between structure, use, economy and form.

*Greg Lynn*

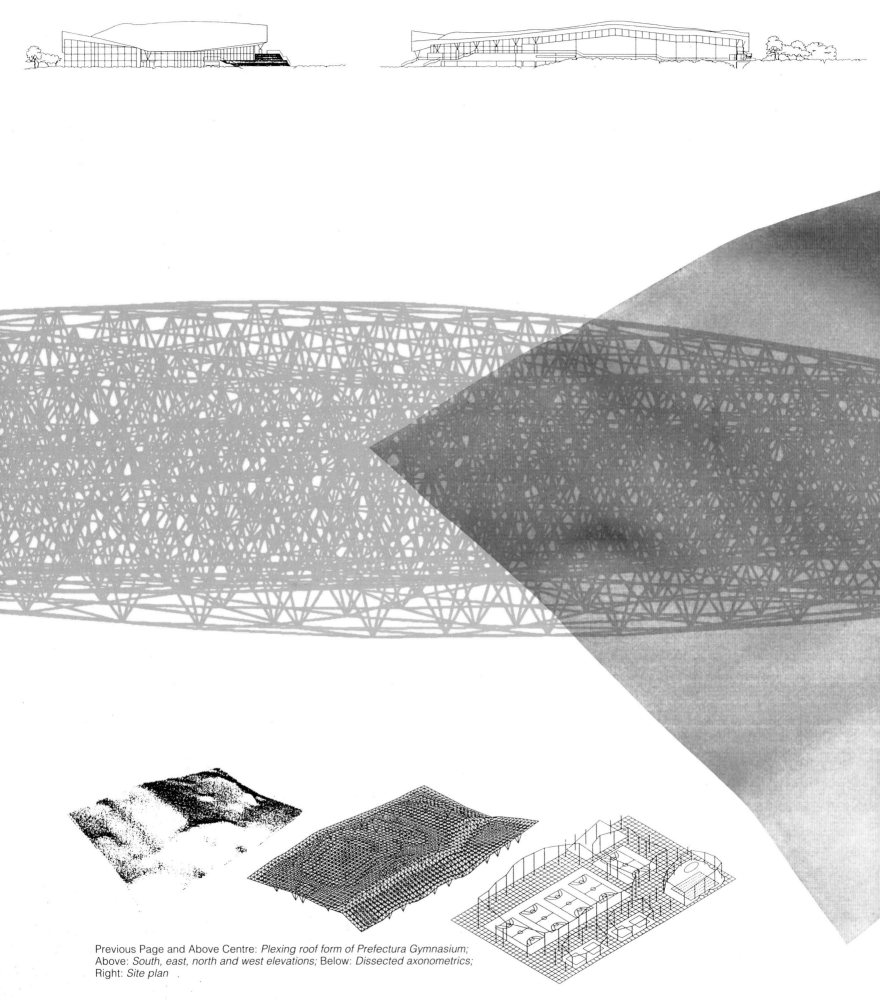

Previous Page and Above Centre: *Plexing roof form of Prefectura Gymnasium;*
Above: *South, east, north and west elevations;* Below: *Dissected axonometrics;*
Right: *Site plan*

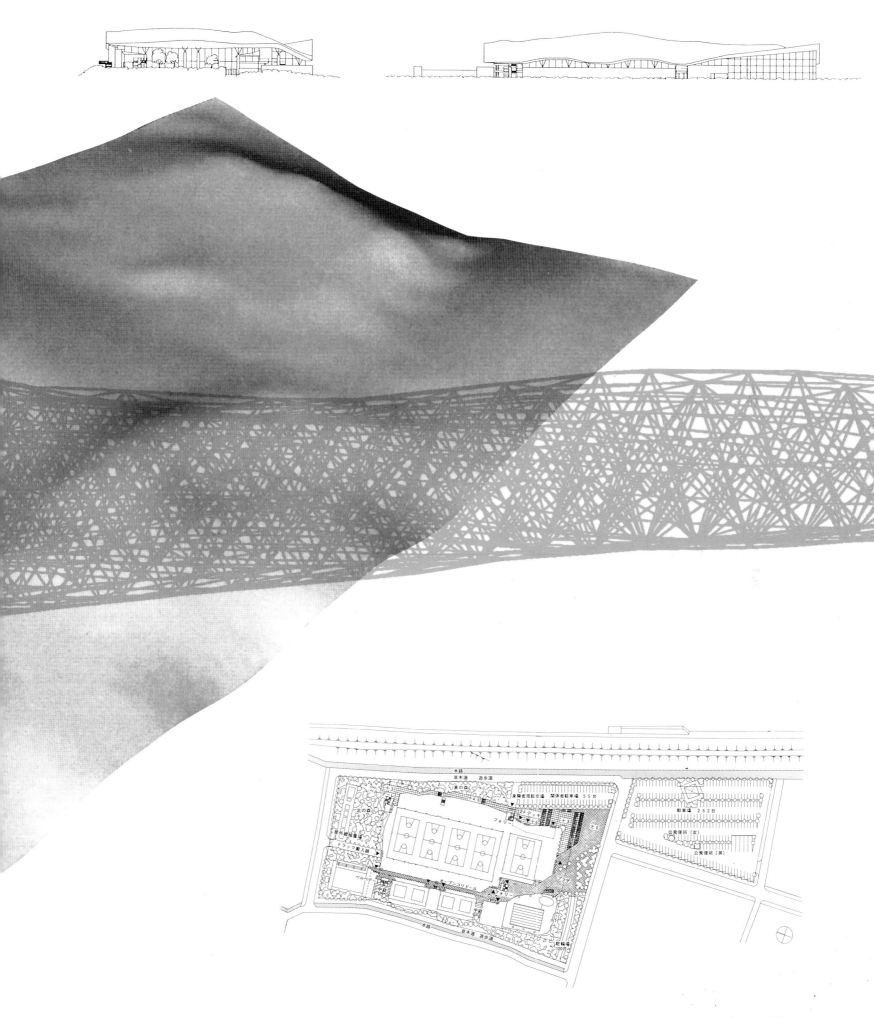

# GREG LYNN
## *STRANDED SEARS TOWER*

This project is a response to an ideas competition held for the city of Chicago: the American city which has the richest tradition of competitions for architectural monumentality. Along with the airport, the corporate office tower has been the primary vehicle for innovations in urban monumentality in Chicago and the United States in general. This project attempts to reformulate the image of the American monument by reconfiguring the existing dominant icon on the Chicago skyline and the tallest free-standing building in the world: the Sears Tower. The existing Sears Tower is disassociated from its context in order that it can stand as an icon. It establishes itself as a discrete and unified object within a continuous and homogeneous urban fabric. This project attempts to affiliate the structure of the tower with the heterogeneous particularities of its site while maintaining monumental status. The monument must maintain its presence while remaining flexible enough to exploit possible involvements with the particularities of context. By laying the structure into its context and entangling monolithic mass with local contextual conditions, a new monumentality emerges from the old forms.

'Buildings are no longer obelisks, but lean one upon the other, no longer suspicious of the other, like a statistical graph. This new architecture incarnates a system that has ceased to be competitive, but is compatible; where competition has disappeared for the benefit of correlations.'

In *The Order of Simulacra* Jean Baudrillard describes a new paradigm for the contemporary office tower in the United States. The previous paradigm of competitive verticality was supplemented with a desire not only for excessive size but for excessive numbers. The Twin Towers, New York inaugurated this tendency toward multiplicity through double identity. Duplication reinforces self-identity of the identical twins as they merge into a singular monumental structure. The response of the Sears Tower to this new (York) paradigm, lay not only in exceeding the height of the Twin Towers but in exceeding its duplicity.

The Sears Tower internalised its multiplication by dividing differentially into the record nine towers which Fazlur Kahn termed the 'bundled tube'. Where the identical Twin Towers duplicate, the differentiated Sears Tower proliferates. 'The basis of the Sears Tower is the bundled tube. In the Tower, nine contiguous tubes, in essence nine towers 75 feet square, make up the 50 storey base of the building. Their tubes are interlocked; thus each tube helps to support its neighbour.'

The 225 foot square footprint is made up of nine 75 foot square tubes; two of which are 650 feet in length; two are 860 feet in length; three are 1,170 feet in length; and the last two of a record 1,450 feet in length. Each tube is striated into five structural bays yielding another 25 tubes per tower. Each of these 225 independent structural bays is subdivided into three five-foot window bays yielding another nine-square tube within each structural bay for a total of 2,025 tubes. The bundled tubes are a multiplicity; as a construction that is simultaneously one and many. The Sears Tower is at once single and multiple as if it were a strand: a collection of 'fibres or filaments twisted, plaited or laid parallel to form a unit.' This strand is both a system of interwoven filaments and a singularity capable of further twisting or plaiting into a larger or more complex yarn, thread, rope or cordage.

This project reformulates the vertical bundle of tubes horizontally along a strand of land between Wacker Drive and the Chicago River's edge adjacent to the existing Sears Tower. To engender affiliations with particular local events, the rigid geometry that dictated the exact parallel relations between tubes was rejected for a more supple description. Through a geometry that is more supple, the nine contiguous tubes accommodate themselves fluidly and flexibly to the multiple and often discontinuous borders of the site. The relations between tubes are not exactly parallel. These supple deflections allow connection to take place which would have been repressed by a more rigid and

reductive geometric system of description. Although the increments of the floor plates are oriented perpendicularly to the surface of the drawings in general, the particularities to the river's edge, roads and sidewalks often deflect any single ideal orientation in favour of multiple oblique orientations. The deformations of twisting result from the external forces within the context. These more supple systems are the techniques employed in the surveying of land forms, in fluid dynamics and other empirical sciences which cannot reduce matter to purely geometric or ideal quantities. The nine initial strands untangle themselves further to align to finer grain local conditions by bifurcating along the lines of their structure and fenestration. The context provides these lines of bifurcation to the tubes and these become potential lines for the projects proliferation into the site. A single body begins to become multiplicitous because of these lines of development imposed from the outside. The bundled tube is a potential paradigm for a multiplicitous monument. It is an assembly of micro-systems which constructs an icon which is provisional. Upon close examination the unified image of the monument unravels into heterogeneous local events. Irreducibility to any single type and the potential to participate with external systems are the characteristics of a stranded and supple urbanism. The Stranded Sears Tower is neither discrete nor dispersed but rather defers any single organisational idea for a system of local affiliations outside itself. The strands exploit possible connections with and between adjacent buildings, sidewalks, bridges, tunnels and landforms. These connections are not accidental but unpredicted as they result from the combination of the disparate systems of the 2,025 bundled tubes with the existing site. The resultant image is neither monolithic nor pluralistic but is of the now supple and flexible internal order of the 'bundled tube' that is differentiated by the external forces of the river's edge, the Chicago grid and the vectors of pedestrian and transportation movement.

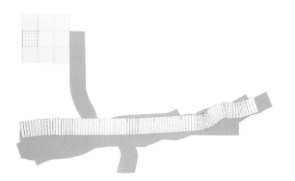
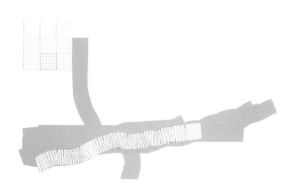

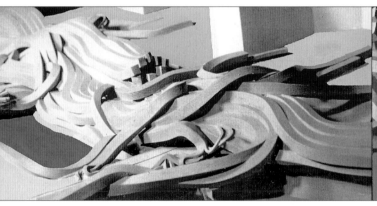
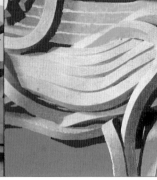
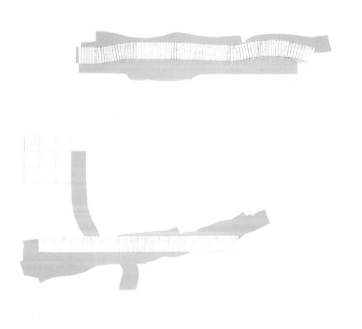
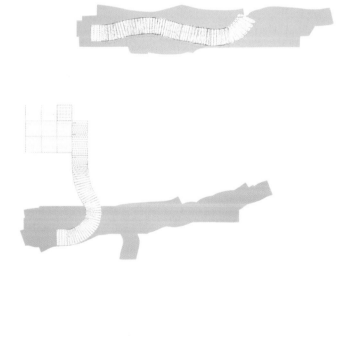

Previous page: *View of model*; Above: *Plans, sections and views of model*

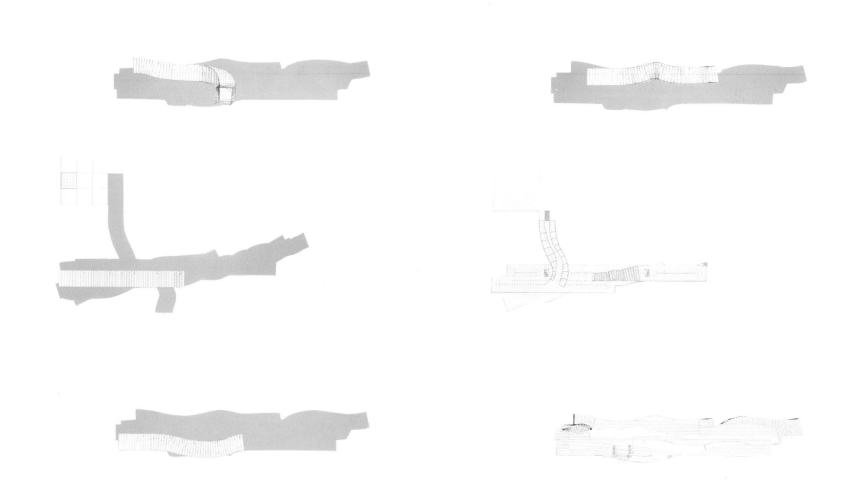

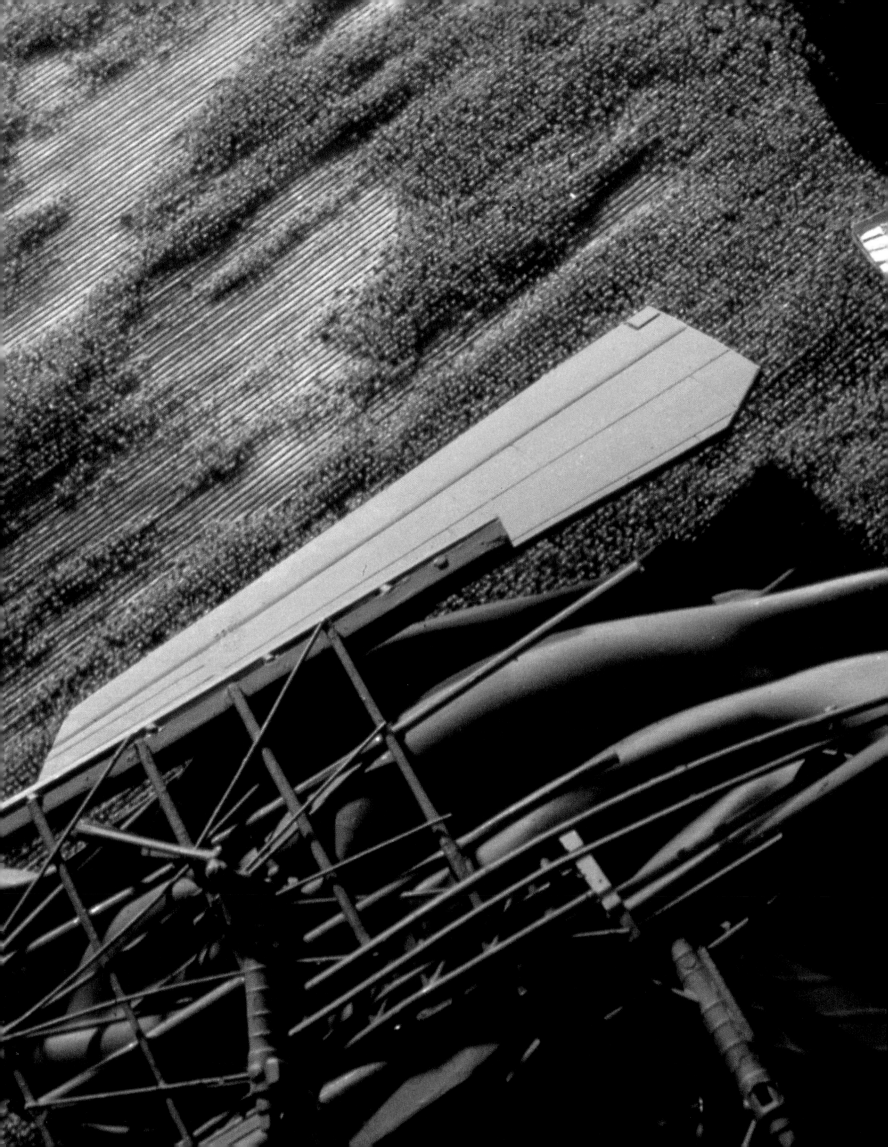

# RAA Um
## CROTON AQUEDUCT

### Site

The site is located along the New York City water supply infra-structure: A branching linear system of reservoirs, aqueducts and tunnels which stretches from rural upstate New York to the dense network of city water mains. Our definition of site is both unconventionally broad (encompassing over 250 linear miles) yet extremely precise – a vertical and regional cut tied together by a single purpose and administered by the City. By taking the entire water supply system as site, we are given a Regional Cross Section encompassing the rural areas of collection reservoirs; control chambers and holding reservoirs throughout Westchester County (suburban and small town context); and distribution sites within the city.

### Process

We have chosen three sites which exemplify distinct conditions: Croton Dam in upper Westchester (rural); Tarrytown interchange (suburban); and Highgate in East Harlem (urban). Realising the necessity to focus further in order to develop credible architectural proposals, we have developed in detail Site 2: Tarrytown Interchange (where the New York State Thruway interrupts the Aqueduct).

### Justification

Any architect working on a site characterised by the extreme dimensions, exceptional demands and high architectural quality of the water supply infrastructure, must necessarily submit to the same criteria and seek to create an architecture adequate to what is already in place. Hence the importance of giving visibility not only to the public dimension of these works, but also to the associated issues of ecology and conservation. Everything associated with the water supply system must respond first to the criterion of necessity, as manifest in the double thematic of (functional) imperative and (aesthetic) indifference.

### Area Rule

The operation devised, as a result of detailed design work on specific sites, is referred to as the Area Rule: rather than follow the strict linearity of the given system and string together a series of isolated, discrete architectural objects, we have developed the interventions on the basis of existing property lines, articulated surfaces and contiguous areas. Surfaces fold up and form structures, blurring the strict division of architecture and landscape. The notion of the public realm proposed here is thus not dependent upon monumental objects. Instead we propose a new condition of surface; an open field for active participation; and a new network of public programmes.

### Programme

The project proposes as its primary strategy programmatic grafts: readings of the site and context developed through a mapping procedure, which seeks to uncover shifting site histories, patterns of land use, and changing articulations of public and private uses as encoded in place names and street designations. Michel de Certeau has noted the uncanny persistence of meaning in place names:

'. . . these names articulate a sentence that his steps compose without knowing it. Numbered streets and street numbers (112 St or 9 rue St Charles) orient the magnetic field of trajectories just as they can haunt dreams. . .

What is it then that they spell out? Disposed in constellations that hierarchise and semantically order the surface of the city, operating chronological arrangements and historical justifications, these words slowly lose, like worn coins, the value engraved on them, but their ability to signify outlives its first definitions. A strange toponymy that is detached from actual places and flies high over the city like a foggy geography of 'meanings' held in suspension, directing the physical perambulations below . These constellations of names provide traffic patterns: they are stars directing itineraries.

Linking acts and footsteps, opening meanings and directions, these words operate in the name of an emptying out and wearing away of their primary role. They become liberated spaces that can be occupied. A rich indetermination gives them, by means of a semantic rarefaction, the function of articulating a second, poetic geography on top of the geography of the literal, forbidden or permitted meaning. They insinuate other routes into the functionalist and historical order of movement. Walking follows them: 'I fill this great empty space with a beautiful name.'

### Cinematic Grafts

The final steps in the design work consist in going back to the map of the overall site and applying the area rule in a consistent manner. Given the detailed vocabularies developed in the design work for the Tarrytown Interchange, we were able to increase the realism of the proposal through the use of aerial photographs (a 'sampling' process of typical terrain) and to expand the scope of the investigation to encompass the full range of sites as originally proposed. Architectural models are not seen as scalar reductions for individual projects, but as nomadic 'props' to be used in multiple contexts and interchangeable combinations. Working in a very direct manner with the particularities of the site, a field of complex and unexpected exchanges develop as a result of these grafts, suggesting in turn a further reprogramming of the architecture, and a redefinition of the site itself. This 'putting into play' of the multiple possibilities of the elements has, we feel, enormous potential: a 'structure' as fluid and suggestive as the water supply system itself.

*RAAUm: Jesse Reiser, Stan Allen, Polly Apfelbaum, Nanako Umemoto*

WHITE PLAINS ROAD

ON AQUEDUCT

SOUTH

BROADWAY

TOLL PLAZA

TAPPAN ZEE BRIDGE

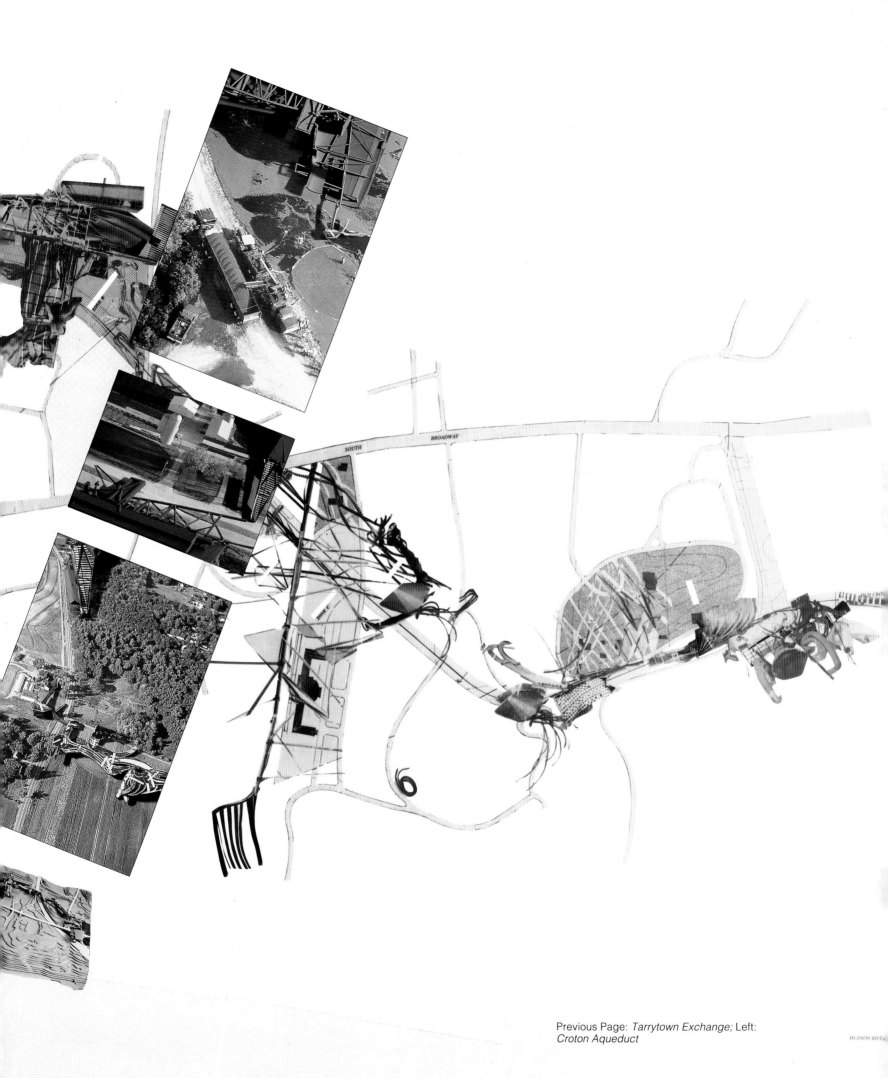

Previous Page: *Tarrytown Exchange;* Left:
*Croton Aqueduct*

# STEPHEN PERRELLA
## COMPUTER IMAGING
### Morphing and Architectural Representation

When one considers the complex spatiality described in the following interview involving the film *Terminator 2*, it is conceivable to maintain that such advances in digital technology affect cinematic temporality and enable new forms of spacetime. Suspending but not dismissing an analysis of the movie's technophobic/fatalist narrative, a closer consideration of its production techniques may reveal astonishing possibilites for contemporary architecture. The technology available to achieve cinematic effects has developed rapidly over recent years and instigates questions about culture, desire and its implementation in electronic technology, especially since many advances originate in the military industrial complex's research and development. The complexity made possible by these new practices may constitute an uncanny convergence between non-foundational theory and ordinary imaging practices. Considering modern culture's emphasis on visuality, 'everyday practices' as it is used here is fairly inclusive.

The context for this cinema/computer/ body interface analysis begins with the cinematic fundament of 24-40 or more frames per second to create real time illusion. Innumerable theses exist surrounding the technical circumstances that constitute cinematic temporal illusion but for the purpose of this discussion it is consequential to examine such basic technical facts and their impact on the illusion of reality given their geometric relations to time. Much theory has also been spun around the possibilities of superposition and montage as a means to surpass the limitation of the frame-gap-frame production sequence of film, avant-garde film of the 30s, through to contemporary French new wave and new German film notwithstanding. These genres reveal specific attempts to emphasise structural transparency or the superposition of one image over another, creating shocking or abrupt juxtapostions. Architect Stanley Allen recently described this condition paradigmatically as *'The Cinematic Eye:*

The engineer-monteur is an architect who builds with images. Place is created out of fragments distant in time and space: by constructing 'with intervals' he recognises the gap, the lag, which must now be built into the fabric of time and space. The metropolis produces a new subject: the montage eye capable of constructing a new reality out of the barrage of fragmentary, contradictory and obsolete information which characterises the modern city.'[1]

Between the spaced configuration of modern cinema, a transitional technology with a long and perhaps marginalised significance involves cartoon animation. Brian Boigon,from the School of Architecture, Toronto has argued for the inclusion, into architecture, of qualities of animism such as those which may be found in cartooning. This is made possible by the cartoonist imparting an intuitive connectivity contingent with the violated laws of realism. A further analysis of the geometries of cartoon animism would reveal glimpses of what is currently available to the mutations of realism.

The repressed phenomena excluded from each frame in the characterisation of modern film include change, time and *becoming*. Philosopher Mark Taylor eloquently unfolds this struggle between identity and difference in philosophy since Hegel (albeit in a critique of Structuralism) explaining that, 'since temporal change resists systemisation, systems can be constructed only by *excluding* time.'[2] The breakthrough achieved in *Terminator 2*, is an interframe, interstitial geometry-morphing. The importance of morphing lies in the capabilities of mutation and the transplacing of one image into another. The meta complex encompassing the interstitial geometry/smooth space involves the derivation of geometry from the actor's body with that of a virtual actor in the computer, which is then mapped into the cinematic frame-by-frame structure. This special effect construct has strong resonances with the problematics facing architectural representation and realisation (in that the architect transforms thoughts

into two dimensional form then into three-dimensional form). A similar difficulty arises in the gaps between the systems of representation. This brief outline suggests one possible connection between the new interstitial geometrics described in contemporary morphing and architectural practices. It seems reasonable to suggest that as technology affords increasingly sophisticated methods of complexification and pervades more deeply into everyday imaging practices, the boundaries between the real in architectural terms and image/ effects will become further delimited.

**Notes**

1. Stan Allen formulations, 'Projections: Between Drawing and Building, Part II: Four Paradigms of Seeing', *A+U Architecture and Urbanism*, London, April 1992.
2. Mark Taylor, *Deconstruction in Context: Literature and Philosophy*, University of Chicago Press, Chicago and London, 1985, p13.
3. Peter Coveney and Roger Highfield, *The Arrow of Time*, Ballantine Books, New York, 1990, p82.

# STEPHEN PERRELLA
## INTERVIEW WITH MARK DIPPE
### Terminator 2

Stephen Perrella: To learn more about geometric complexity we are interested in the computer software that Industrial Light and Magic (ILM) developed for the liquid metal sequences in *Terminator 2* and the 'morphing' effects in Michael Jackson's current video *Black and White*. We understand morphing as the grafting or the superposition of faces/images with a specified number of intermediate frames, but the *Terminator 2* sequences are certainly complex. In the documentary *The Making of Terminator 2*, laser scanning techniques and grids applied to the actor's face and body are the interface between 'reality' and the computer. Could you describe in detail these techniques and focus on their implicit geometries?

Mark Dippe: Morphing as you describe it was developed at ILM for the film *Willow*, for the sequence in which the Willow character tries with a magic wand to reconstitute a good witch who's been turned into a goat. In the sequence she transforms from a goat into an ostrich, a turtle, a tiger, a young woman and finally an older woman. Morphing involves a transformation between objects of completely different shapes, sizes and forms. A traditional technique like the typical wolf/man dissolve isn't enough. In the digital realm we now have the freedom to change the shape of the picture while simultaneously dissolving. That's the essence of the morphing technique, taking two images that are shot separately and, while performing a cross-dissolve between them, changing the shape of both to improve the illusion of transformation.

SP: Does one select particular control points on the first face/image and then determine their counterpart control points on the next sequential image, with an interstitial range of 50 to 5,000 frames?

MD: Yes. We talked earlier about the role of a grid in the original morph technique, and although it has evolved over the years, it is based on a grid of points. To take an image

of a square, for example, to a circle, a grid of points is imposed over the picture containing the square and a similar grid over the picture containing the circle. That gives you a correspondence between points on each.

SP: The grid is the controlling geometry for the linkages?

MD: Exactly. But to continue, if I take a certain grid point in picture A and move it and leave the corresponding grid point in picture B alone, that will determine how picture A will be distorted as it turns into picture B. That is a direct correspondence and becomes a unique mapping between the two images. This is how the original morph worked: a point-by-point grid correspondence with the freedom to move any of the points in picture A or B with the computer distorting them back to the ideal grid, which can then be cross-dissolved. That correspondence and manipulation give you the changing form. It's mostly moving the grids. The computer doesn't know what the picture is, it has no knowledge of the image. It only knows grids, and as the grid points move it takes the underlying picture and distorts it as the grid is distorted.

SP: How is the liquid metal effect more complex than this?

MD: We now have a whole new generation of morphing ability. The basic principle of morphing as it was used in *Willow* around 1988 has been used repeatedly and is now just one small tool in our spectrum of capabilities. We use the previously described morph all the time but now it's rarely the only thing used to accomplish an ILM effect, and in fact determines a rather small proportion of the total effect. *Terminator 2* is a good example of the next level of what some people call morphing; we don't call it morphing because it's really more distinct. *T-2* involved creating a believable, life-like human form. One quality of human forms, of any living form, is that they are

difficult to represent in traditional computer animation because they are soft and have tissue that reacts and changes in very subtle ways. For instance, when we run, our muscles shake each time our feet hit the ground and impact our thighs. These soft-tissue, muscle and bone dynamics of living creatures in motion are very difficult to model because conventional computer graphics are essentially Euclidean; everything is rigid, polygonal and flat.

SP: Current architectural researchers are interested in the middle ground between the organic and the Euclidean that is considered 'supple.'

MD: Organic forms don't obey the Euclidean rules in which computers excel. Computers can calculate perfectly straight lines but with human forms nothing is perfectly straight; there are only recognisable unique shapes. The other side of the coin is that people can recognise a real human face, even though they can't describe it. We might be able to draw it, but we can't quantify the shape easily.

SP: One might add that living organisms have a certain vitality over anything mechanical that furthers the computer modelling problematic.

MD: One of the aesthetic dilemmas in computer animation is that an algorithmic process can be stiff and inorganic. In *Terminator 2* we were very aware of these limitations and even the movement of the chromed liquid-metal man with a metallic feeling had to be life-like. The principle used here also relates to the grid. We knew that if we projected a perfect grid on our actor Robert Patrick's body and filmed him moving with a painted grid on his body, the grid would distort in the same way as his body tissues did when he walked, ran or performed. So he was made to stand still for hours like a figure on a crucifix while we projected grids on him and then make-up artists copied them meticulously around his body; parts of which the projection didn't cover, so the make-up artists interpolated them. We then took Robert into daylight to analyse his motion again. This became our reference to study how his tissues moved in an organic, supple manner. Our digital actor would move the same way. We worked with an analogy between the real world and our virtual world. With a real set, a real camera and a real actor on the one hand; and on the other a computer camera, a computer set and computer actor. Our objective was to make them match perfectly. We can put a computer actor into a real set or a real actor into a computer set. We're good at creating computer cameras that match real cameras and computer sets that match real sets. Things that are manmade, like buildings and chairs, are easily handled; but trees and flowing water are more difficult. We had our actor perform many different movements – running, walking, dancing and fighting scenes: different dramatic actions that were to occur in the film. They were filmed with two cameras simultaneously from two perpendicular views, a front view and a side view. The cameras were synchronised to photograph frames in unison. We then took the two pieces of film and input them into the computer to produce perfect side and front views. We also had all the data on the cameras and the lenses and built an exact duplicate on our computer of the real filming situation. We had two computer cameras with exactly the same lenses etc, then we placed our computer actor the same distance from the two cameras, made him walk and run at the same speed as the real actor, and then finally compared the two.

SP: So you built an interstitial model in virtual reality.

MD: We concentrated here on the mixture of reality and virtual reality. For me that's almost natural. We've always concentrated on augmenting things or growing them. Greater percentages of an image are being generated on a computer, but still there's always a portion that is photographed or obtained by some other means.

SP: Your work can be looked at in another way, in that it problematises real perception – what we see in the movies and in natural perception is altered by virtuality. We might also consider the space between virtual and real as one of displacement: where neither the virtual nor the natural remains intact but each problematises the other.

MD: Lately, images are no longer pure – in cinema, photography or almost anywhere. The camera itself is of course an interpretation of reality, but images are being manipulated further. There used to be a notion of the image as truthful, the veracity of photographs. It's a moot point now because they are always manipulated. The idea of special effects seems anachronistic; eventually it may be accepted as natural. This seems unusual because all images are 'real'. They are always manipulated or created, changed or altered, yet somehow real.

SP: That is a condition that we might consider as hyperreality.

MD: In this hyperreality we built our virtual man in a virtual set, with a set of references to make sure our digital actor behaved like the real actor. Having completed his model we had essentially created the character of our digital actor including his animation and behaviour. We knew what he would do in any situation, just as a writer would. We were able to anticipate how the T-1000 would sit, walk and get up and how his head would rise out of a floor. At that point we began working on the actual shots, and the initial phase of creating the T-1000 lasted at least two months.

SP: Did the research that you were doing in any way influence the script?

MD: No, but I would say we had a great impact on the film's look. In film-making the content must always come from the story. The director, James Cameron, was and still is the only major director who has any sort of sensitivity to, or compassion for, the new aesthetic possibilities of digital film-making.

SP: The documentary on the film portrayed the director's vision of how to go further with the man-machine relationship. Can you articulate the liquid-geometry sequences?

MD: We had created the T-1000 character to go through a transformation that breaks down into five stages, each with its own model that could be transformed or morphed, from one to the other. This is different from the morph we talked about in Willow because it's a 3-D shape: it's actual geometry, an architectural form in 3-D that can now transform or evolve through five stages. First, was the blob stage: the amorphous, molten liquid blob-form. Second, was the 'silver surfer' form: a very

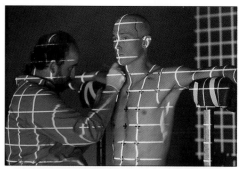

soft, man-like form; smooth like a sand-blasted figure, like the silver surfer in the comic books and like an Oscar award. The third phase we called the soft T-1000: the image of the actor smoothed down but with distinctly recognisable contours of clothing and detail. The fourth step was completely defined metal: he had all of the detail, minus skin or clothing. The fifth stage was reality: the real, skin and flesh actor.

SP: How many interim frames were used between phases?

MD: That depended on the action. The character might take at the most a couple of seconds to transform from one stage to another. Transforming from the stage-one blob to stage five, in the big, grandiose scene where he's a blob on the floor and the camera pulls up and he's slowly changed all the way to the man, took at least five seconds. It varied in the action scenes and he rarely went all the way between the two extremes. He typically went from stage two to stage five. That's how we broke it down. After working with it a while, we noticed there were distinct stages, even a certain logic to it. If he was going to perform a certain action, he had to go through a certain stage.

SP: What kind of geometry occurs in these five phases?

MD: We reduce our models of the actor to a great interconnected web of points, and those point meshes transform in shapes between the stages.

SP: Are those alpha-numeric trajectories, or do you actually see these geometric trajectories connected?

MD: On the computer you can see the model at stage one, then at stage two; and then you can run the animation and watch the model transform and all the points move in space from stage one to stage two. We have an interactive animation system for those views.

SP: You have software that helps you see the phase interfaces?

MD: Yes, we can bring up the point mesh visually on the screen. The ability to bring up these point mesh models interactively on the screen is becoming more common and you can buy various computer model-ling systems that do that. The models we

work with are very dense and complex, so our systems are more high-end than most.

SP: Did ILM develop this software, or do you use standard authoring programmes? How deeply do you get involved with programming?

MD: It is a combination. At ILM we have a software staff of about six people and we combine the best of everything. There is no necessity to invent new programmes, we use whatever will give the best visual results. We have a combination of off-the-shelf software and custom software. The work we do could not be done without custom software. In some sense we are forced to write software to create these kinds of images. I'm an effects supervisor and I sometimes get involved in the design of our software in terms of the functionality needed to achieve the image. To me a central problem is the metamorphosing of 3-D forms. That's the key. Like muscularity, it's transforming in shape and function; but it's moving. It's a living organic being, a character. These things are very complex and many other things also take place. The surface quality changes: maybe from a very shiny metal to a dull, pitted, worn surface; or to a more diffused or a matte, skin-like surface; or even to clothing. The computer can transform very easily between two states. Animating all parameters or all aspects is a natural computer function and very difficult to do physically. In real life a morph like equivalent requires a dissolve between two stages or a very complicated and unique animatronic puppet. That puppet is only capable of a few things — maybe its fingers can grow longer or something — but with a computer it's very easy to transform shapes, colours and everything else.

SP: I've heard rumours that there is work on a virtual reality theme park and also about developing virtual space for audience interaction in movie theatres. When I saw the T-2 video arcade in the theatre lobby, I realised that project was already underway.

MD: They were working on the game when we were working on the set. It was interest-ing. They took some of our grid ideas as a clue. In fact, they had seen the two-camera shot and set-up and the grid on the actor, and they worked with similar ideas for the game designers. They were shooting from two simultaneous cameras to give the game designers references as well. Soon there

will be virtual reality thatchers, where each audience member has virtual reality headsets and can walk around and experi-ence the movie as they like and perhaps be a part of the action. In the San Francisco Bay area there are performances groups like Antenna Theatre where the audience members actually walk around with little FM headsets and are part of the performance. As time goes on the difference between what is real and what isn't real is breaking down. For instance, we can extract some-thing someone didn't like out of an existing film or take an actor out of an old film and put him in a new one.

SP: Can you mention any of the software that you used in the T-2 movie?

MD: For the 3-D morphing or the 3-D transformations we developed a technique called 'make sticky' – similar to Disney-land's Haunted House effect where live-action film is projected on a bust to simulate the act of talking. We have the same idea in 3-D computer graphics. We can make a figure of a man walking and then project a film of a walking man in the computer, where it becomes a virtual projection. The film projection on our computer model resembles the same man walking in the computer. 'Make sticky' entails sticking the picture onto an object. Another technique we developed was called 'sock' in order to create a flexible, supple tissue base for muscular form. We thought of it as elastic bandages vacuformed over a basic constructed rigid form. Workable elasticity was provided, hence the name 'body sock' – now developed into a system to create supple, muscular forms for human bodies, animals or anything. For modelling and animation we use off the shelf Alias soft-ware, along with custom software; for rendering we use Renderman. Silicon Graphics workstations we use exclusively – the same company that makes Iris, Indigo. When T-2 came out the Indigo wasn't around but we have a lot of their machines which vary in price from $30,000 to $250,000. Macintosh is used for paint touch-up. We also use a programme called Photoshop.

*Mark Dippe was assistant effects director on* Terminator 2. *Dennis Muren, who has won many Academy Awards, was effects director and Steve Williams was principal animator*

# HENRY COBB
## *FIRST INTERSTATE BANK TOWER*
## *A Note on the Architectonics of Folding*

Bending is a manipulative strategy of objects. Folding is a manipulative property of surfaces. For example, when we refer to a sheet of paper as being folded we are engaging in an elision. The full statement would be that the sheet of paper is being bent while each of its surfaces is being folded. It is important to understand that the fold in one surface is distinctly separate from the fold in the other. We feel justified, because paper is dimensionally thin, in eliding these distinctions by compressing the statement 'the paper is being bent and its two surfaces folded' into 'the paper is being folded'. However, when we increase the material thickness from that of paper (+/-1/100") to that of building wall construction (6" minimum) we can no longer afford to elide these distinctions: we must acknowledge explicitly that the wall as a constructed object is being bent, and hence that we will achieve an architectonic manifestation of folding only to the extent that we can locate the visible architecture of the wall on a single plane corresponding to the wall's outer surface. Why we might wish to achieve an architectonic manifestation of folding is a matter that with reference to the skyscraper illustrated here, has already been discussed in the Charlottesville Tapes (Rizzoli, 1985): 'Although I have been designing tall buildings for 30 years, these are, I suppose, my first real "skyscrapers". I will acknowledge that I set out quite deliberately in this project to find my own way of making a skyscraper image: these are skyscrapers made by carving away rather than by building up. In this sense they remind me of Roland Barthes' comment that skyscrapers of New York have made it a deep city, not a high one – a city excavated rather than built. This is my fourth building project in Dallas, and it reflects two concerns: a concern about imagery and a concern about place. To my mind they are equally important. Let me first speak about the issue of imagery. Downtown Dallas is a city of box office towers that, owing to the flight path of a nearby airport, cannot exceed about 60 storeys in height. Our clients are understandably

concerned that their project, which is to contain three million square feet of rental office space, should not become lost in this crowd of nearly indistinguishable commercial buildings. They requested a strong memorable image on the skyline; an image that would be intrinsic to the building's form without resorting to fancy hats or applied ornament. The design strategy we adopted to achieve this goal is governed by its own internal logic: a subtractive procedure applied to a prismatic tower 190 square feet in plan and 720 feet high. This "pure prism" is carved from the top down with incisions that adhere rigorously to the geometry of a double square in both plan and section. The resultant twin skyscrapers are identical but appear to be different as one is rotated 90 degrees in plan with respect to the other. Major incisions in the base of each tower reintroduce the diagonal geometry and create a spatial rather than volumetric presence at street level.'

Although the conventional logic of commercial development prefers spatial uniformity, especially with regard to office towers, folding is useful in such buildings because the fold introduces a figure to a surface which animates both the totality of the form and the individual units of which it is composed. An architectural manifestation of folding on the surface of the building not only engenders the appearance of bending in the overall shape of the building, giving it a distinct urban identity, but also introduces differentiation into the repetition of the typical office units. In the First Interstate Bank Tower, every floor-plate has a different identity. Moreover, the interior spaces below sloping surfaces have been the most sought after by the occupants as they provide the greatest identity through their differentiation.

The primary purpose of this note is not to argue why we would desire the architectural manifestation of folding, but to explicate how it can be achieved through a rigorous architectural treatment of materials and space. In the First Interstate Bank Tower the fold has been developed as an architectural response to the contingencies

of commercial development. Here, the fold is considered from within a discipline of materiality and does not begin with an ideology of folding.

1 An architecture of folding is by definition an architecture of surface. Therefore, the first requirement is that the constructional elements that make up the surface to be folded must be assembled in such a way that they are manifested only on that surface. This is more of a challenge than it may seem, as the components of buildings by necessity have varying depths yet the fold can occur at only one surface. So, if a fold is to occur at the scale of a building rather than the scale of a piece of paper, it has to be assembled out of pieces which have depth in themselves and are set into a structure with depth also. When giving architectural form to these methods of construction through a strategy of folding, all constructional elements have to be reduced, in terms of their expressive capacity, to a single surface.

2 Buildings exist at a scale so large that they cannot be monolithic like a single piece of paper which is folded or a single stone that is carved. Buildings must be constructed out of pieces. Inevitably, there are joints between these pieces. A fundamental rule for an architectural manifestation of folding is that the folding must never occur at a joint between the elements which make up the surface to be folded. A joint is a void between two pieces and cannot be folded. Any fold which coincides with a joint is not a fold but the manipulation of two separate pieces. A fold does not exist in the interval between elements but describes their shared surface. The pleasure of the fold is that it occurs on a shared surface that has the ability to unite elements through manipulation. The fold both flattens and animates; it folds elements together on a continuous plane while differentiating the same surface.

3 The logic of construction suggests that the building components which make up a surface are typically orthogonal; whether the glass panels that actually constitute the surface or the metal frames that support the

glass. If the building components are indeed orthogonal in their organisation, one way to dramatise vividly the act of folding is to locate the fold on a diagonal. A diagonal fold (in a direction oblique to the orthogonal grid of construction) is inevitably more eloquent than an orthogonal fold (in a direction parallel to the orthogonal grid of construction) which lacks the unpredictable drama of uniting constructional elements with a system oblique to their own order.

The three fundamental principles applied to the design of this skyscraper are that the disparate constructional elements are given architectural expression on only a single plane; that folds occur on the surface of those elements and never in the joints between elements; and that folding occurs whenever possible in an oblique orientation to the orthogonal order of construction.

To respect and accord with the above procedures a rigorous curtain wall system was developed that was capable of being folded. The key to the building lies in the development of two types of mullion systems: solid frame and joint frame. The building's surface is organised into 6'x12' panels mounted precisely flush with bright aluminium frames. Between the frames are constructional joints – the method of assembling the facade. Within each 6'x12' frame are four panes of glass; each pane framed by an aluminium extrusion painted to match the glass. These frames have joints in between. All folds occur on the frames. This allows for folding within the panels rather than at the joints in between, without literally having to bend the glass.

The fact that the folds occur on metal is less significant than the fact that they never occur at a major joint between elements. All folds occur within panels; either on green orthogonal mullions or on green diagonal mullions which are introduced for the diagonal folds. This allows the curtain wall manufacturer to prefabricate the major panels and therefore all of the folded conditions within the shop, rather than assembling them piece by piece on the building – assuring accuracy within the geometry of the folded elements. Within each large frame there are at least four and as many as seven separate panes of glass. These large panels are then assembled in the field in the same manner as the adjacent unfolded orthogonal panels.

*First Interstate Bank Tower: Previous Page, Floor plans and overall view; Above: View from under highway; Right: Orthogonal fold; diagonal fold, one direction; diagonal fold, two directions*